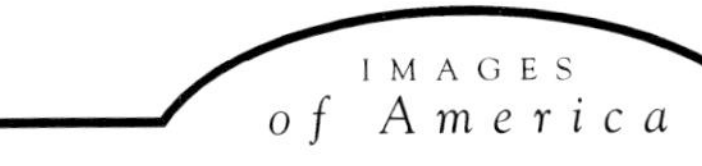


# The Swedes of Greater Brockton

# About the Authors

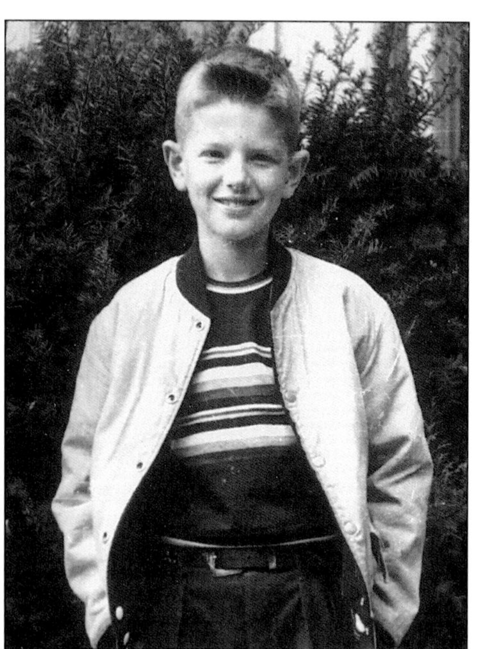

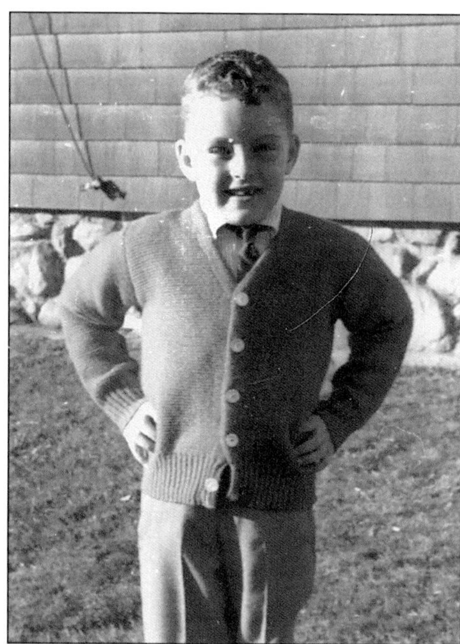

*Left:* Lloyd F. Thompson, a kid from Tribou Street, grew up in the Swedish neighborhood of "honse-backan." He played in Brockton's first Little League and Pony League. A graduate of Boston University, he went on to become a vice president of the international engineering firm of Camp Dresser & McKee, a partner in the architectural firm of Symmes, Maini & McKee Associates, and president of Marketing Strategies Incorporated, a firm he co-owned with his wife, Wilette. He is a member of the Lutheran Social Services of New England Foundation Board of Directors and a former legislative and press assistant to Congressman Hastings Keith. *Right:* James E. Benson was born in Brockton, lived briefly on Hillberg Avenue, and grew up in West Bridgewater. A graduate of West Bridgewater High School, he earned a bachelor's degree in history from Muhlenberg College. Benson is chairman of the First Evangelical Lutheran Church Archives Committee and chairman of the West Bridgewater Public Library Board of Trustees. Employed in the retail lumber business for 26 years, he is currently manager of purchasing and business development at Mahoney's Building Supply in Mattapoisett.

IMAGES
*of America*

# THE SWEDES OF GREATER BROCKTON

James E. Benson and Lloyd F. Thompson

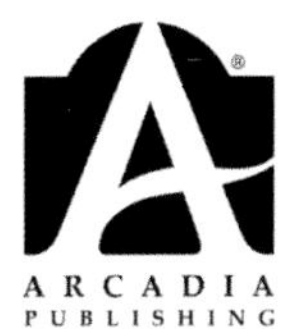

ARCADIA
PUBLISHING

ISBN 978-0-7385-0851-1

Published by Arcadia Publishing
Charleston, South Carolina

Printed in the United States of America

Library of Congress Catalog Card Number: 2001088722

For all general information contact Arcadia Publishing at:
Telephone 843-853-2070
Fax 843-853-0044
E-mail sales@arcadiapublishing.com
For customer service and orders:
Toll-Free 1-888-313-2665

Visit us on the Internet at www.arcadiapublishing.com

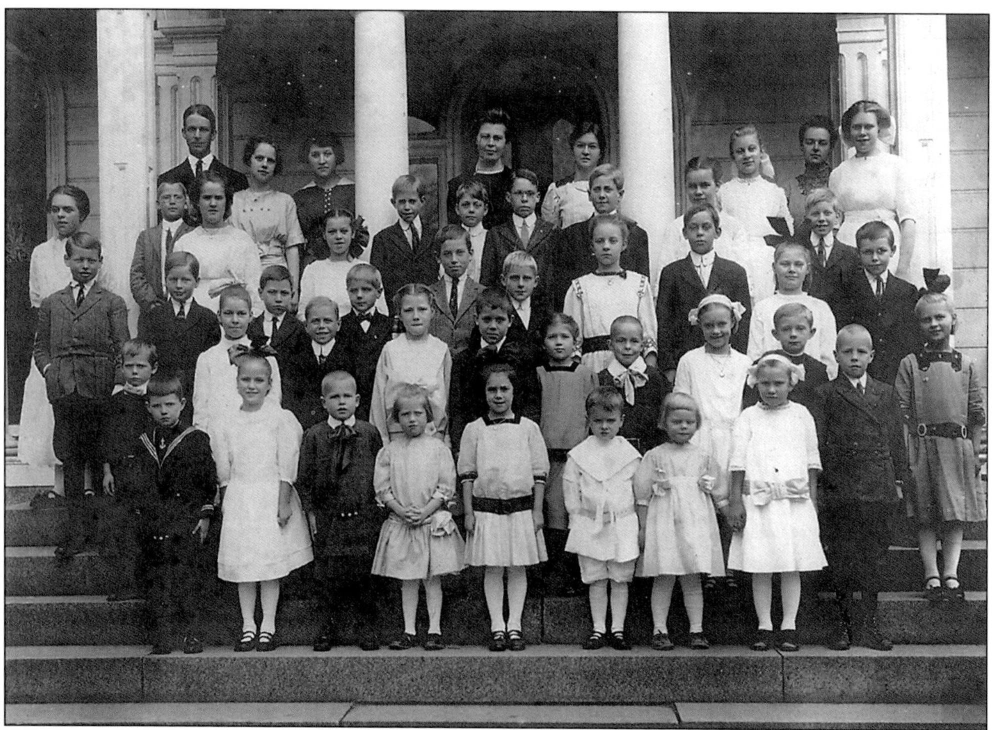

Among the many charitable activities of the Swedish Lutheran Church was the operation of the Orphans Home in Avon. Shown in this 1913 photograph are matron Amelia Rabinius, (back row center), cook Amelia Johansson (back row, left of the column), hired man Gustaf Edstrom, and five staff members (back row) along with their 39 charges. The fine appearance of the children bespeaks the care they were provided.

# Contents

# ACKNOWLEDGMENTS

Most of the photographs in this book, which date from 1867 to the 1950s, are from private collections and church archives. The authors gratefully acknowledge the generosity of the families and institutions that shared their knowledge, history, and captivating photography.

For putting up with the archival intrusion and for her splendid efforts in editing and proofing the manuscript, we thank Wilette Thompson.

We also give special thanks to the following individuals: Carolyn Anderson, Dolly Anderson, Stanley A. Bauman, Marge Anderson Benvie, Gladys Bergstrom, Elsie Burgesson, William Bystrom, Eugene Carlson, Warren Carlson, Curtis Holm Chase, Verna Chubbuck, Charlotte Cotter, Phyllis Pearson Cousins, Edward N. Dahlborg, Joan Hillstrom DiMarzo, Pamela Dunbrack, Davida Lawson Easton, Greta Edson, Laverne Gustafson Ekberg, Gary Eliasson, Hartley Erickson, Hulda Hackenson, Avis Holmstrand Evans, Ruth Goransson Fitzpatrick, Roy Franzen Jr., Bertil Froeberg, Vilma Pearson Hall, Susan Froeberg Heng, Carl Holmander, Everett A. Johnson, Gerald Johnson, Lester E. Johnson, Lester R. Johnson, David and Ellen Johnson, Ruth Emberg Johnson, Robert A. Kane, Dorothy Dahlborg Kendrew, Evelyn Benson Lagerval, William F. Larson, Robert Lindgren, Esther Lundin, Mildred Lundin, Lynne Martin, George Moberg, Eleanor Sondeen Morlino, Jean Muncy, Carl Olson, Allan Ortendahl, Jane Ostlund, Irene Ozelius, Elaine Parks, Dana Anderson Perkins, Russell E. Perkins, Roger Peterson, Lennart Plahn, Brenda Redmond, Jeanette Johnson Reed, Elaine Peterson Sawler, Donald Seablom, Nancy Bolinder Shaw, Robert Sigren, Margaret Silva, Helen Snook, Janet Studley, Shirley Studley, Marjorie Benson Sullivan, Harold Swanson, Walter Swanson, Marie Syverson, Jane Anderson Taylor, Dr. Robert Thompson, Francis Trojano, Phyllis Wasson, and Ellen Anderson Werner.

We would like to thank the following organizations for the generous use of their archives: Community Covenant Church (East Bridgewater), First Evangelical Lutheran Church (Brockton), Prince of Peace Lutheran Church (Brockton), the West Bridgewater Public Library, the Brockton Historical Society, the Easton Historical Society, and the Vega Social Club (Brockton).

—James E. Benson and Lloyd F. Thompson

# FOREWORD

Just 18 years after the Pilgrims landed at Plymouth, a small Swedish colony was established in Delaware. Numerous descendants of these pioneers served in America's fight for independence in 1776. John Hanson of Maryland, whose grandfather was a founder of that colony, was elected president of "the United States in Congress assembled" in 1781, thus preceding George Washington as the highest office holder in the new nation. Two years later, Sweden extended diplomatic recognition to the new nation, thus beginning our fruitful relationship with the United States.

During times of domestic crisis in their homeland, America became a haven for Swedish people, as for countless others throughout the world. Along with their traditions and culture, the Swedes brought their penchant for hard work, a determination to succeed, and the necessary skills to help build their "new" land.

When my countryman Daniel Lawson of Frostorp arrived in Brockton (then North Bridgewater) in 1844, he was the only Swede. At age 23, he immediately plied his trade as a shoemaker and enthusiastically entered American life. In a very real sense, Mr. Lawson was the magnet that drew others to Brockton and formed a cradle of Swedish culture that grew and flourished. In all walks of life, the Swedish contribution to the region of Greater Brockton has been great, and a justly proud legacy remains.

The accomplishments of all Swedish Americans continues to strengthen the historic bonds between our two nations and promises a future of limitless possibilities.

I salute the Swedes of Greater Brockton.

—Hon. Jan Eliasson, Ambassador of Sweden

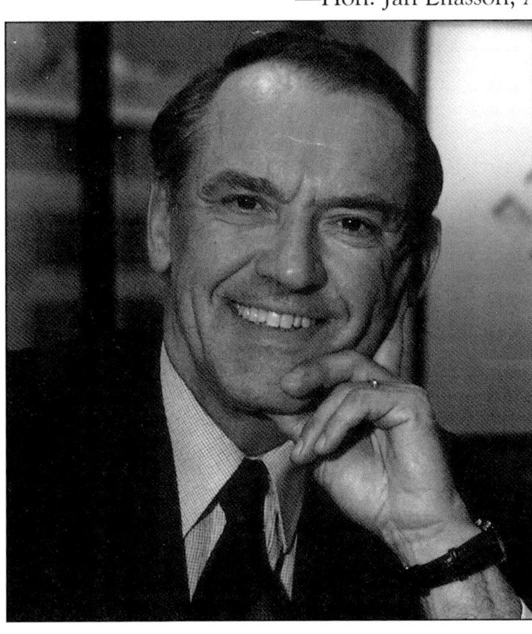

# INTRODUCTION

This volume contains more than 200 vintage photographs that will evoke thousands of memories. The authors have attempted to highlight the people, places, and events that helped to form the fabric of the Swedish community in the Greater Brockton region and its impact on the community at large. Although the book is far from a comprehensive history, many little-known facts are presented, along with insights into the lives of the pioneer Swedes and their descendants.

Beginning with the Swedes' heart-rending decision to leave home and family, this book allows the reader to travel vicariously with these émigrés on a journey to America, on to their destination, and into their homes and businesses.

A handful returned home, not being satisfied with the conditions they met. Those who persevered were to realize their dreams.

Although no specific history of the Swedes of this region exists, it is clear from newspaper accounts, business directories, church records, and family histories that the Swedish immigrants were generally welcomed. Even though most did not speak, read, or write English when they landed, the overwhelming majority was literate, thanks to the Swedish Elementary School Act of 1842. One of their first challenges, therefore, was to learn their adopted language, and mastery came easily.

The upward mobility of the Swedes was steady, and their influence was significant, as these glimpses of history illustrate.

Businessmen and bakers, pastors and politicians, florists and farmers, shopkeepers and servants, educators and entertainers, shoeworkers and soldiers, laborers and lawyers, machinists and masons, and fathers and mothers all contributed to the well-being of this region.

To them, we dedicate this book.

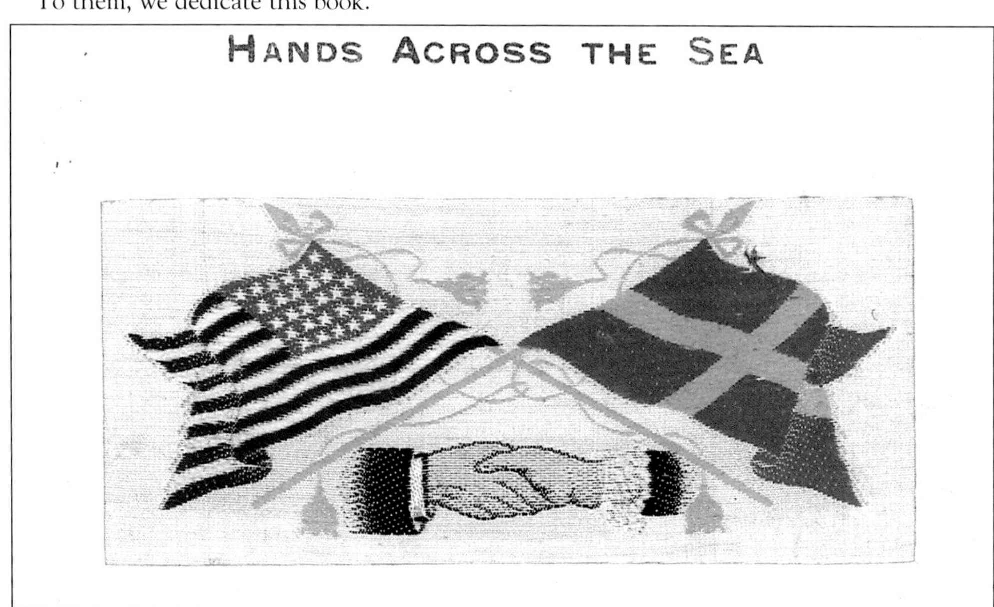

# One

# The Homeland and Journey to America

The words to the immigrant's song "Hälsa dem därhemma" eloquently reveal the feelings of those leaving their homeland for an uncertain future in America: *I den stora tysta natt star jag här vid skeppets ratt, under himlens stjärnehär, man pa post mig satt.* "On the deck I stand at night, when the stars above are bright, far away from friends and home, lonely here I roam." Imagine you are 16 years old or even 30, a passenger on an old ship crossing the Atlantic on storm-tossed seas, heading for a foreign land where the first people you will meet will be somber immigration officials. Then it is off to your destination to meet your sponsor, another stranger. Or, maybe you are lucky and have a relative awaiting your arrival. You do not speak the language or know the customs. You have little money. You have just left behind your parents, brothers, sisters, aunts, uncles, teachers, and friends. Chances are that you may never see them again.

This was the plight of many of the early Swedish immigrants. Their reasons for leaving were similar to those found throughout Europe: agricultural failures, political and religious discontent, and social crises. There was also the great promise of opportunity for all in America. The migration to Brockton began in 1844 and intensified between 1880 and 1920. Determined and adaptable, the Swedes made their way into the new society, left a positive mark in their community, and made a better life for their children. For the overwhelming majority, the promise of America was fulfilled.

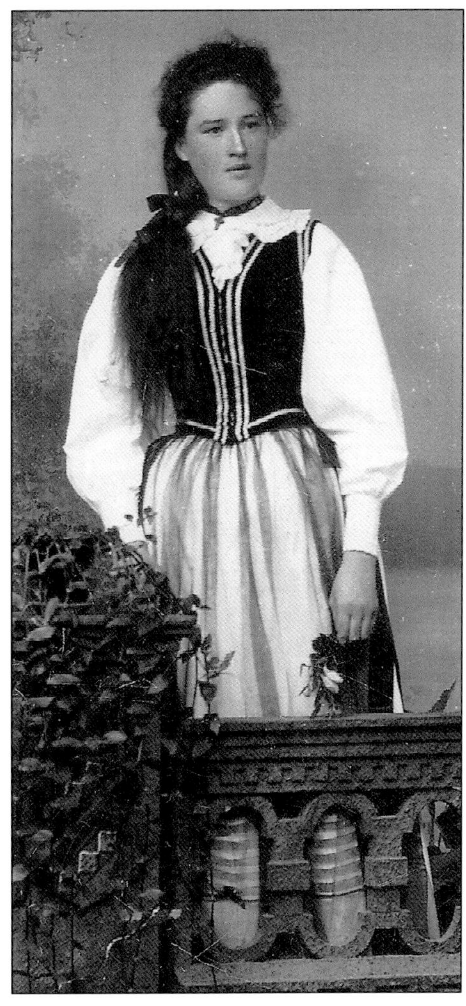

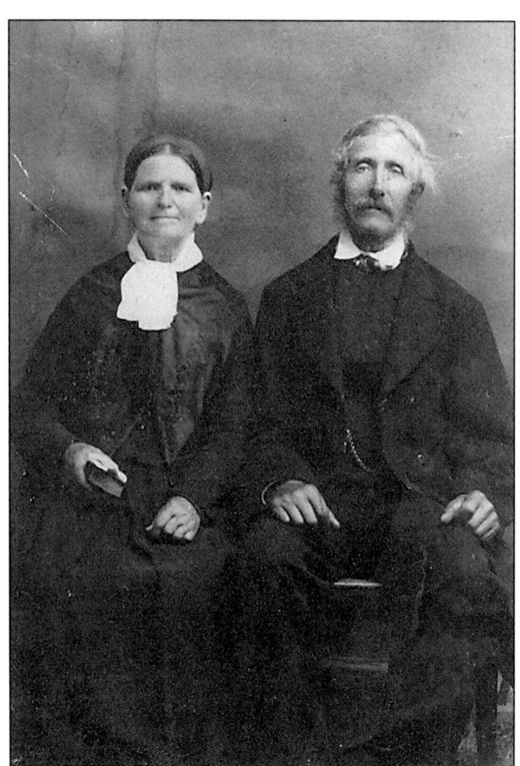

Johannes Max, a former soldier in the Swedish army, and his wife, Anna Lena Johansdotter, pose for photographer S.J. Johnson in his studio in Oskar-shamn in 1876. Shortly after the death of Johannes Max, Anna Lena, at age 80, made her way to Brockton to live with her son Abel Max, a shoeworker and a leader in numerous Swedish lodges in the city.

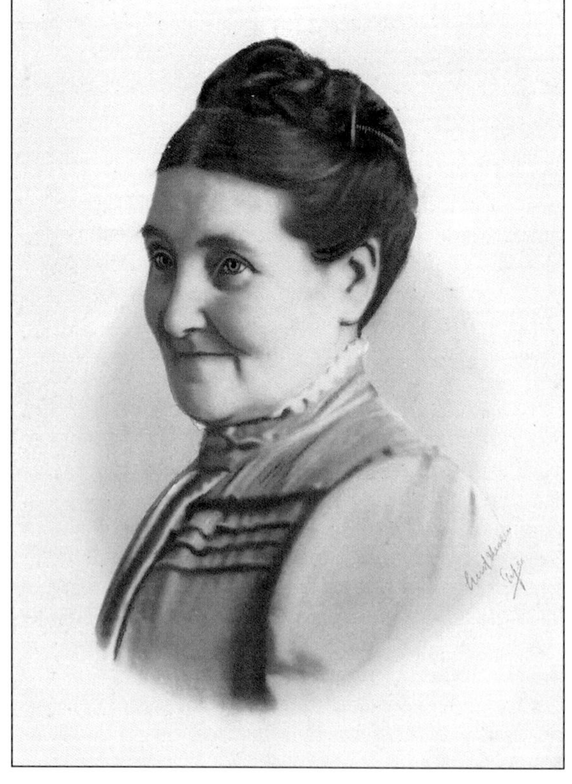

Seeking a new life in America meant leaving behind parents, siblings, and friends. Johanna Augusta Holmstrom Ericsson, born in the 1840s in Gavle, saw her three daughters immigrate to Boston in the 1890s, while two sons remained at home. The immigrant's story is one of great hope and also of anguish.

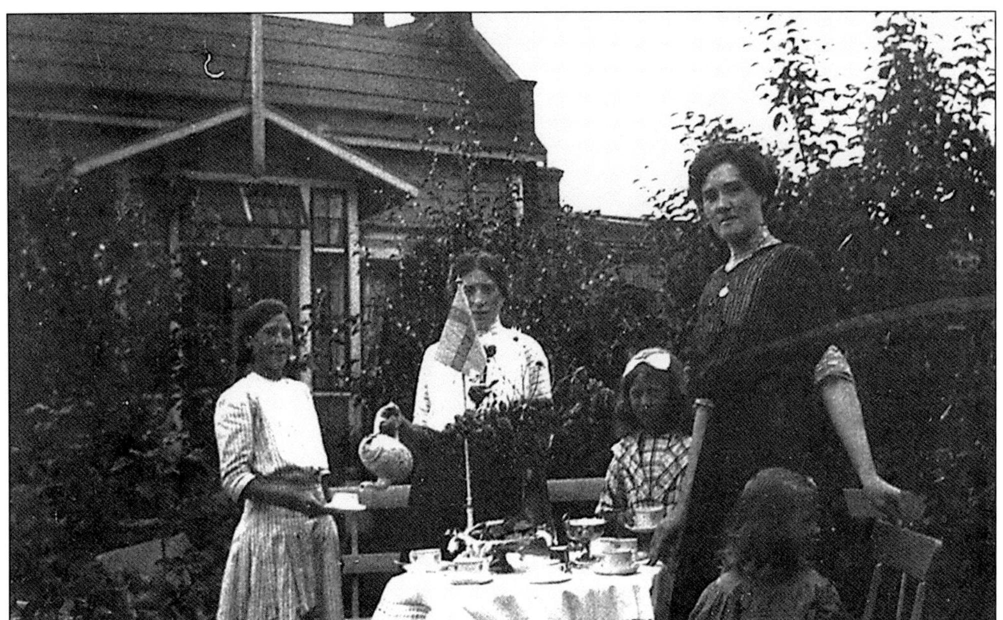

The family homestead in Asarum, Blekinge, is the setting for a "bon voyage" tea party given for Hilma Ottosson by her mother and three sisters. This was a bittersweet occasion, however, as Ottosson would see her family only once again, although she corresponded with them frequently until the 1950s. Note the Swedish flag proudly displayed on the table along with a bouquet of fresh flowers.

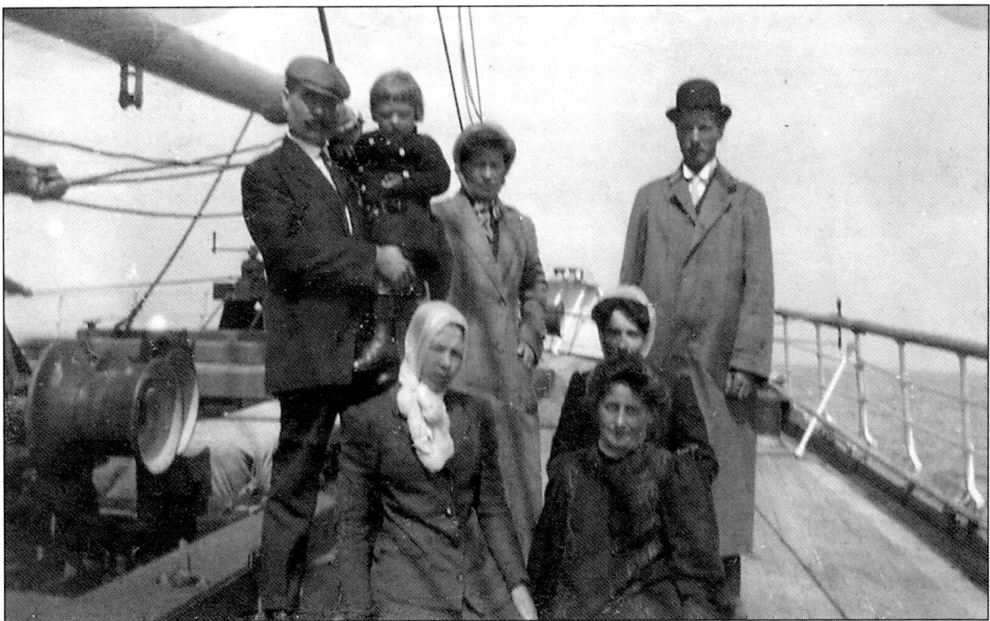

Making their way to America, Swedish émigrés pose during a May 1902 Atlantic crossing. Kneeling in front of the gentleman sporting the derby is Hilma Ottosson, who (at age 21) left her home in Sweden to seek opportunity in the Brockton area. For a period of time, she resided at a boardinghouse at 18 Denton Street in the Campello section of the city. She later met and married Carl Victor Erickson. They had two children—Martha Vivian and Hartley.

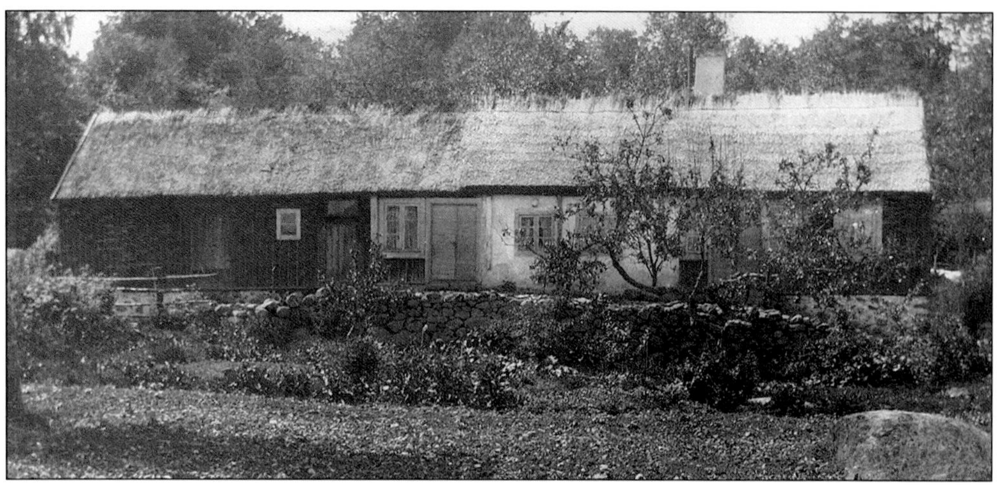

The Bengtsson homestead in Gammalstorp, Blekinge, was typical of the Swedish tenant farm of the 1880s. Many Swedish farmers emigrated for the promise of a better life and the lure of land ownership. To those from Blekinge, known for its farmlands and close proximity to the ocean, New England was an ideal destination.

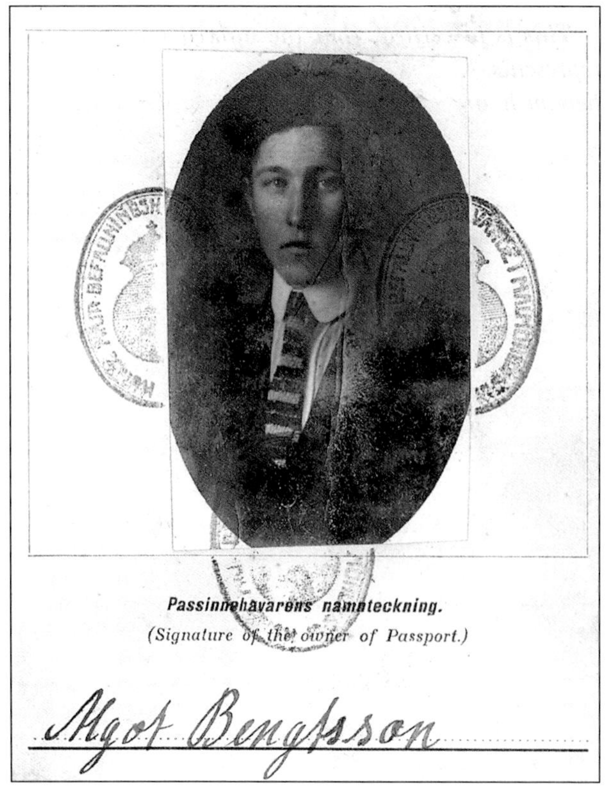

**Passinnehavarens namnteckning.**

*(Signature of the owner of Passport.)*

Algot Bengtsson

Shown here is a page from the Swedish passport of 17-year-old Bror Algot Bengtsson, issued on March 26, 1923, in Malmö. He landed at Ellis Island and then proceeded by train to Brockton in April of that year. On arrival, the young man immediately enrolled in evening classes at Brockton High School to learn English and American history. In addition, he attended the Americanization class at the Swedish Methodist Church. He established residency in West Bridgewater in 1930 and Americanized his surname to Benson at the time of his naturalization in 1934. Trained as a stoneworker by his father, Mr. Benson operated a mason contracting business until his death in 1969.

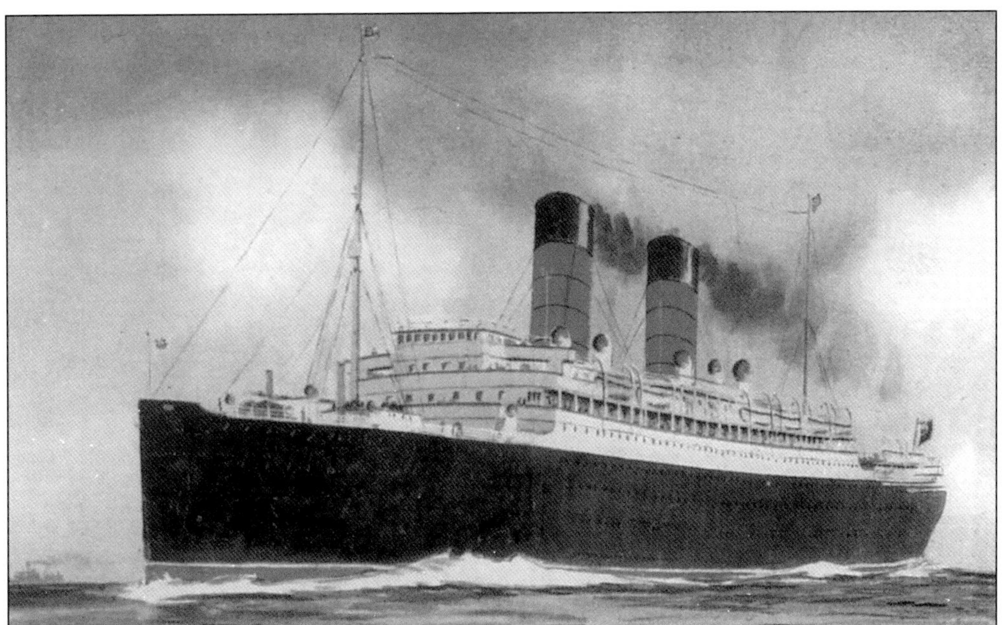

The RMS *Franconia* (shown) and *Laconia* were two of scores of ships that carried Swedish émigrés to America. Other vessels that played a key role in the 20th-century emigration included the ships of the Swedish American Line—the SS *Stockholm*, SS *Drottningholm*, MS *Kingsholm*, and MS *Gripsholm*.

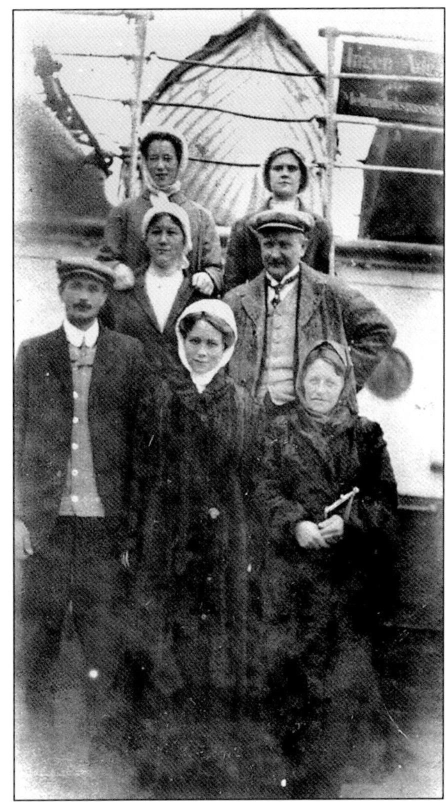

In 1914, Gerda (Lundin) Bergstrom and her sister Anna Lundin sailed to America aboard the HMS *Lusitania*. At 2:07 p.m., May 7, 1915, less than one year after their crossing, the *Lusitania* was hit by a torpedo from German U-Boat 20. Some 18 minutes later, the ship slid below the waves off the Irish Coast with a loss of 1,198 lives, of whom 128 were American citizens. In this view, Anna Lundin is standing in front. Gerda Bergstrom is seen in the back row on the left.

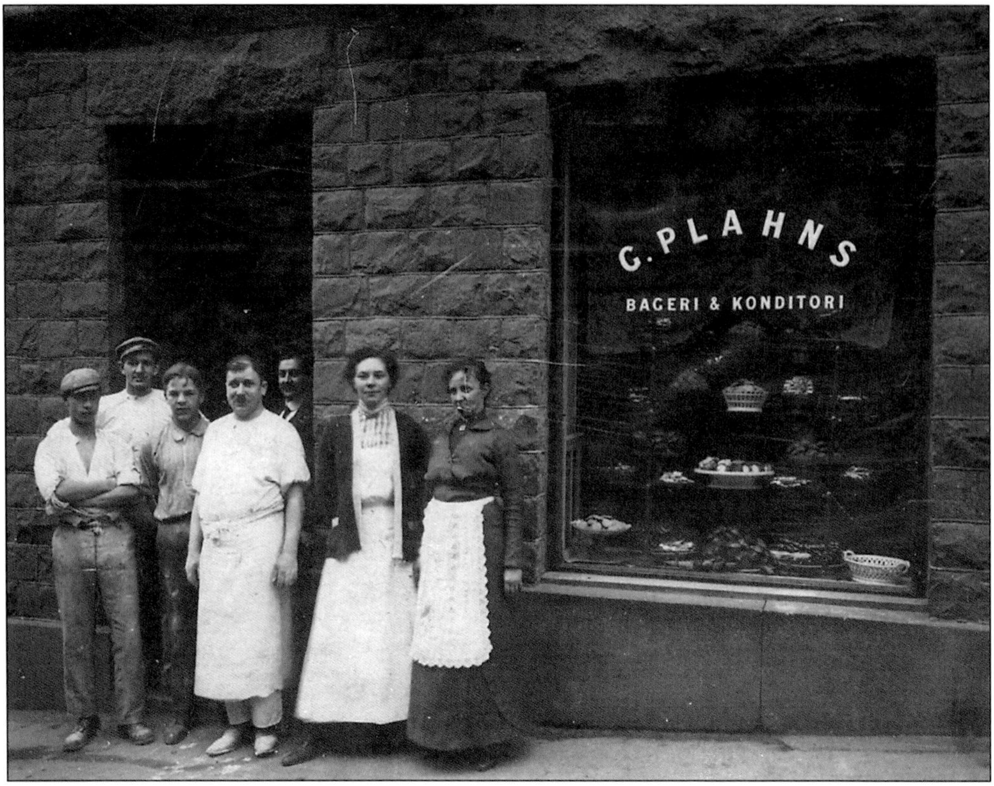

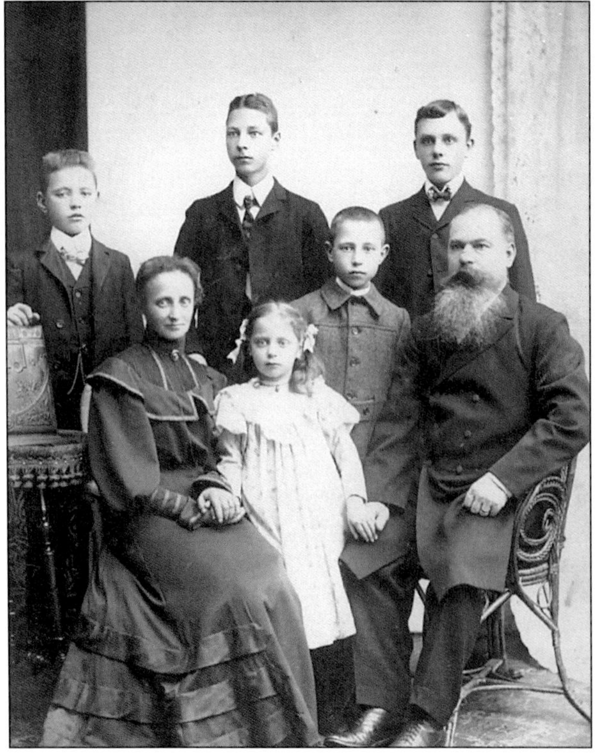

Gustaf Plahn and his wife, Elin, operated a large bakery in Stockholm in the late 19th century. Young Fritz Brynholt Waldemar Plahn (in the buttoned overcoat next to his father) journeyed to Brockton in 1903 at age 16. A responsible youth, he became "custodian of liquors" at the Osgood Hotel, 99 Warren Avenue. He later became a machine operator at Campello Nail-Less Heel on First Street. For many years, Fritz was custodian and function coordinator at Vasa Hall, a center for Swedish businesses and social events.

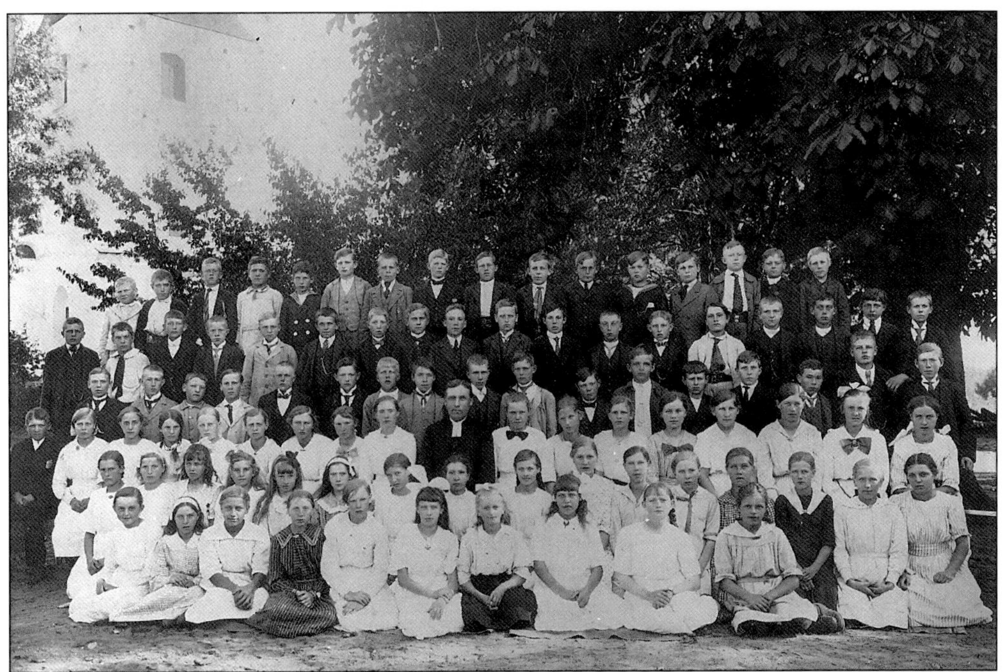

The pastor sits at the center of 94 graduates of the 1919 Confirmation class of Gammalstorp Kyrkan, Blekinge. At the age of 15, boys and girls were confirmed into the faith, a rite that continues today in Lutheran churches throughout the world. Photographing these events was a tradition brought to Lutheran congregations in America.

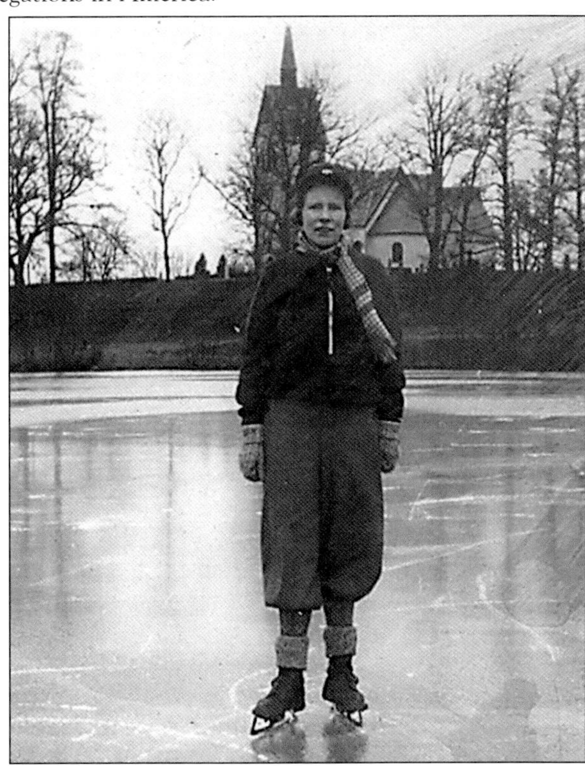

Taking time from her skating, Elsa Johansson poses with the Lutheran church in Jarsnas, Prastgard, as a background. A college graduate, she taught the fine arts of weaving and embroidery.

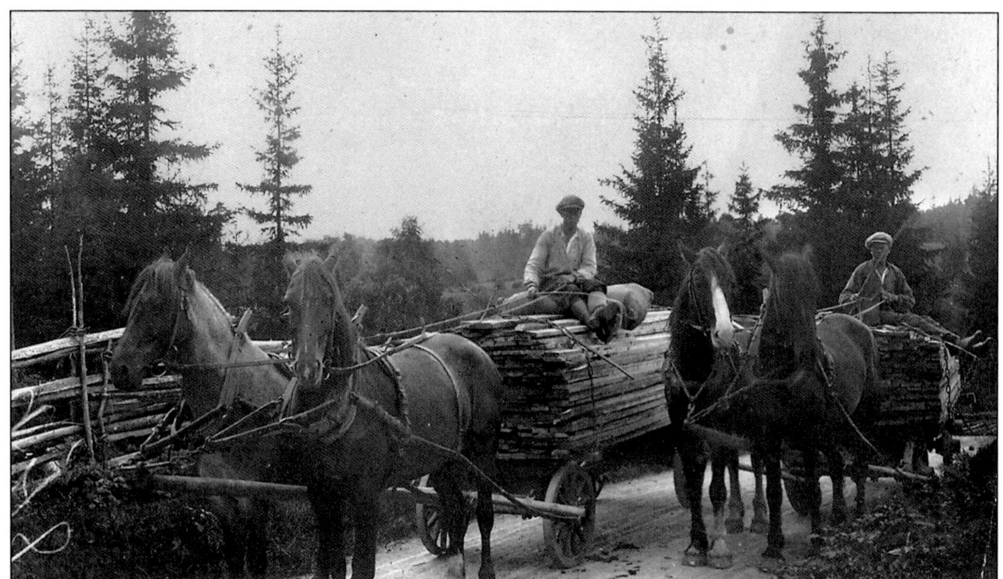

Logging and lumber production was an essential activity on the Hellstrom farm in Husqvarna, a large and productive dairy farm known for the high quality of its milk and cheeses.

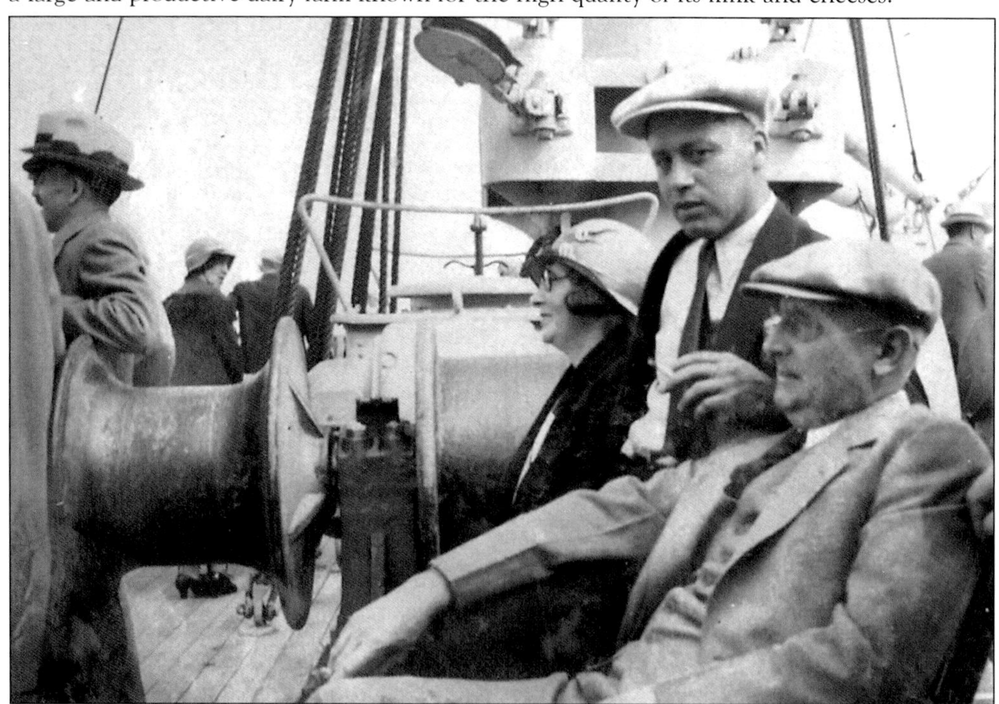

In 1929, Bror Gunnar Emmanuel Hellstrom sailed for America aboard the *Gripsholm* to seek his fortune in America. At Ellis Island, he was told by officials that the first syllable of his surname was not a good word in English; thus, his name was changed from Hellstrom to Hillstrom. A highly skilled machinist, he learned his trade in the large sewing machine factory in Husqvarna. In Brockton, he lived for a time at Emilson's Boarding House on Laureston Street. Hillstrom enjoyed a 40-year career as a machinist, mostly in the employ of Brockton Tool & Die Company of Easton.

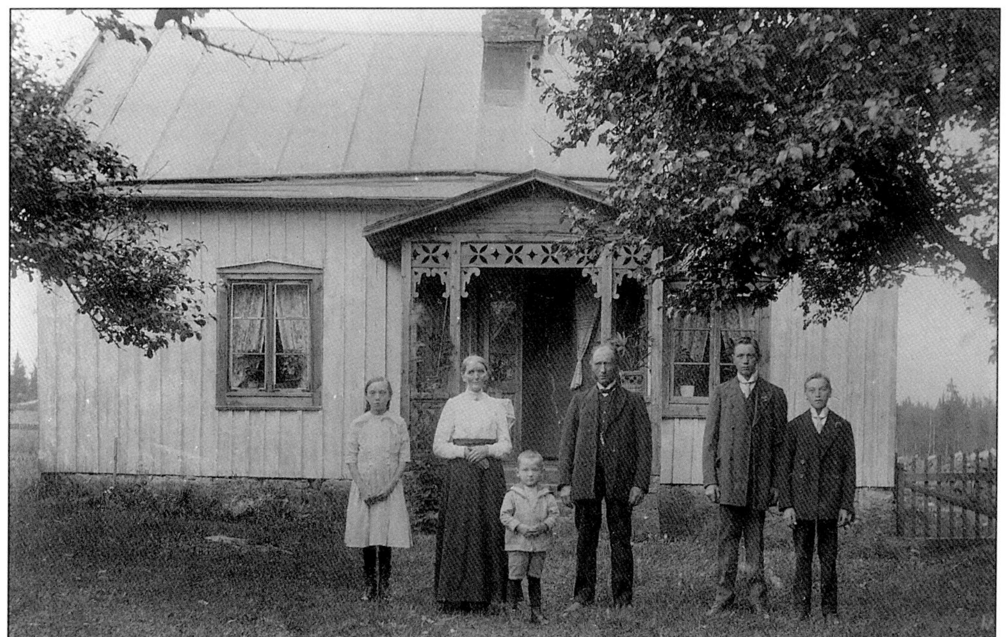

The Goranssons pose proudly at their home in Hultet, Småland. They are, from left to right, Gerda, Ida Marie Bengstdötter, Arvid, Goran Magnus Anderson, Carl, and John.

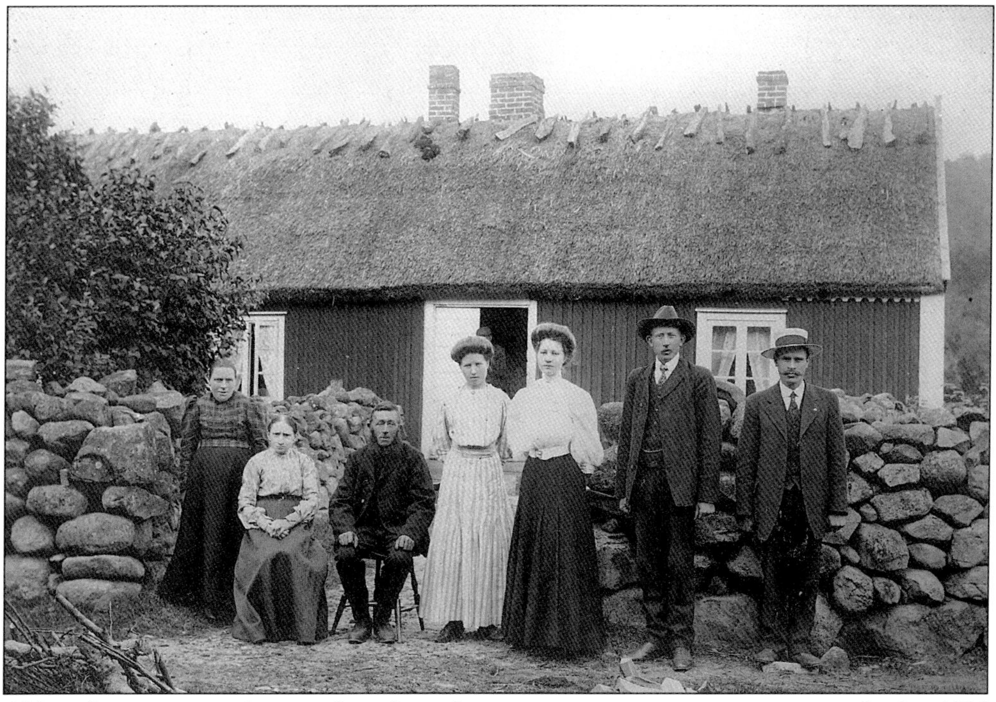

Although it is not evident on these faces, homecomings were a joyous occasion. In this 1906 photograph, the Hakanssons gather in front of their home in Jokarp, Blekinge, to celebrate the visit from America of three children—Anna, Per, and Nels. From left to right are Hanna Svensdotter, Elsa Hakansson, Bengt Hakansson, Selma, Anna and Per Bengtsson, and Nels Hansson.

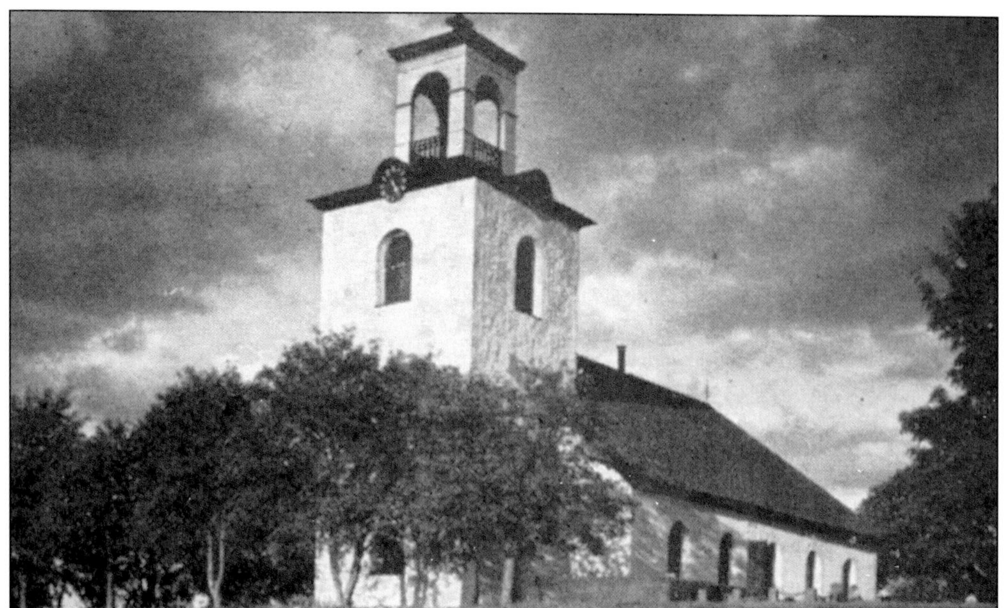

Built in 1791, the Nässjö Gamla Kyrka (Old Church) is where Isak Petter Nilsson Lagerstedt served as parish clerk and organist in 1828. (The length of his tenure is uncertain.) Earlier, according to a note in the family Bible, he played the organ in King's Chapel and was given the name "Lagerstedt" by King Oscar. Petter's sons Samuel Sebastian and Issac Magnus immigrated to Brockton in 1884 and 1887, respectively. Settling in Campello, "SS" (as Samuel was known) was employed as a clockmaker. Issac was employed as a farmer.

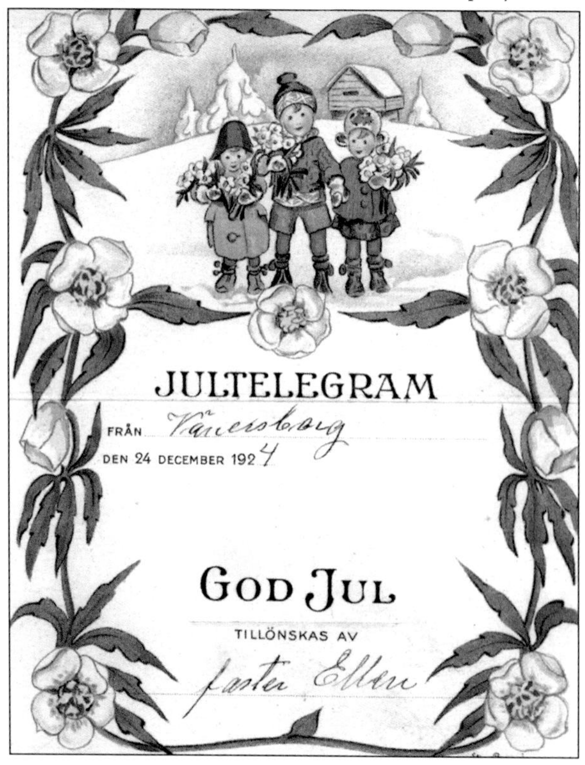


Strong ties were maintained with the old country, as expressed by this Christmas greeting card from a family in Sweden to relatives in Brockton. Even today, Swedish Christmas cards are sold in the region.

# *Two*

# THE CHURCHES

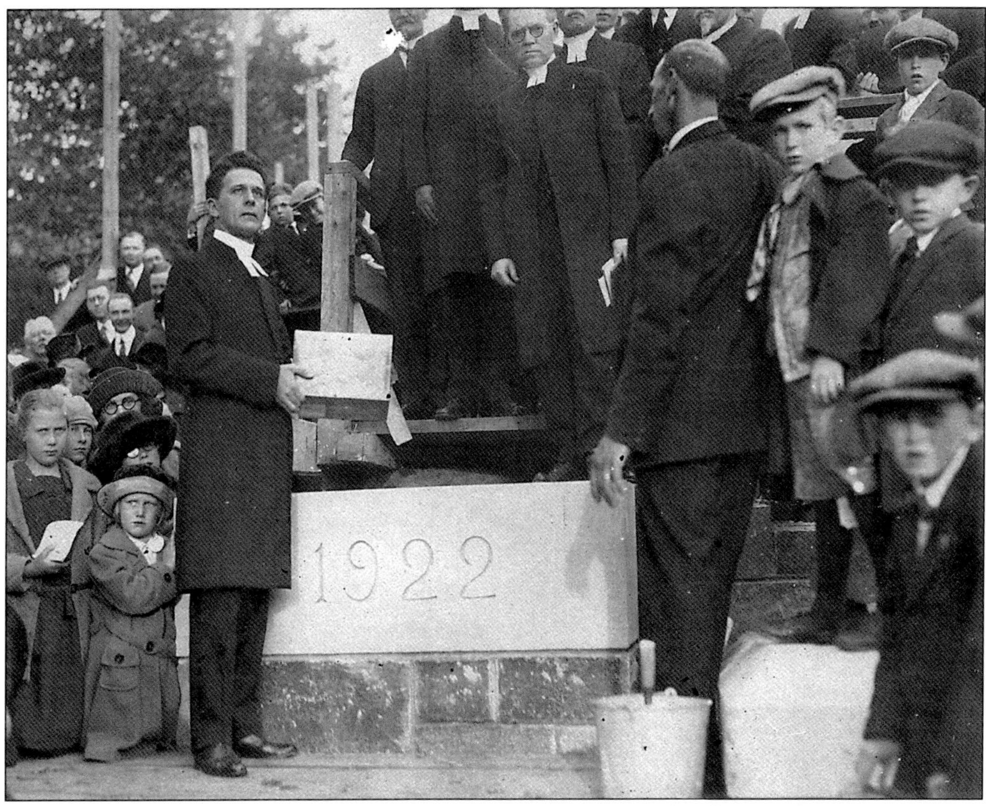


The strength and vitality of a community often lies within its churches. Such was the story of Greater Brockton's Swedish settlers. Faced with numerous obstacles, they found a common bond in the church. In Sweden, the state church was Lutheran, and all citizens were members. In this new land, the constitutional separation of church and state created opportunities for Swedes to form churches of denominations other than Lutheran. These new congregations were the centers of both religious and social life. Outreach, a term in wide use today, was practiced daily through numerous benevolent societies, orphanages, and pastoral visits to the sick and bereaved.

North Bridgewater, in 1853, was the scene of the first religious service among the Swedish immigrants. It was conducted by Pastor Olof Gustaf Hedstrom, founder of Swedish Methodism. In 1867, area Lutherans began holding services and formed the first Swedish congregation in New England, the Bethesda Swedish Lutheran Church. Within 30 years, the Campello neighborhood was host to three additional Swedish churches of different denominations—Baptist, Congregational, and Methodist. Also, the area was home to the Scandinavian Salvation Army. All were clustered within two city blocks. In the Montello section, a second Lutheran church was later established. These foundational congregations—though shaped by time, merger, and relocation—remain vital cornerstones of their communities.

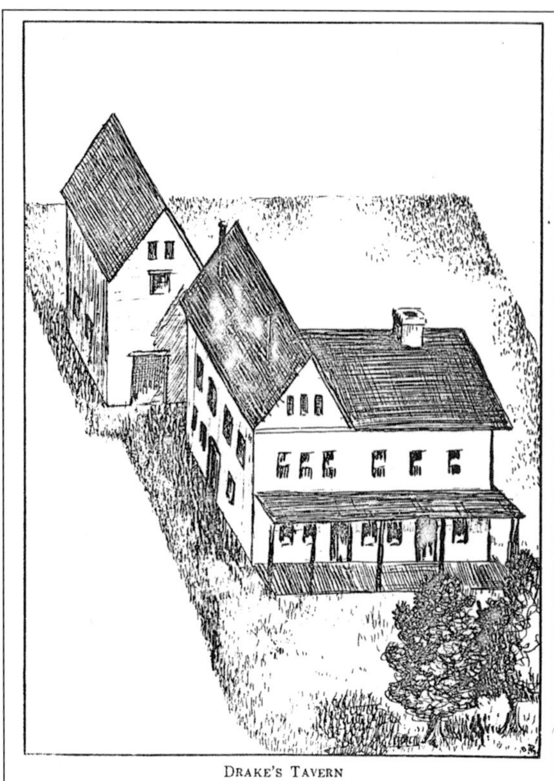
DRAKE'S TAVERN

As unlikely a place as any for a church to have its beginnings was Drake's Tavern. This establishment, owned by Postmaster Aaron Drake and later known as the Salisbury House, was located on the northwest corner of Main and Tremont Streets. Drake's was the first home to three of the Swedish churches in Campello—the Lutheran, Congregational, and Baptist. For a number of years, services were held in a large room on the second floor.

On Sunday, November 13, 1870, Brockton (then North Bridgewater) was host to the world-famous Swedish soprano Christina Nilsson. The *Gazette* announced that "for once our town may felicitate itself on the exquisite pleasure of sharing in a musical feast with the prominent cities of the land." Performing for the benefit of the fledgling Swedish Lutheran Church, the concert was held before an overflow crowd at the Church of the Disciples (Unitarian). More than $2,000 was raised for the construction of a new church. As an interesting footnote, the Old Colony Railroad put on a special train to transport Mlle. Nilsson from Boston to Brockton. The return trip to Boston, some 20 miles, was made in as many minutes, something of a record in these early railroading days.

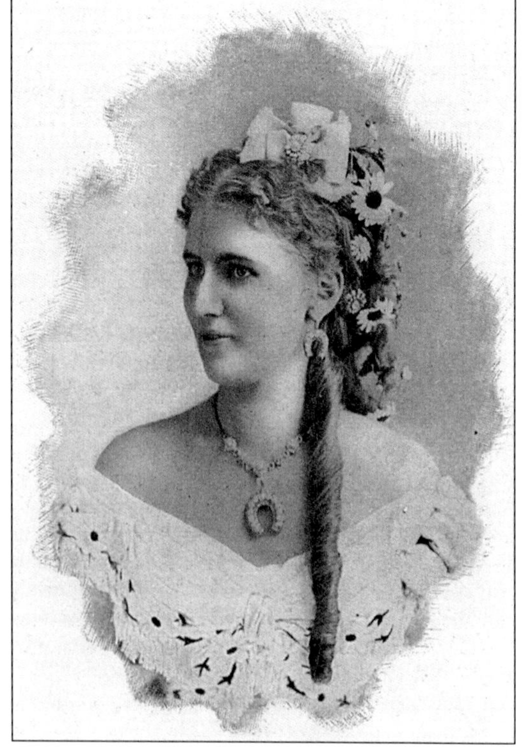

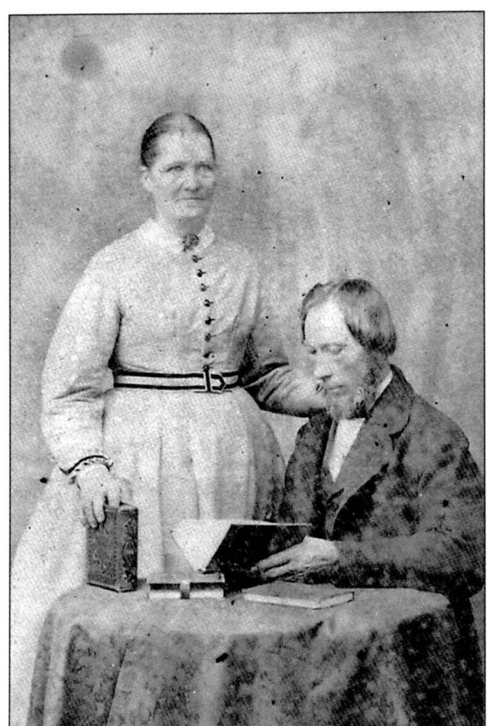

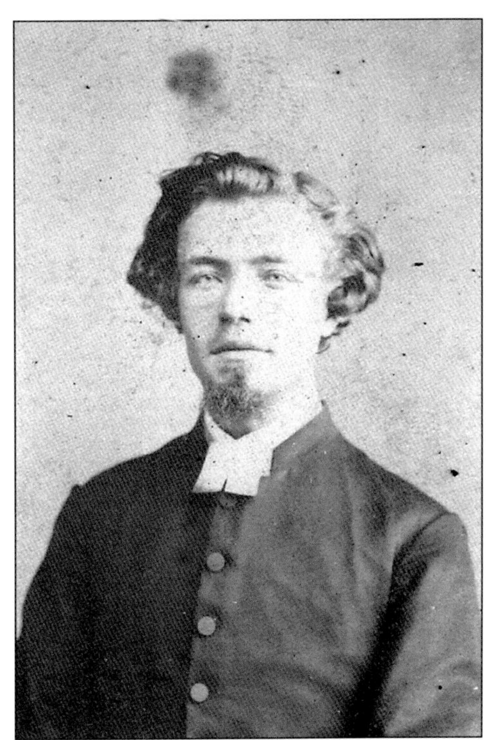

Among the early Lutheran lay leaders was Peter Blomstrand (above left, with his wife). It was Blomstrand who was responsible for Henric Oliver Lindeblad (right) being the first Swedish Lutheran clergyman to serve a congregation in New England. Lindeblad was called to serve in June 1869 and was given an annual salary of $825, plus a Christmas Day offering.

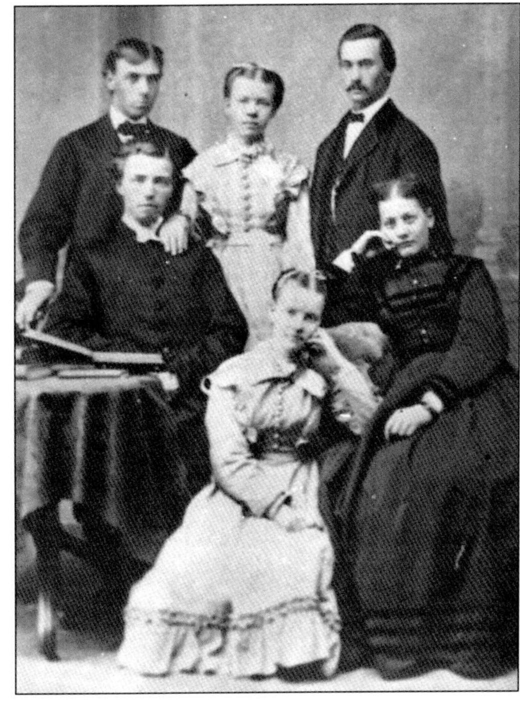

The first Swedish young people in New England to be prepared for their First Communion were confirmed on October 17, 1869, by Pastor Lindeblad. The confirmands were four members of the Bengtsson family—Anton Rudolf, Amanda Maria, Jennie Mathilda, and Hilda Wilhelmina—and Oscar Johnson.

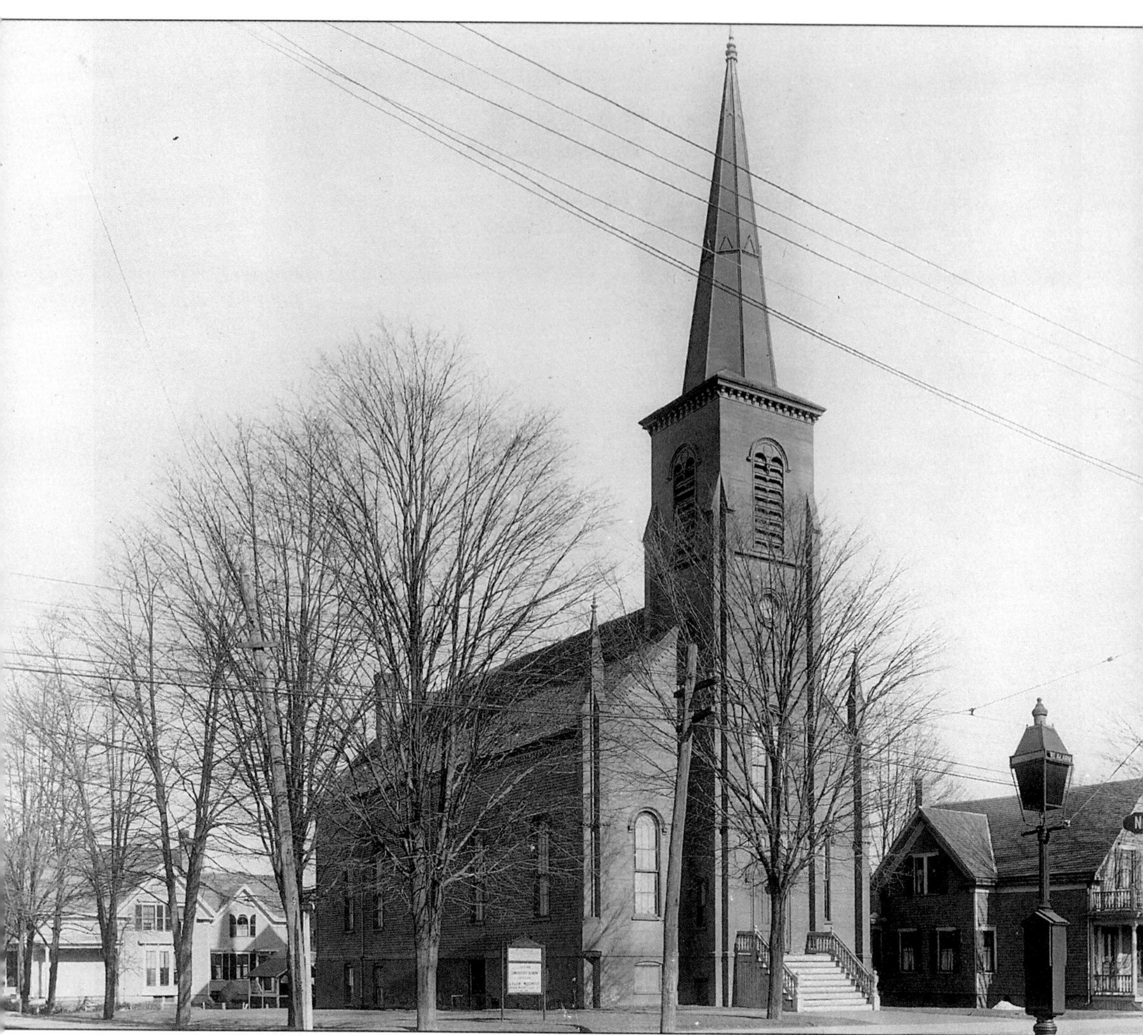

On January 1, 1870, Brockton's first Lutheran congregation voted to erect a church, and a double lot was purchased on Main Street from W. Kingman for $500. On Sunday, February 12, 1871, the new building was dedicated. The construction cost was $8,097.80, and the debt carried was $2,067.96. In 1881, the main structure was lifted from its foundation and a full basement and assembly hall was installed underneath at a cost of $1,830. In 1888, the growing parish built their parsonage adjacent to the church. In 1907, continued growth caused the congregation to begin raising funds for a new building and, eight years later, a building committee was formed. Delayed by World War I, construction of the new granite structure started in 1922 on the same site. It should be noted that the architect called for the foundation stones of the old church to be incorporated in the new, thus building the future upon the labor and faith of those early pioneers.

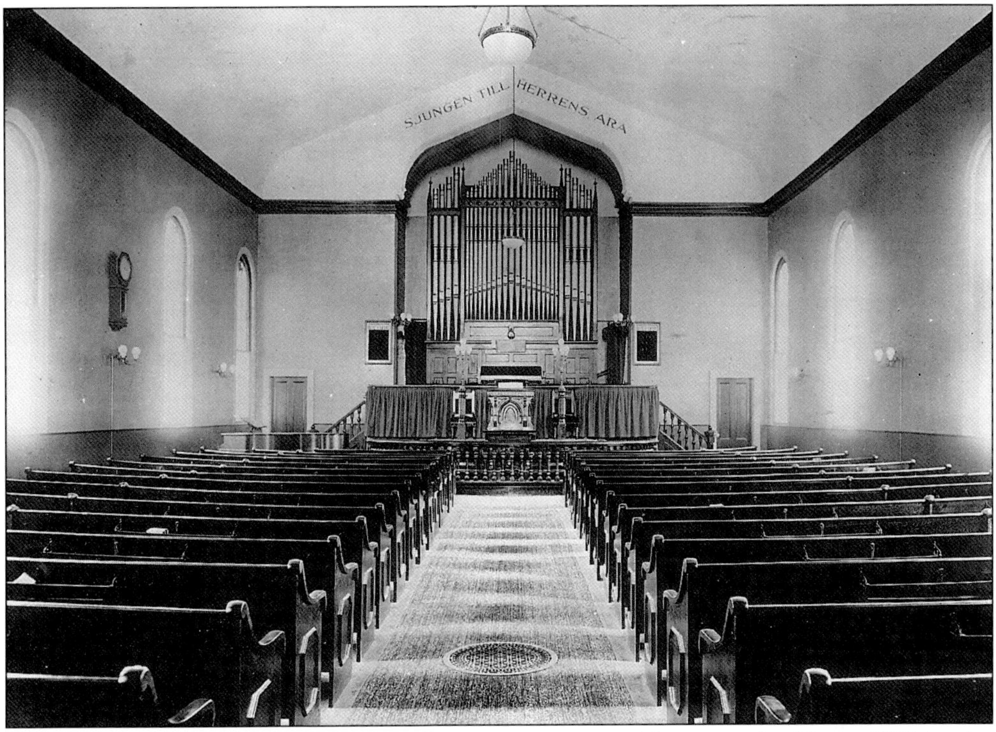

This photograph and the one on the opposite page were sold as a set for 50¢ in 1922 by the Lutheran Brotherhood to help raise money for the new church building. The pipe organ, which had been installed in 1890, was sold in 1922 to the Abington Universalist Church for $500. The last service in the old church was held on April 24, 1922. The next day, the structure was razed, the spire falling point first and piercing the sidewalk while parishioners watched with tearful eyes.

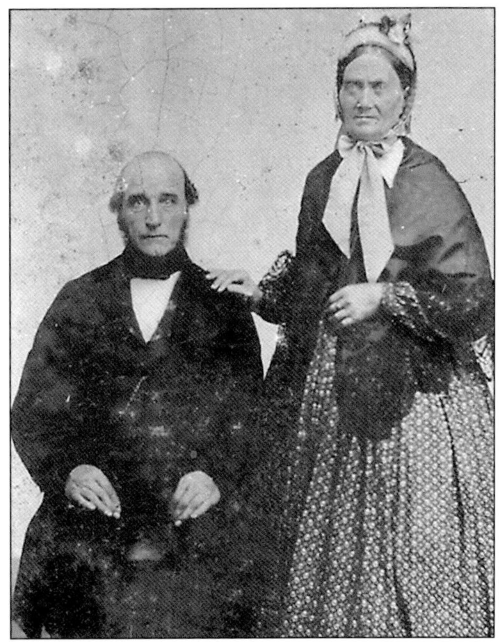

On September 4, 1870, a small group of Swedish immigrants laid the cornerstone of the first Swedish house of worship in New England. This photograph of the Youngquists, along with many others, was sealed in a copper casket and placed in that stone. Some 52 years later, in a ceremony at Keith Hall, that container was opened. The contents were found in excellent condition.

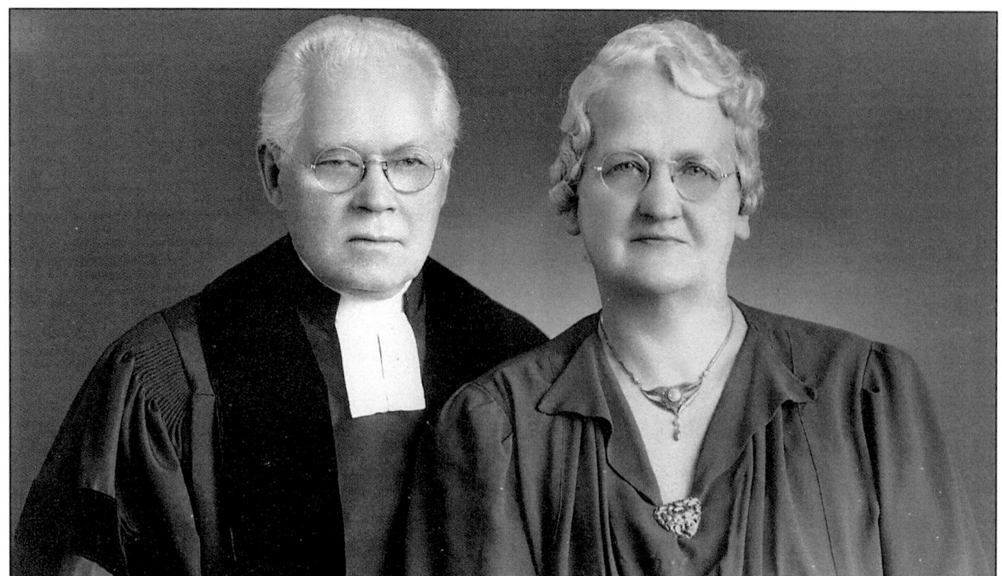

Resigning his post as president of Upsala College in New Jersey, Peter Froeberg and his wife, Annette, arrived in Brockton on October 8, 1918, to begin a ministry that would last for more than 35 years. Arriving at the height of the influenza epidemic, Dr. Froeberg would shepherd the congregation through two world wars and a depression, while increasing membership to 1,500 people and erecting a grand new edifice.

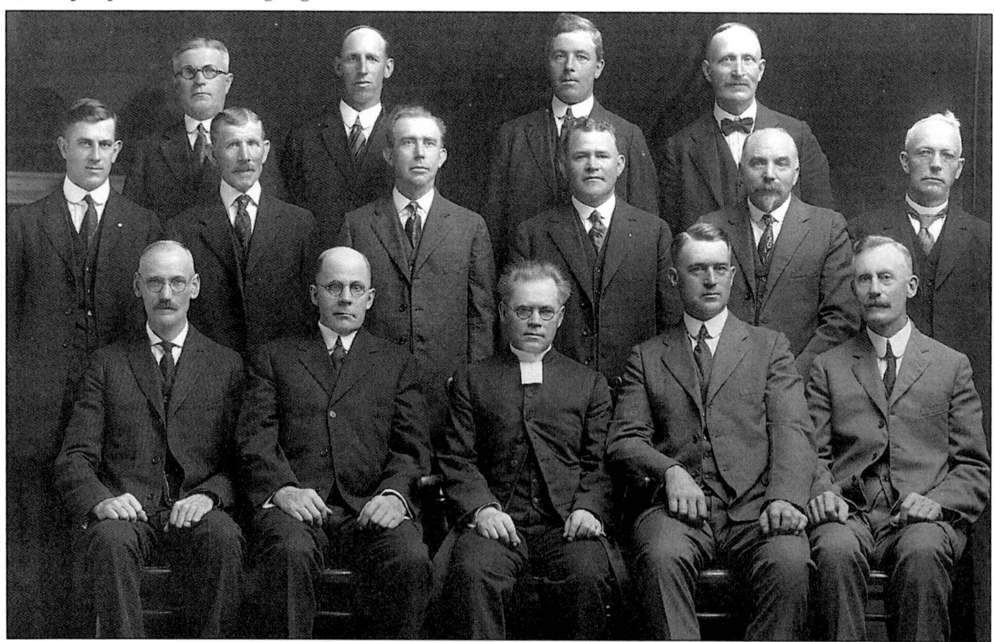

Many prominent businessmen and tradesmen made up the committee appointed to oversee the construction of the new Swedish Lutheran church building. From left to right are the following: (front row) C.W. Otto Lawson; J. Emil Johnson, treasurer; Dr. Peter Froeberg, chairman; G. Arthur Moberg, secretary; and John Warme; (middle row) J. Eric Winberg; Magnus Anderson; Hjalmar Freberg; Robert Peterson; Paulin Peterson; and Andrew Swanson; (back row) Robert Mansbach; Carl Johnson; Ivan Johnson; and Hokan Johnson.

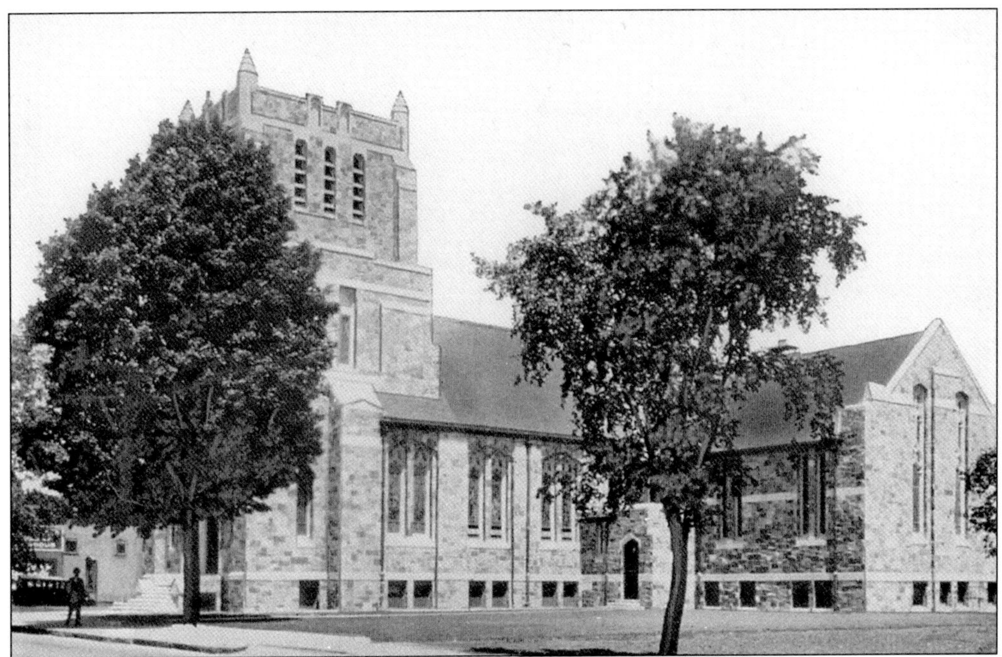

The imposing new edifice of the First Swedish Evangelical Lutheran Church was designed by architect Charles Coveney, a partner at Brigham, Coveney, & Bisbee of Boston. The building contract in the amount of $99,201 was signed on April 26, 1922. The cornerstone was laid on October 15, 1922. The first service was held in the vestry level on September 30, 1923.

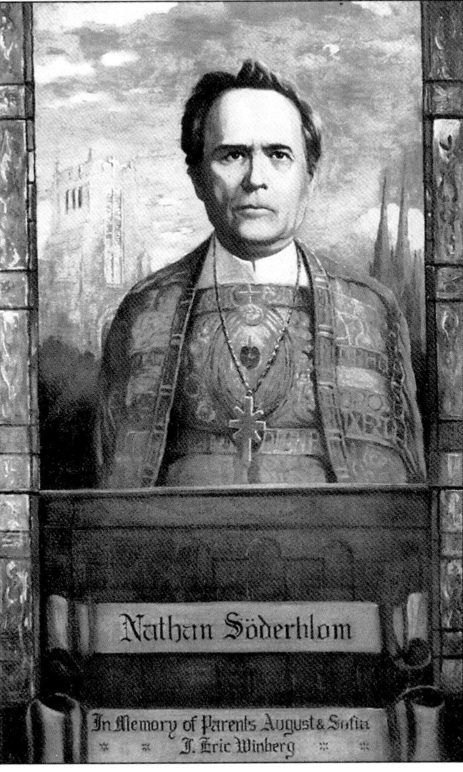


On Thanksgiving Day, November 29, 1923, Archbishop Nathan Soderblom (primate of the Church of Sweden) dedicated the new church structure. More than 1,600 people crowded the new building to witness this impressive ceremony. This painting of Soderblom, in a window niche in the nave, was given by J. Eric Winberg in memory of his parents. The archbishop received the Nobel Prize for Peace in 1930.

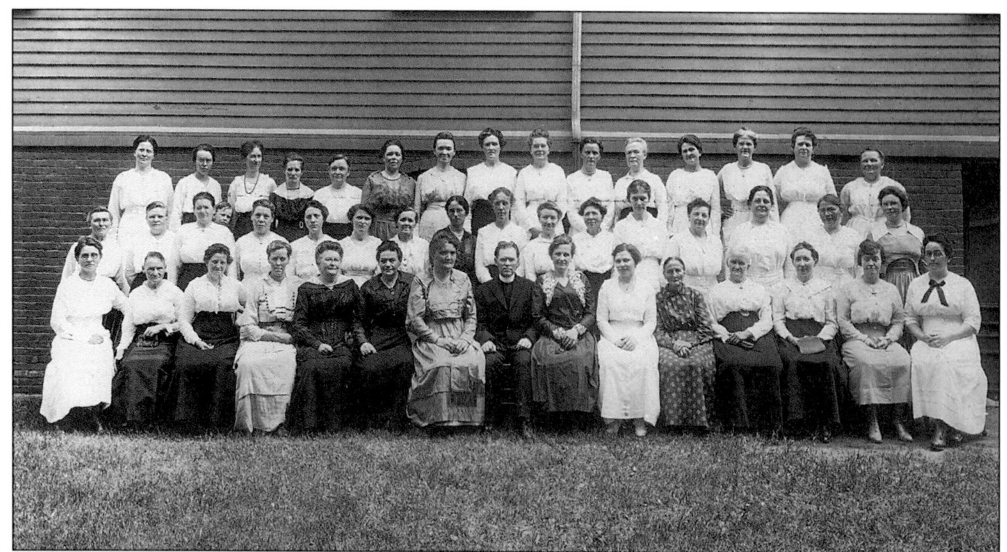

This *c.* 1919 photograph shows the Missionary Society beside the old building. By 1925, this group consisted of about 125 women instrumental in raising funds for the new church.

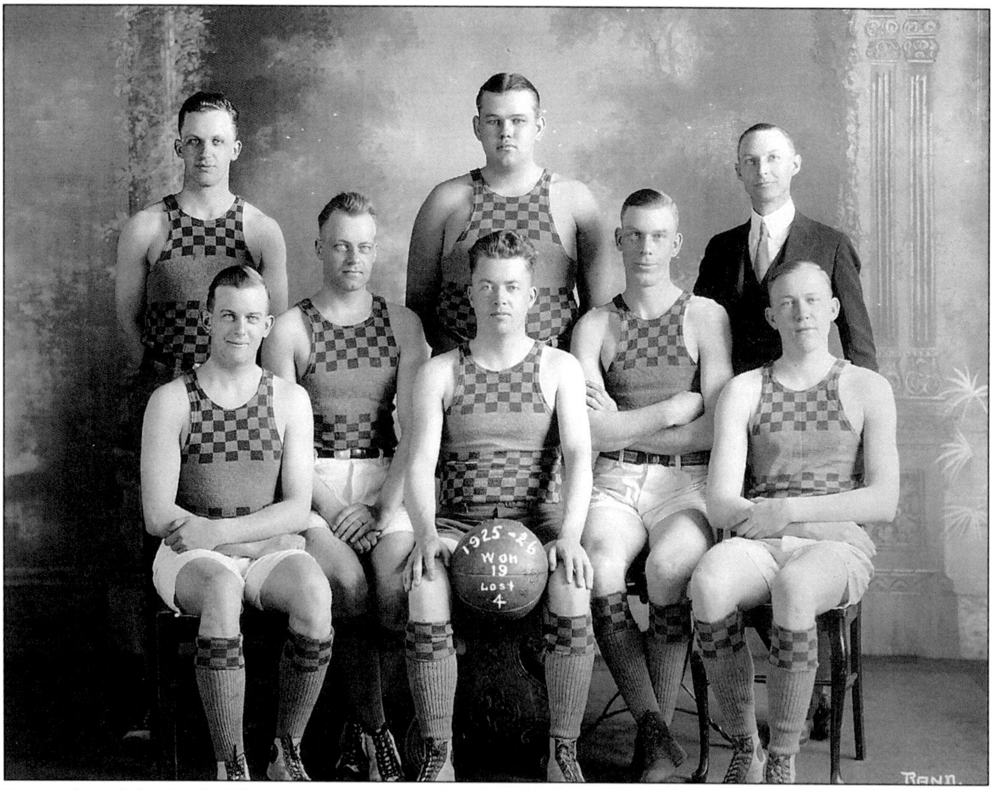

Inter-church basketball league games were played at the YMCA, South Congregational gymnasium, and other locations throughout the city. Shown wearing stylish uniforms and high-tops is the 1925–1926 championship team. They are, from left to right, as follows: (front row) Carl Sondeen; Arthur Hollertz; and Helge Persson, captain; (middle row) Ragnar Paulson and Carl Johnson; (back row) Walter Hollertz; Oscar Holmberg; and Waldemar Jacobson, manager.

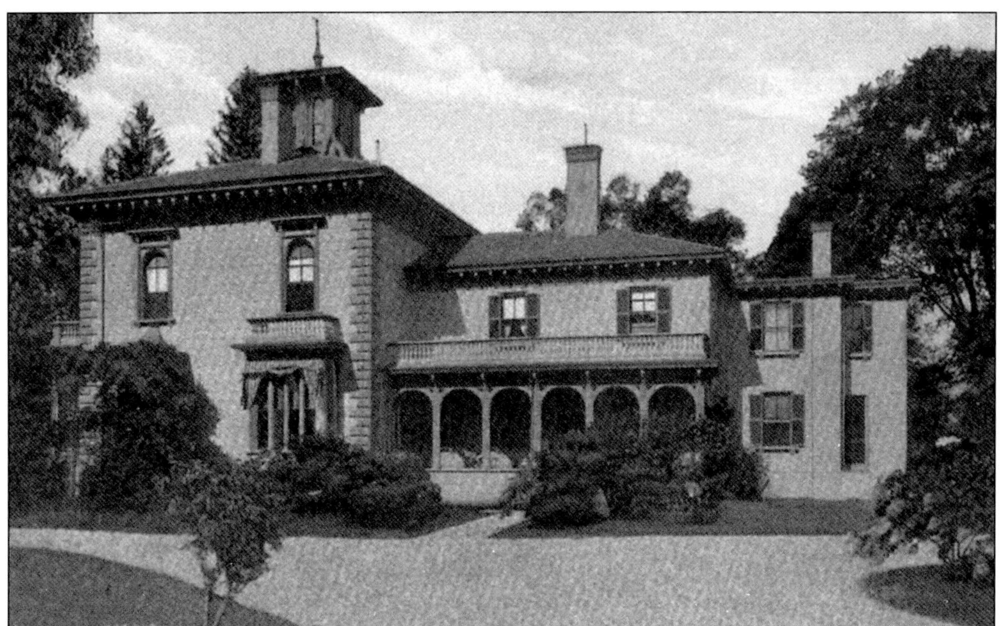

Founded in Avon in 1907, the Lutheran Children's Home and Orphanage was an institution of the Boston Conference and, later, New England Conference of the Augustana Synod. Dr. J. Alfred Anderson, a pastor of First Lutheran, was a founding member of the home and its first treasurer. Amelia Rabinius served as the matron from 1907 to 1938. She was a pillar of strength to the institution and to the Gethsemane Lutheran Church in Montello. A nurturing home to hundreds of boys and girls for five decades, the home was forced to close in the 1950s due to social changes.

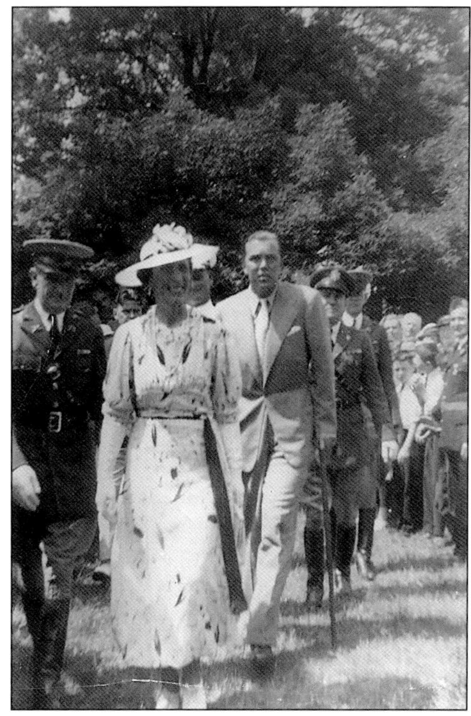

The tercentenary year of the arrival of the first Swedes in America was 1938. In celebration, the royal family toured the United States and included Brockton on its itinerary. Crown Princess Louise and Prince Bertil greeted local Swedes at a joyous celebration held at the Lutheran Children's Home in Avon on Sunday, July 10, 1938. Dr. Peter Froeberg officially greeted the royal visitors, and hundreds lined the motorcade route from West Bridgewater to Avon. It was a momentous event in the lives of the local Swedish Americans who still held a great affinity for their ancestral home.

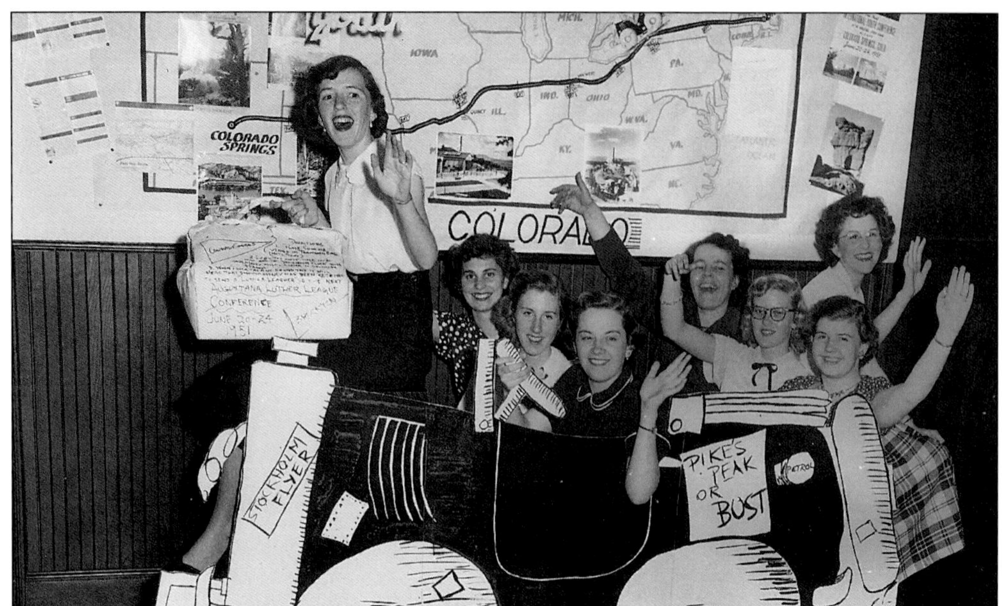


"Pike's Peak or Bust" was the cry of these young women from First Lutheran in 1951. Colorado bound for a youth convention of the Augustana Synod are, from left to right, Marjorie Anderson, Grace Sigren, Marion Nelson, June Hollertz, Gertrude Forsstrom, Lois Oberg, Jennie Freberg, and Inez Johnson. Young people have always played a vital role in the life of Swedish churches. (Stanley Bauman photograph.)

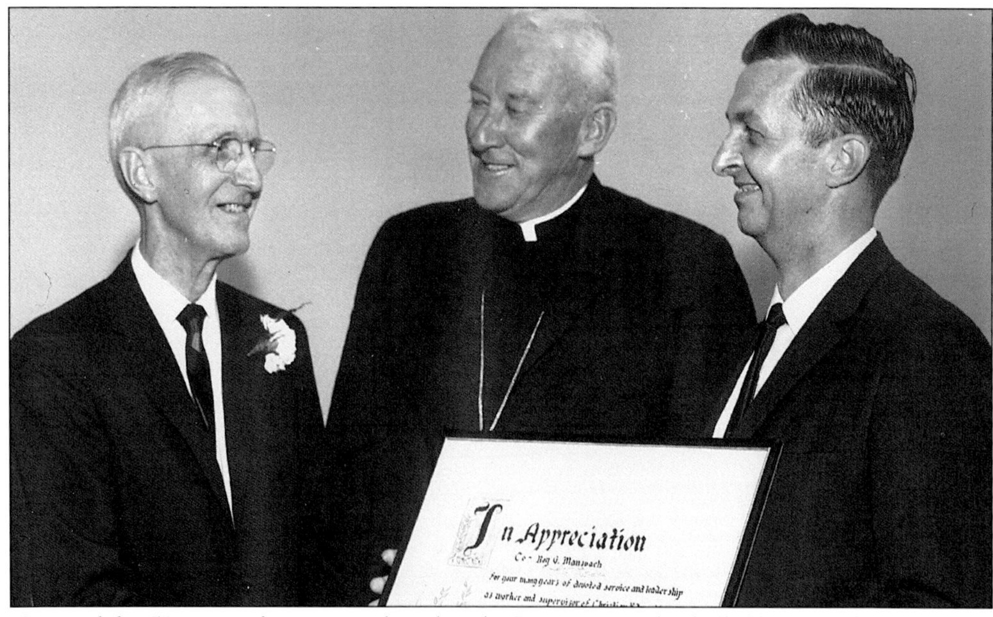


Honored for 50 years of service to his church, Roy G. Mansbach (left) was a dedicated and inspirational leader. A Sunday school superintendent and teacher, he was also the author of numerous devotional booklets, a contributing writer to the *Lutheran Companion* magazine, the composer of several hymns, and a poet. Much of his working life was spent as the "Swedish salesman" at Atherton's Furniture Company. Making the presentation are the Reverend Dr. O. Karl Olander and Alden Anderson Jr. (Stanley Bauman photograph.)

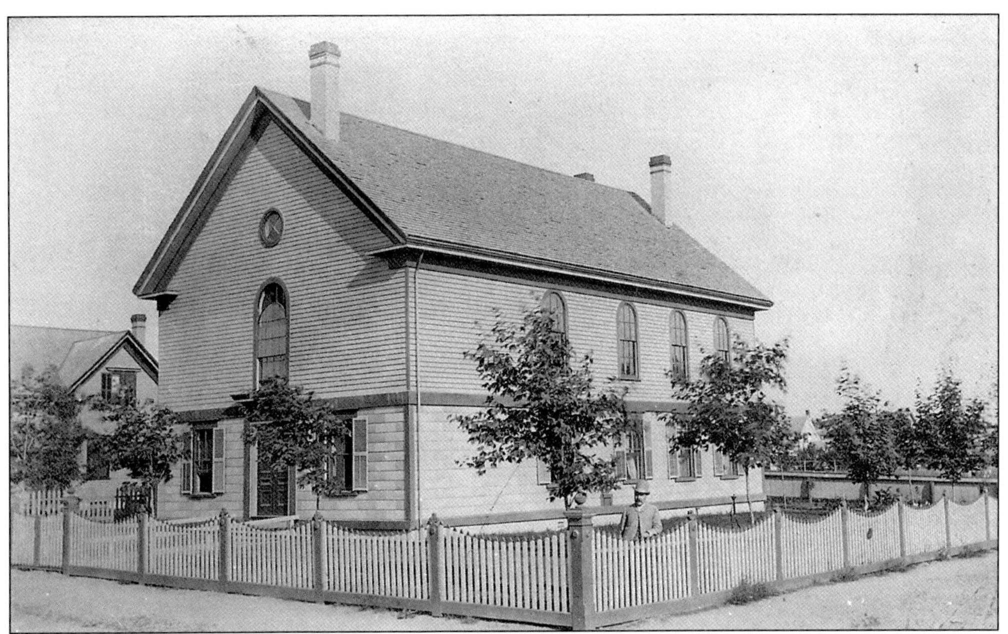

In 1881, the first permanent home of the Evangelical Independent Mission Church in Campello was constructed at the corner of Laureston and Nilsson Streets. Seven years later, to make way for a new structure, the building was sold and moved to a nearby location at the corner of Denton and Nilsson Streets. For many years, it was occupied by the Scandinavian Salvation Army and, today, is home to the St. George Lodge, AF & AM.

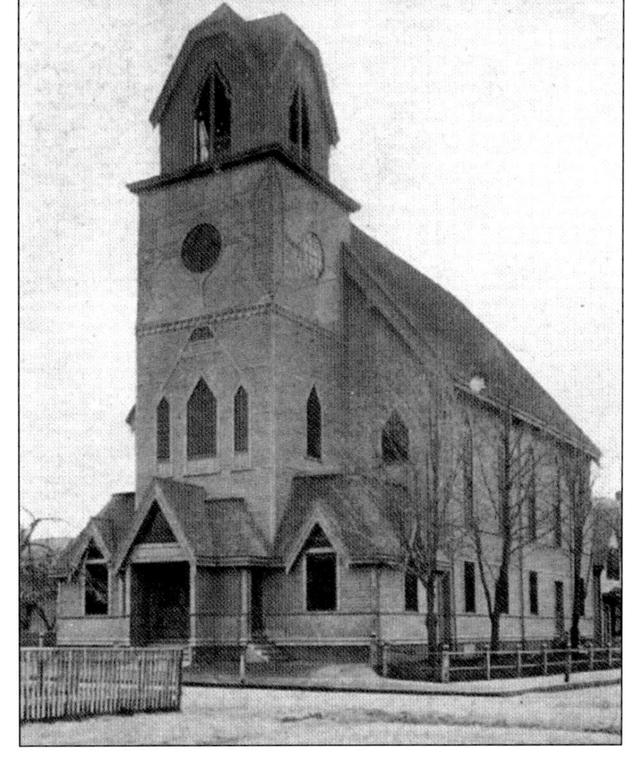

During construction of its new house of worship, the congregation received permission to change its name to the Swedish Evangelical Congregational Church of Brockton, a name that remained until 1949. The church is now located in East Bridgewater and is known as Community Covenant Church.

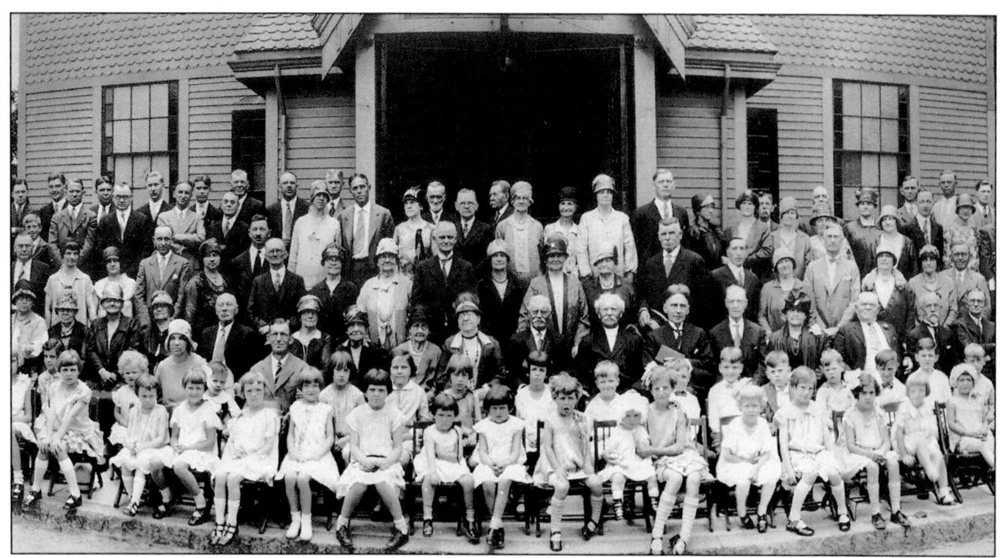

Members of the Swedish Evangelical Congregational Church assemble for a Sunday morning photograph *c.* 1929.

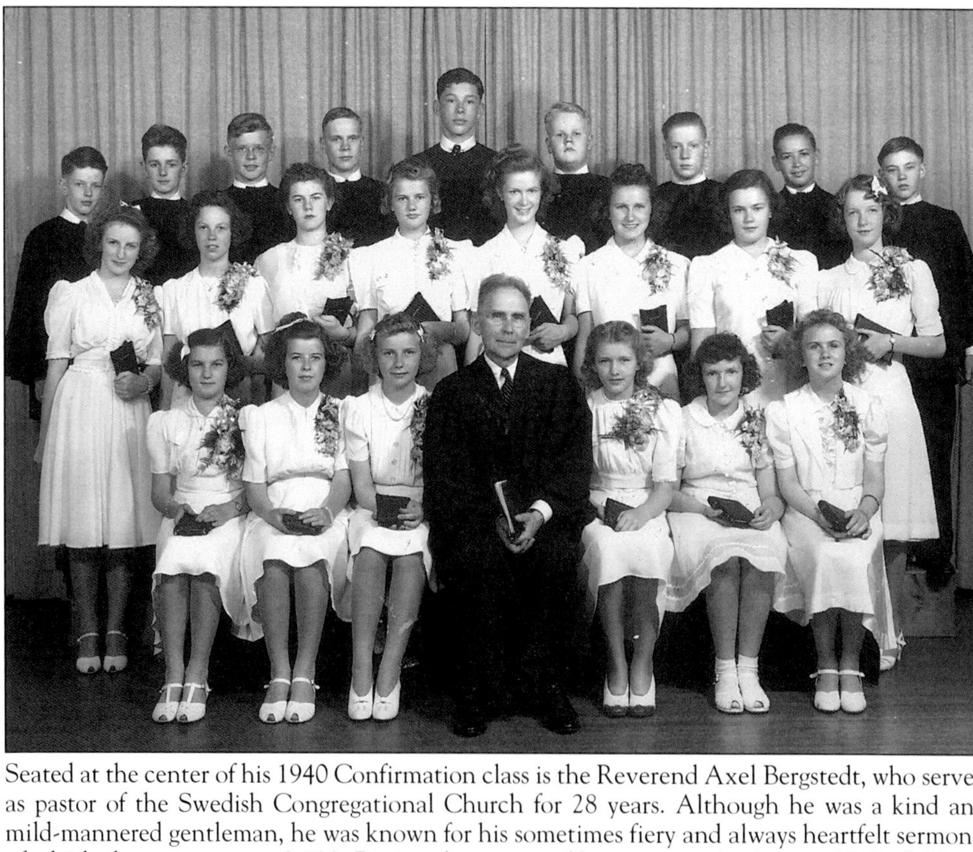

Seated at the center of his 1940 Confirmation class is the Reverend Axel Bergstedt, who served as pastor of the Swedish Congregational Church for 28 years. Although he was a kind and mild-mannered gentleman, he was known for his sometimes fiery and always heartfelt sermons, of which there were some 2,400. During the course of his ministry, he baptized 392 children, married 448 couples, officiated at 644 funerals, and made 8,288 visits to the hospitalized or shut-in members of this congregation. He retired in 1947.

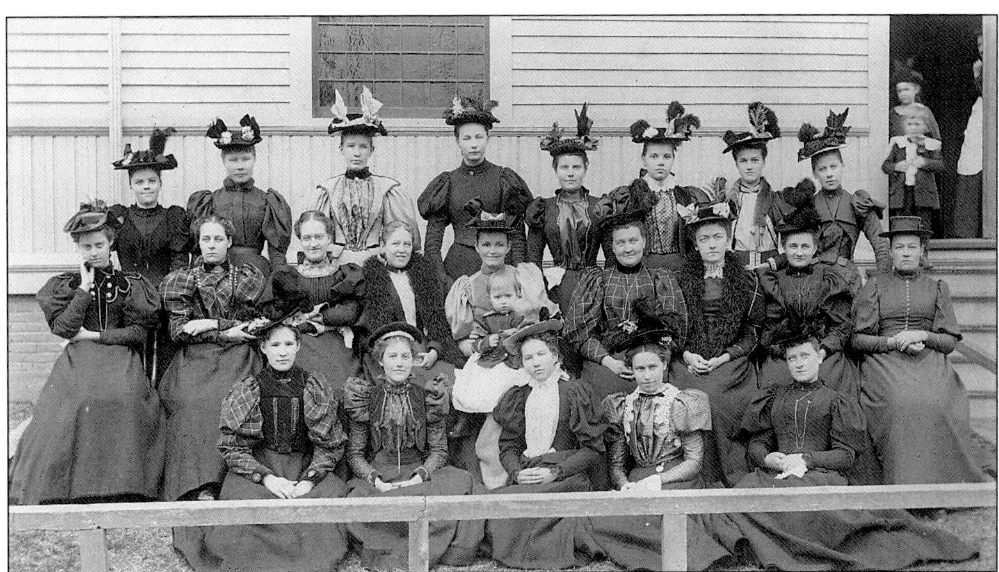

Elegantly dressed, these Swedish Congregational ladies pose in their stylish dresses and hats. The young onlookers seem somewhat astonished by the goings-on. Although the event and date were not recorded, the names of the ladies are, from left to right, as follows: (front row) Amanda Franzen, Jennie Abrahamson, Esther Gustafson, Edith Newberg, and Hanna Benson; (middle row) Maaora Cook (believed to be the proprietor of Cook's Boarding House), Ada Hultman Johnson, Ida Bergman, Anna Steele, Mrs. J. Dahlborg and child, Augusta Nelson, Ellen Bogren, and Mrs. August Swanson; (back row) Hanna Johnson, Augusta Nelson, Mrs. Otto Lawson, Anna Hallberg, Freda Nelson, Hilma Johnson, and Mrs. Gust Anderson.

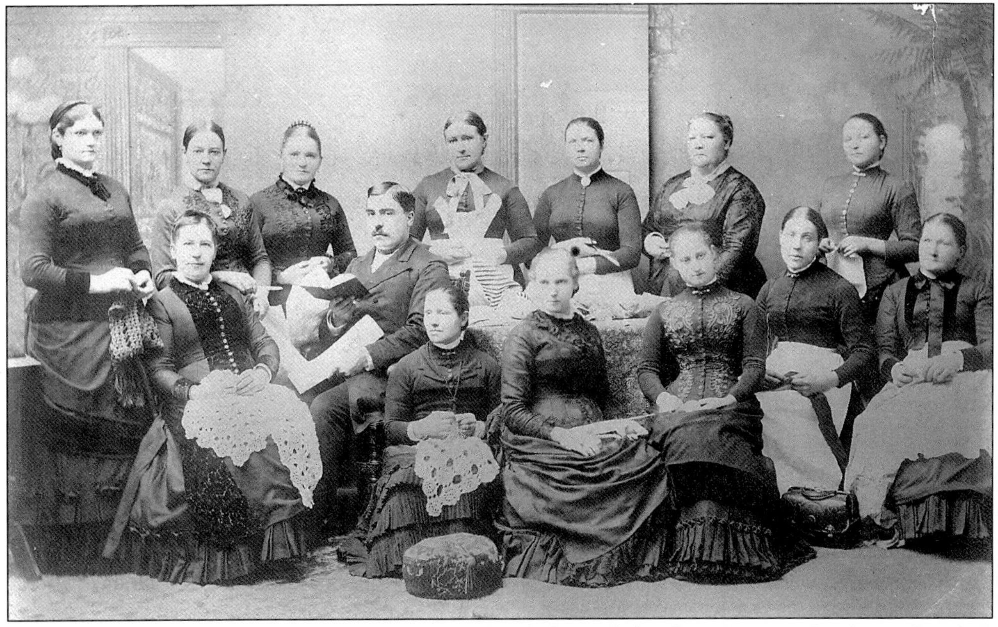

The Reverend Axel Nordin is seated with the ladies of the first Sewing Circle at Swedish Congregational Church. Much of the crochet and other work painstakingly produced by this group was used in charitable efforts. The embroidered bodices and finely pleated skirts were a true fashion statement in 1885.

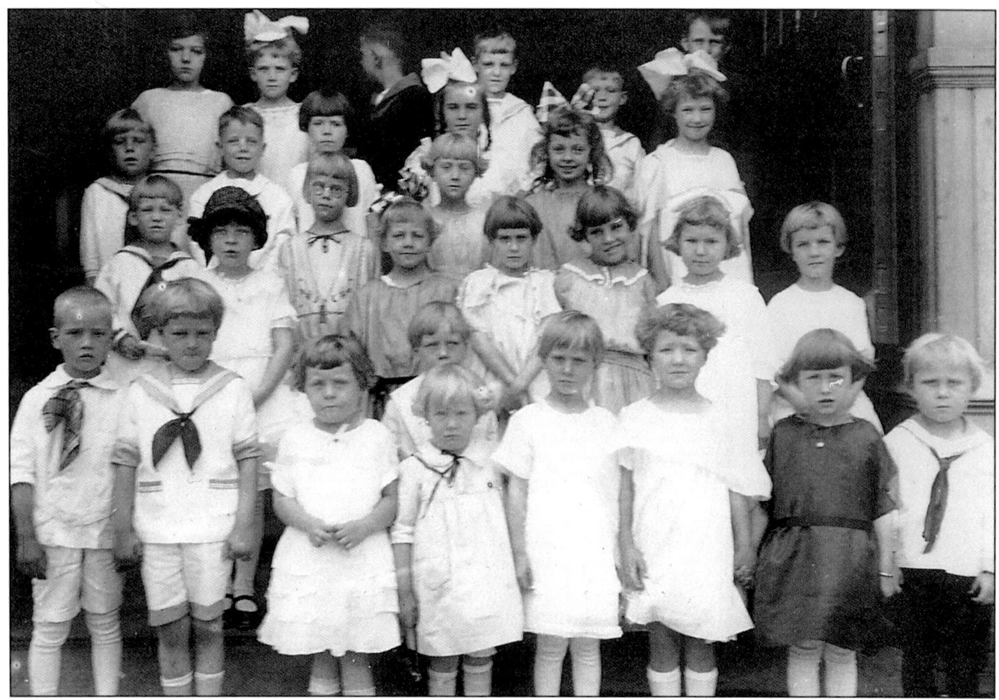

Shown here is the 1920 Sunday school class of the Swedish Congregational Church. Two members of this class would marry brothers from the adjoining town of East Bridgewater. Merriel Thompson (fourth row, second from the left) married W. Nelson Perkins. Dana Anderson (second row, second from the left) married Nelson's younger brother, Alfred Perkins. Both weddings were performed at "Swedish Congo."

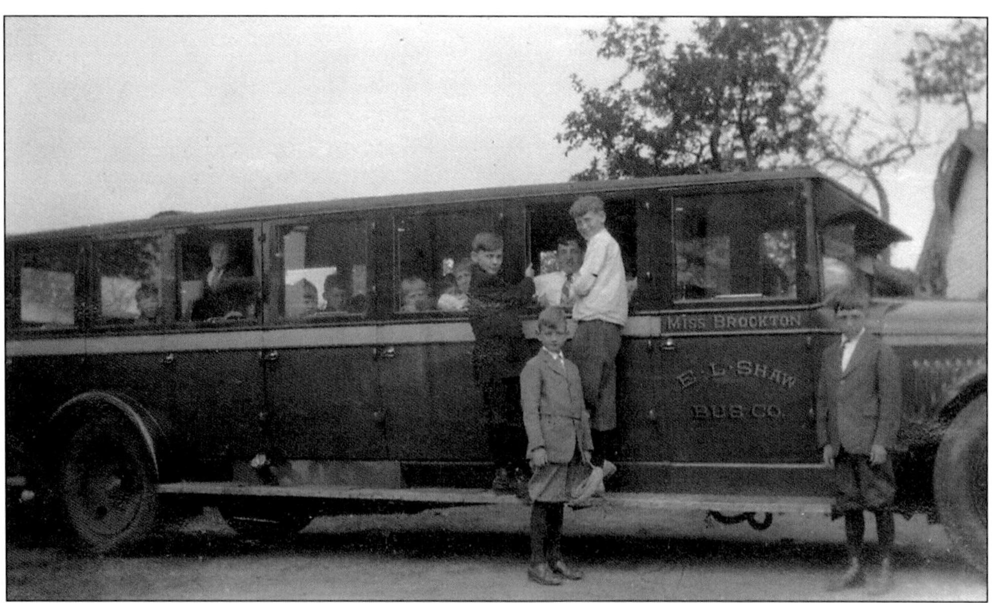


Children from the Swedish Congregational Church boarded this bus, the "Miss Brockton," and traveled to Cromwell, Connecticut, where the church maintained an orphanage.

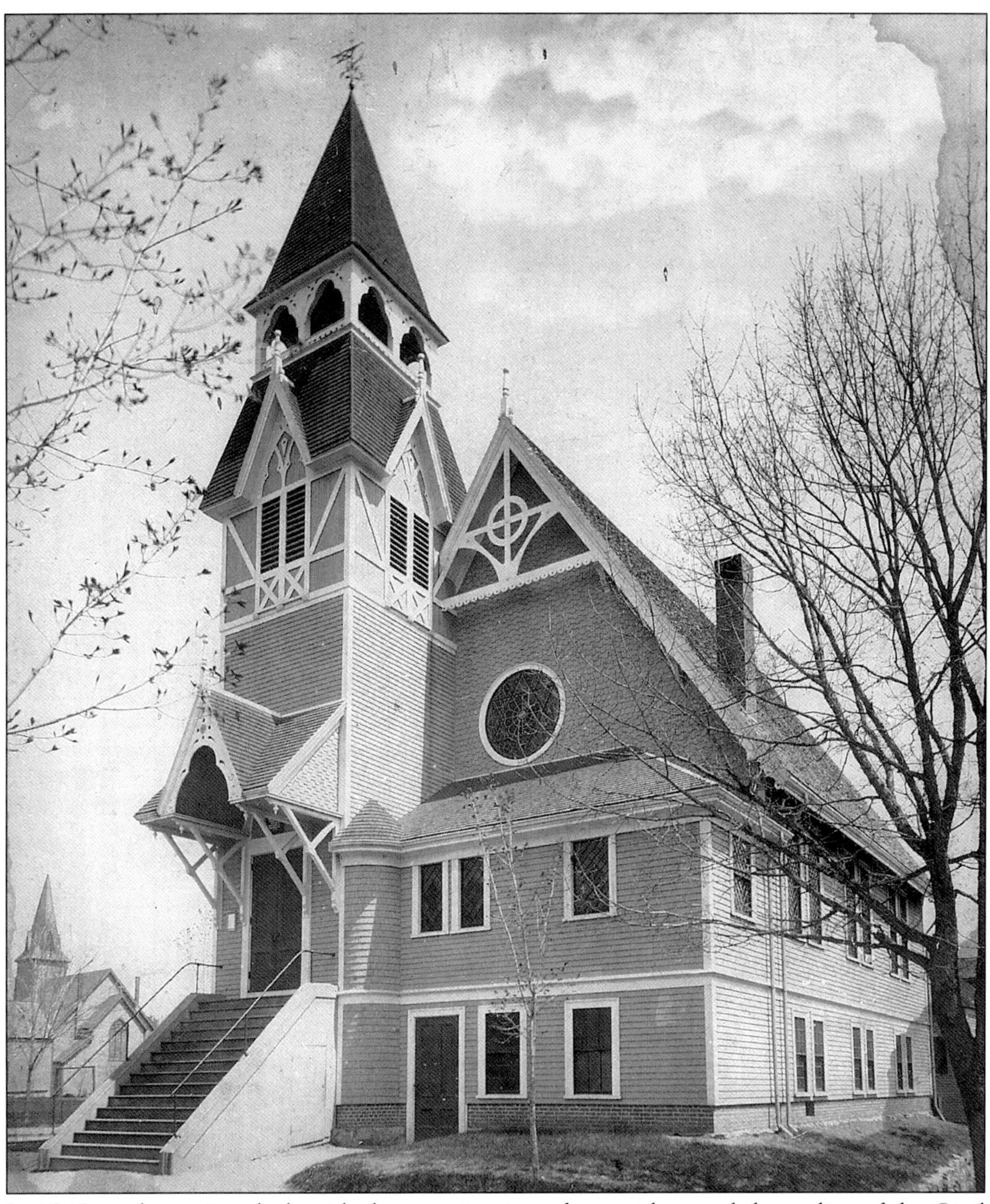

In 1865, as the nation dealt with the assassination of a president and the ending of the Civil War, the first Swedes arrived in North Easton. These immigrants, drawn by employment opportunities at the Ames Shovel Works, brought the Lutheran faith with them. During the early 1870s, Pastor Anders Hult traveled from Campello to hold services in the homes of these early pioneers. Services were later held at McCarthy's Hall and Williams' Hall. In October 1890, the Swedish Evangelical Lutheran Church Society was formed. It was incorporated on March 22, 1892. Known as the Swedish Evangelical Libanon Lutheran Church, the congregation erected its first building at the corner of Williams and Jenny Lind Streets. The land was purchased in August, and the building was dedicated that fall. A.M. Benander became the first pastor in 1897 and, in 1898, Mrs. Frederick Lothrop Ames donated the pews. In 1908, the building was severed in two and 16 feet was added to the middle to accommodate the growing parish. Today, the church is known as Holy Trinity Evangelical Lutheran.

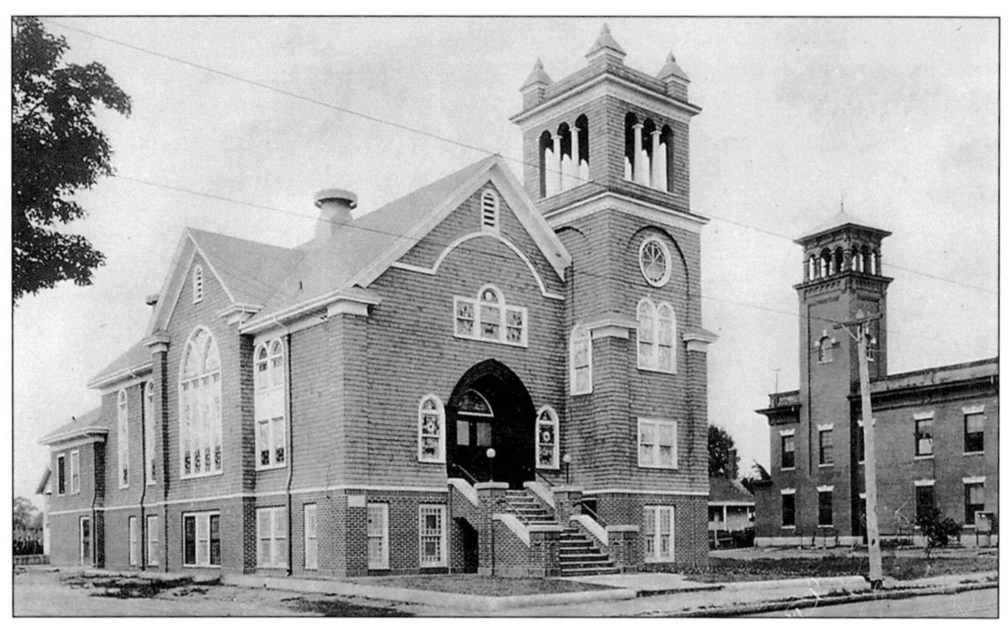

Meeting in living rooms in the Montello section of Brockton and, later, at the home of Axel Kling, the Swedish Evangelical Lutheran Gethsemane Church was incorporated on July 16, 1895. The first church was constructed on Ames Street in late 1895. The lower level of the present church, on Main Street, was built in 1911. The superstructure was added in 1922–1923. The charter members were Mr. and Mrs. N.P. Olson, Mr. and Mrs. Gustaf Polson, Mr. and Mrs. Axel Berglund, Mr. and Mrs. Axel Kling, Mr. and Mrs. L.P. Peterson, Mr. and Mrs. Nils P. Bolin, Mr. and Mrs. M.P. Johnson, Mr. and Mrs. John Anderson, Mr. and Mrs. August Peterson, Mr. and Mrs. August Swanson, Mr. and Mrs. John Polson, Mr. and Mrs. Charles H.L. Kahler, Mr. and Mrs. John Peterson, Charles Pearson, Ludwig Lundvall, and Ann Lundvall.

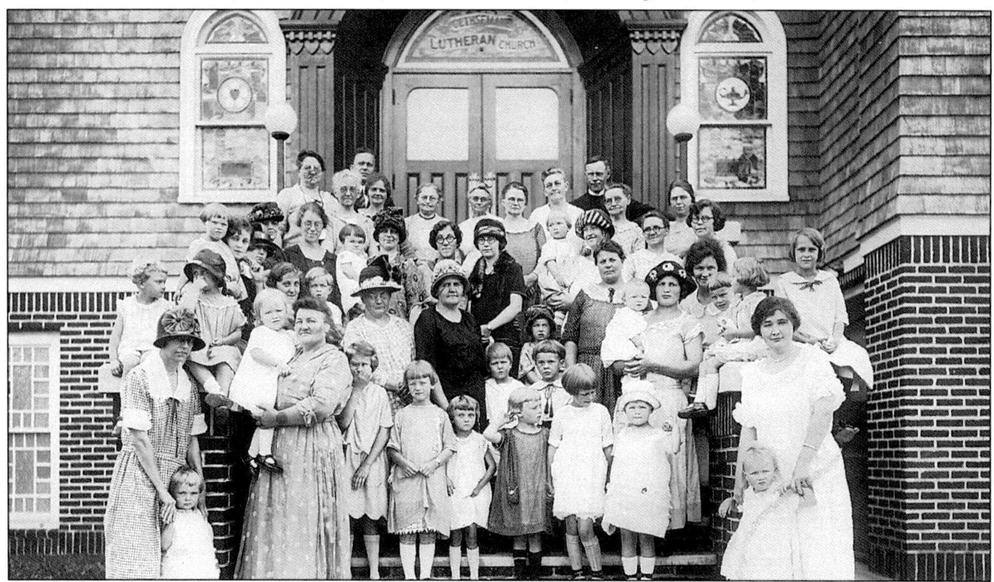


Shown in this photograph are the ladies and children of the Cradle Roll shortly after the completion of the new church. The young girl being held by Emma Youngren (front row, second from left) is Helen Snook, church archivist and historian.

"A big-hearted fearless leader" was a description from a congregational history of the Reverend William Frendberg. Arriving from New York on March 1, 1922, where he had been pastor of the large Gustavus Adolphus Lutheran Church, Frendberg wasted no time in completing the building that had been started in 1911. The new church was dedicated on September 16, 1923. Frendberg married Ansie Miller, a member of the congregation, and, on June 5, 1931, resigned his post for another call.

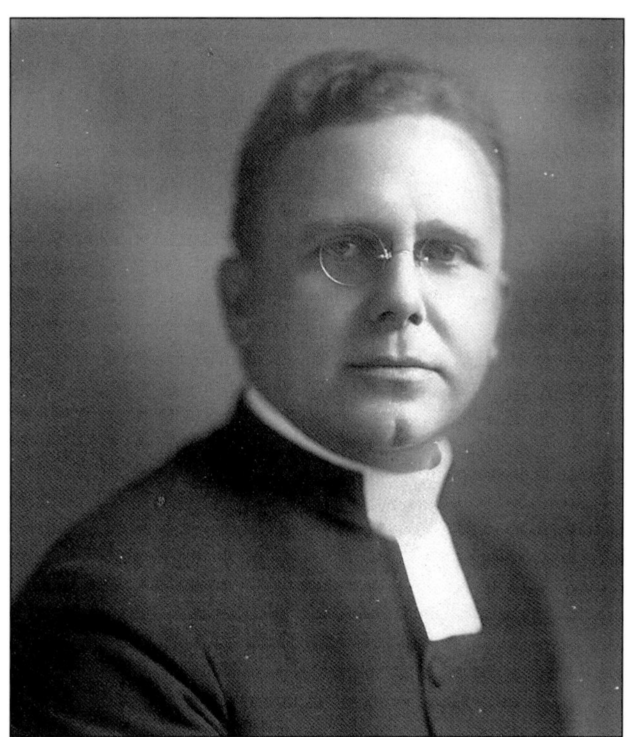

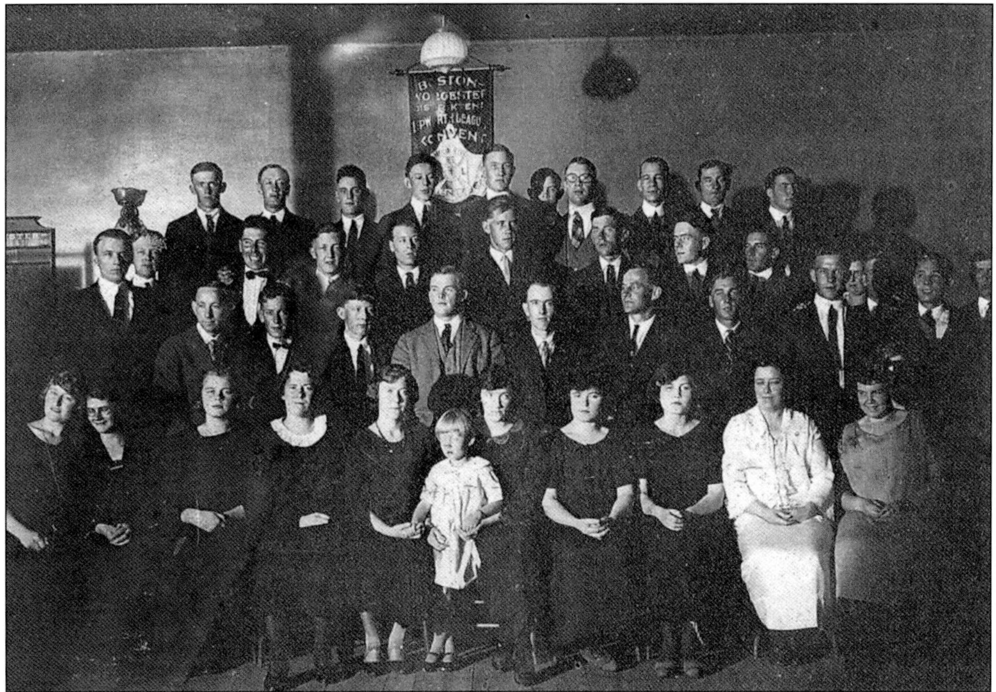

Learning to speak and write English and learning the ways of their new homeland was a priority for Swedish immigrants. Shown in 1923 are 38 graduates of an evening Americanization class taught at the Swedish Methodist Church. Many of these men and women would spend their days performing various jobs at local shoe factories.

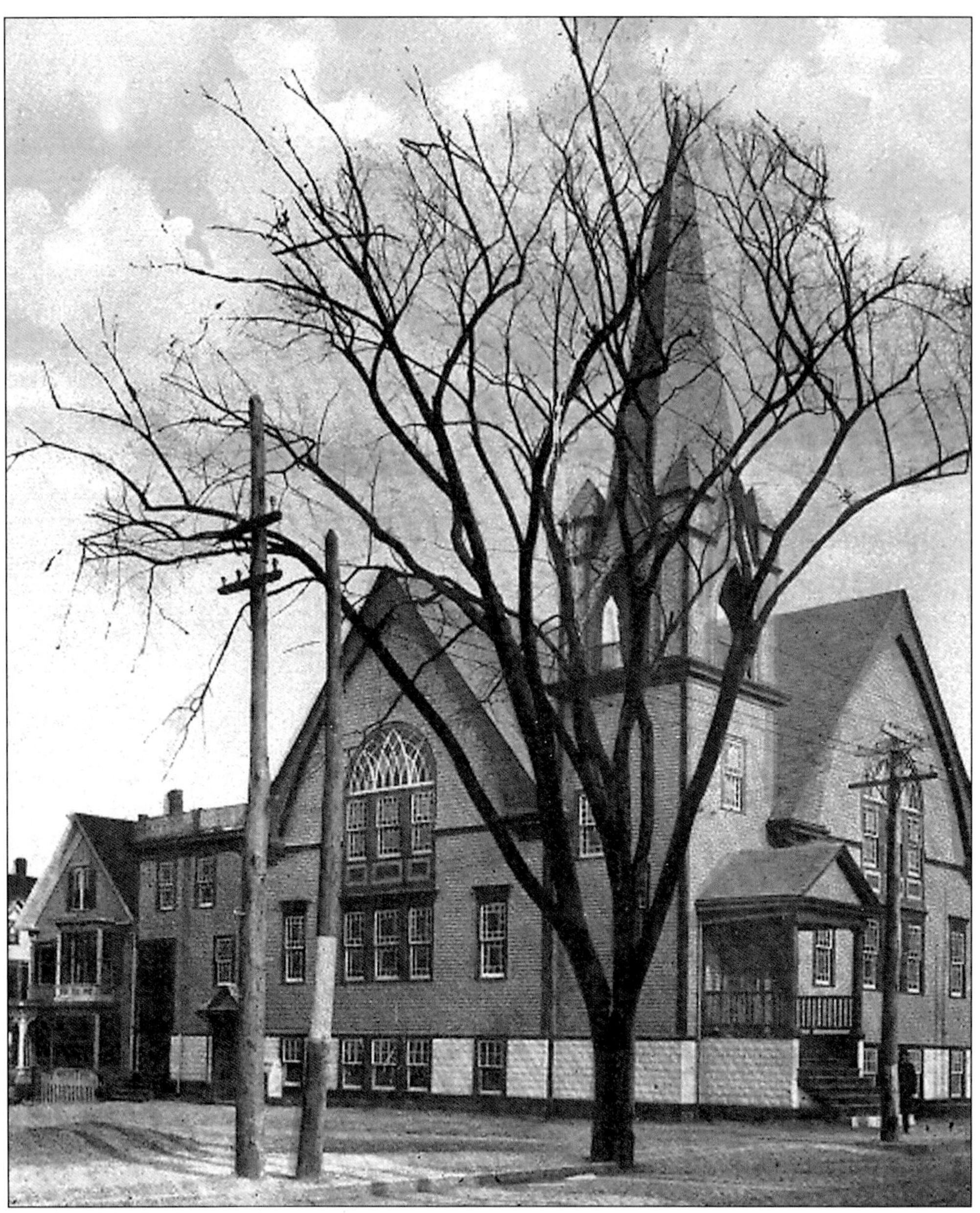

The Swedish Baptist Church was one of five churches established in Brockton by Swedish immigrants between 1867 and 1895. Pastor A. Tjerlund was the first preacher to serve the congregation and, under his direction, the church was formally organized on July 24, 1883. There were 11 members. The first church building was constructed in 1885 at the corner of Main and Grand Streets. The facility shown here, constructed on the same site, was dedicated in February 1903. This house of worship served its parishioners until 1958, when the parish relocated to a new building on the former estate of Harold Keith, a son of shoe industry magnate George E. Keith. Groundbreaking ceremonies took place on October 13, 1957. Among those participating were Hjalmar Peterson (mayor), Edward Ekstrom (chairman of the board of trustees), Henry Hanson (vice chairman of the Swedish Baptist Church), and Clifford Carlson (chairman of the board of deacons).

# Three

# People and Pastimes

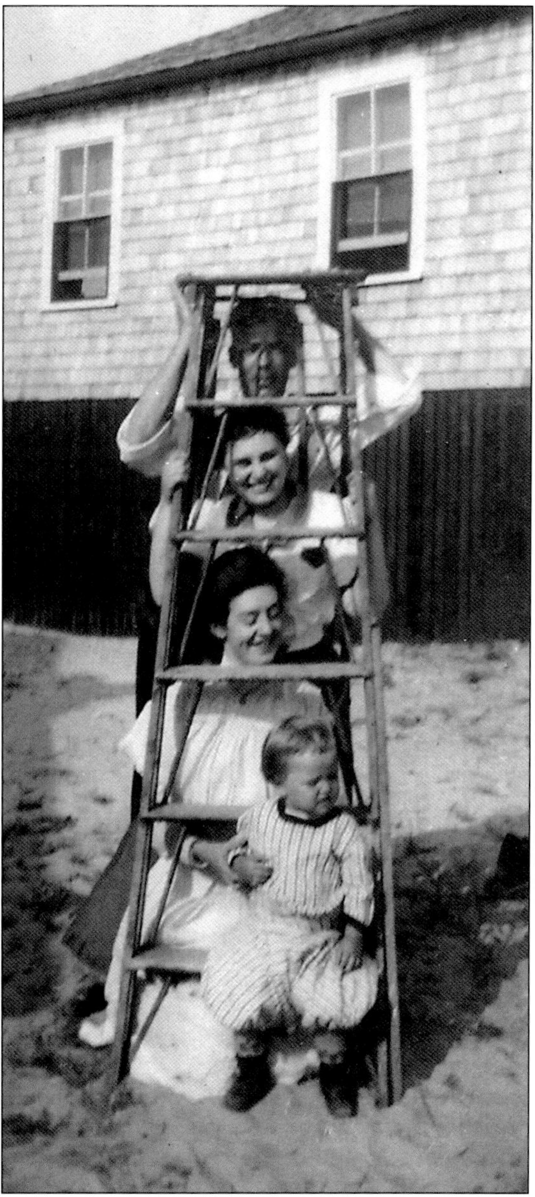

In the July 8, 1896 edition of the *Brockton Times*, the growing population of Swedes was noted as "a progressive people and among the best citizens who have come to these shores. Their homes and property are kept in the best of condition, and the majority own their own homes. They are industrious, hard-working and a temperate class, and as a rule, a people who make everything right as they go forward." Already making their mark, the Swedes had formed businesses and entered the work force as skilled craftsmen. Many of the women and girls were employed as domestics by well-to-do families. Others worked as stitchers in the factories. Some ran grocery stores. Married women, for the most part, remained at home, raising the children and running the household.

The times were not always good, but there were always good times. As the six-day workweek gave way to five and a half days and then to five, there was more time for leisure. Families gathered for backyard picnics or traveled to Scandia Park, Highland Park, or Field's Park for a day of fun. Some had cottages along the South Shore and invited their friends to visit. Area farms such as Hillstrom's, Walborg Johnson's, and Eric Winberg's were also the settings for large gatherings, complete with plenty of food, music, and games for the children. It was also a good place just to sit and talk. Above all were the neighborhoods. Friendly and clean, most of the yards contained flower gardens. The lawns were mowed and the houses neatly painted. No one was a stranger.

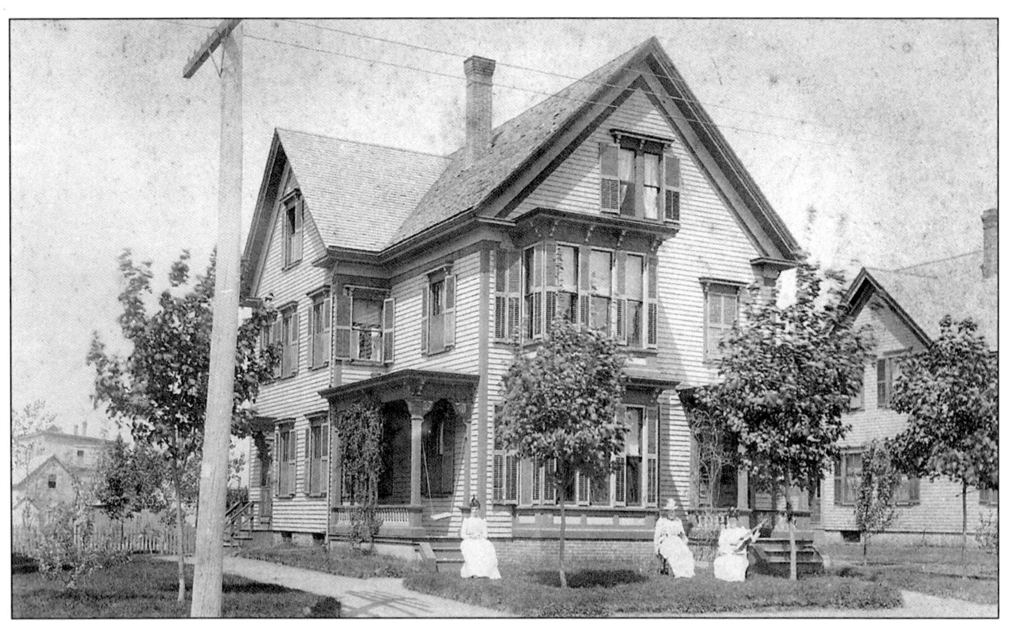

Boardinghouses were the first American homes to many Swedish immigrants. A clean room, Swedish cooking, and a place of pleasant living were promised by Cook's, Emilsson's, and similar establishments.

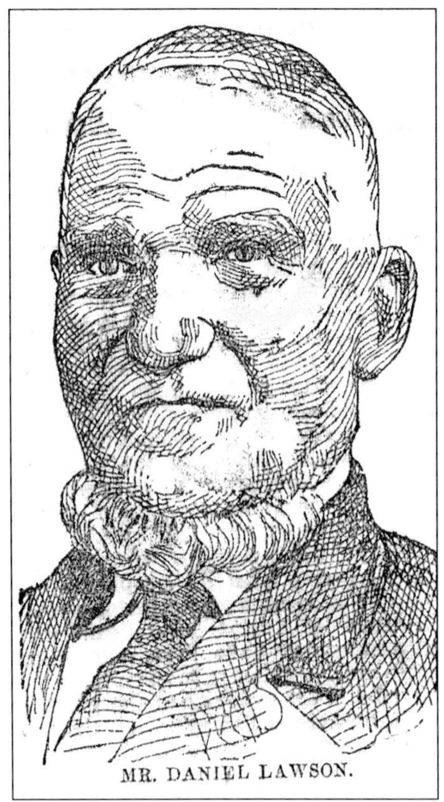


The first Swede to settle in North Bridgewater (Brockton) was Daniel Lawson, who arrived from Frostorp, Sweden, in 1844 on the sailing vessel *Superior*. Finding himself satisfied with his adopted country, he returned to Sweden in 1854 to visit his family and to sing the praises of America. Lawson returned with a wife, Catherine Nordquist, and some 60 of his countrymen. This small group of immigrants was the nucleus of Brockton's Swedish community.

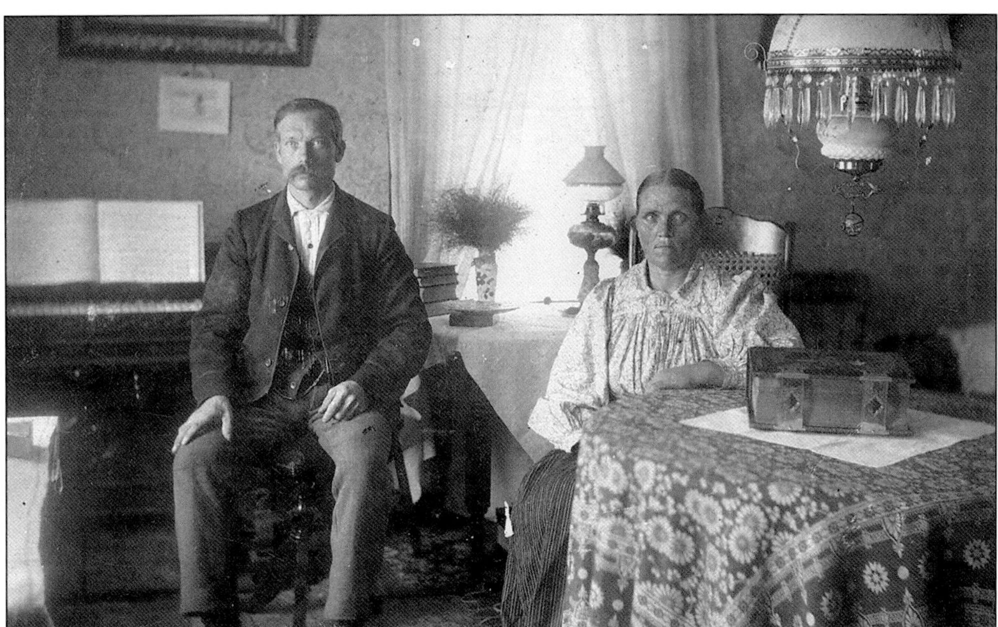

This image offers a rare look at the interior of a working-class home in North Easton *c.* 1900. A cobbler and dry goods store owner, Anders Magnus Helander and his wife, Charlotta, appear to have lived a life of relative comfort. An organ, framed art, elegant Victorian chandelier, and table lamp reflect the material success immigrants had sought, while the presence of the family Bible indicates the deep faith brought to their new land. The Helanders were the parents of Brockton alderman Charles Helander, who served from 1922 to 1931.

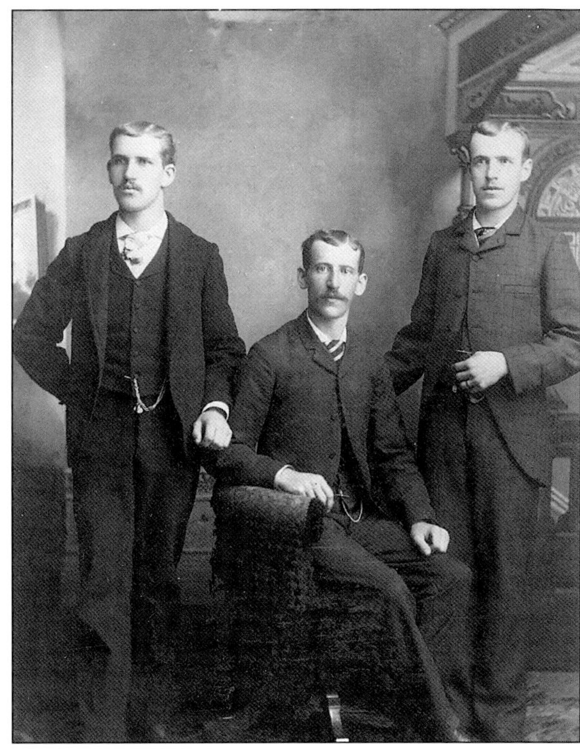

Bakeries were an essential part of the Swedish community, and there was an abundance of them in Campello. One family, well known for its bakeries, was the Lawson family. Pictured here are Carl, A. Herman, and Axel Lawson. Herman established a bakery on Main Street, while his brother Axel chose 26 Nason Street. Competition was friendlier in those days, and many family members operated competing enterprises throughout the community.

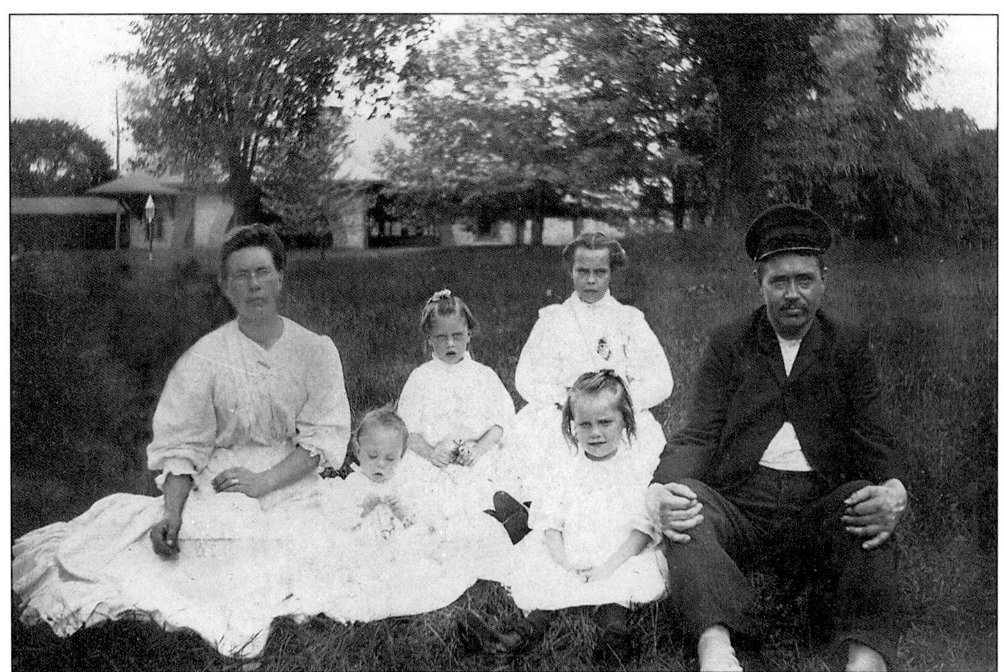

In this May 1909 photograph, John Abraham Anderson poses with his family in front of Old Colony Railroad Station in North Easton, currently the home of the Easton Historical Society. From left to right are his wife, Hilma Josephine (Helander), and his daughters Olga Amollia, Edith Sedonia, Ellen Victoria, and Anna Elizabeth. He worked as a polisher at the Ames Shovel Works in North Easton and was a founding member of the Holy Trinity Lutheran Church.

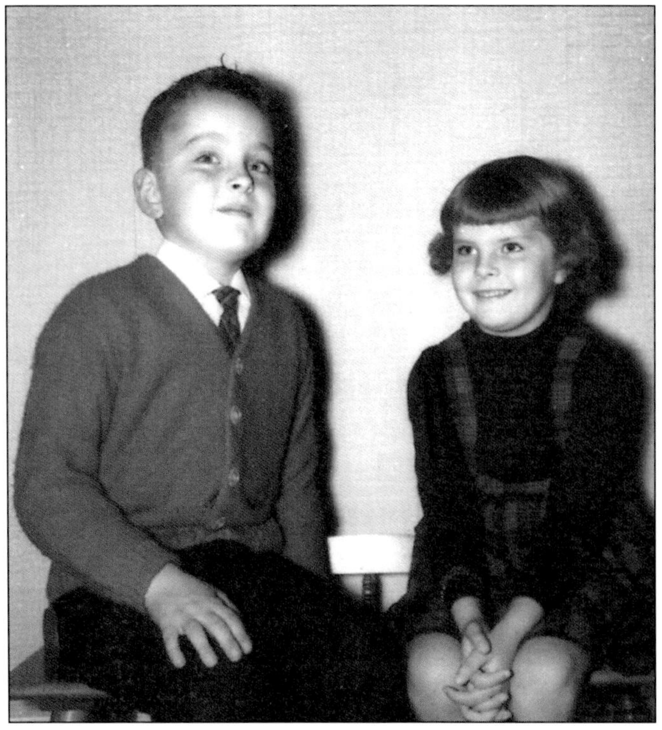

James Edward Benson and his sister Cheryl Ann (grandchildren and great-grandchildren of those in the above photograph) are the embodiment of the dream their ancestors had coming to America—college graduates, well employed, active participants in their church, and contributing members to their community. Imagine what the immigrant shovel polisher would think of his great-great-granddaughter Corinne Packard, a student at the Massachusetts Institute of Technology!

For some 35 years, Rudolph Hackenson managed the delivery of ice for the Brockton Ice & Coal Company. Arriving from Edestad at age 18, he, like many, began his life in America as a shoeworker. In 1913, he met, courted, and married Betty Anderson, from Malmö. Their daughter Hulda, active in the Trinity Baptist Church, was the manager and buyer at the gift shop of the famous Toll House Restaurant.

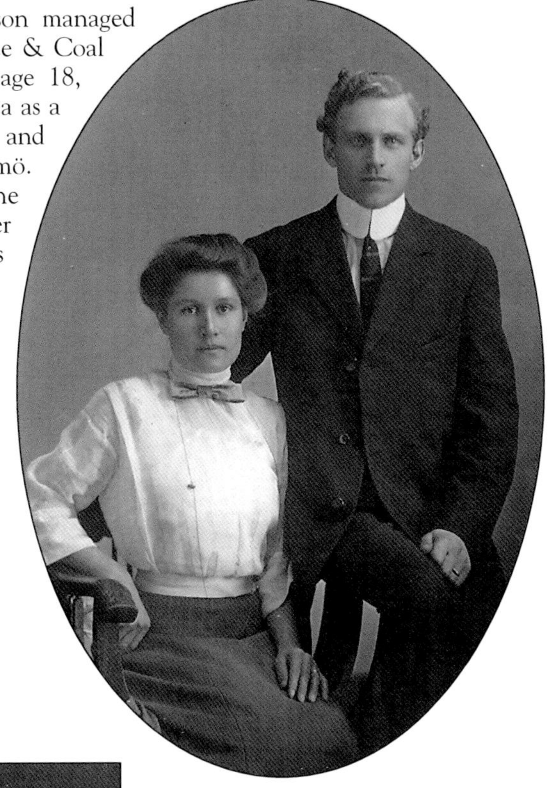

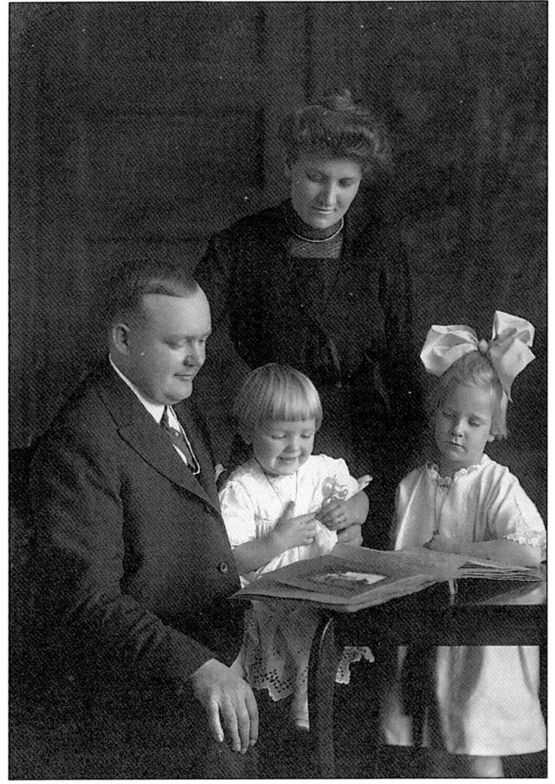

The Swedish immigrants were hardworking people. One such person was O. Philip Pearson, pictured here with his wife, Esther, and his daughters Phyllis and Vilma. According to his children, he was a jack of all trades. When the shoe shops were out on strike or taking stock, he started selling fish and smoking hams and bacon. He also operated a small farm in the Matfield section of West Bridgewater and was employed by the Churchill & Alden Shoe Company and Lawson's Bakery. Esther worked as a domestic and also for the Reynolds Shoe Company.

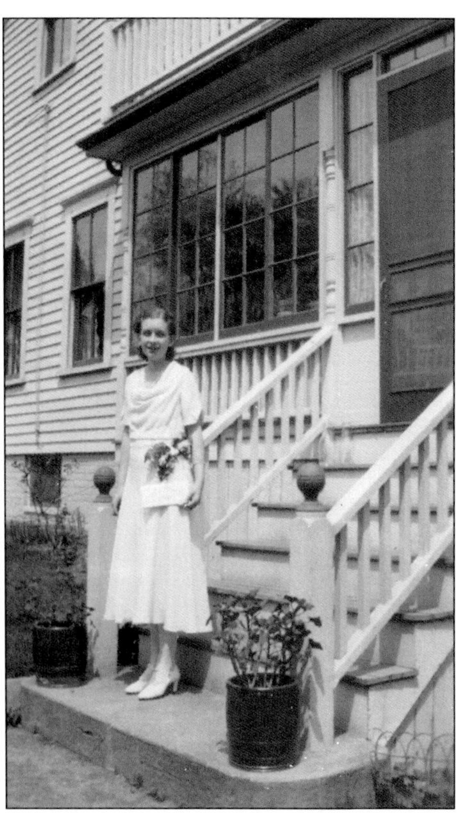

High school graduation day for Dana Victoria (Anderson) Perkins was June 12, 1932. A talented musician with a love of religious music, she concentrated her skills on the organ, playing at the Trinity Baptist and First Lutheran Churches and for 16 years at the Dahlborg-McNevin Funeral Home.

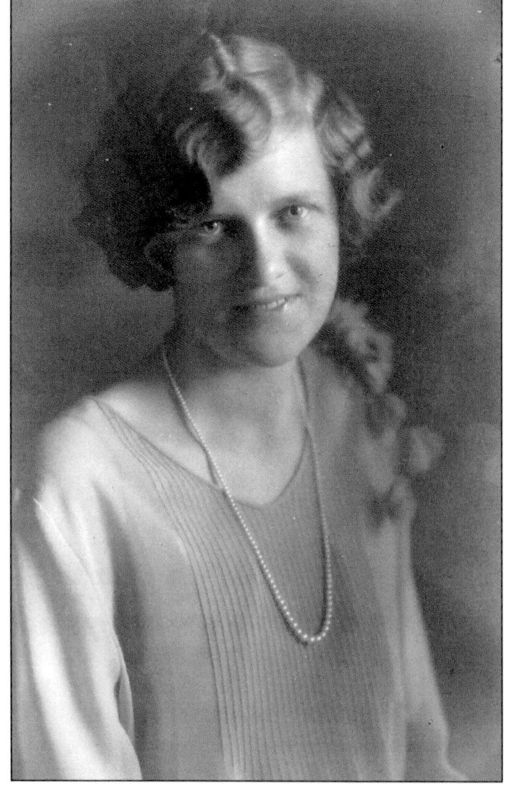

"A beautiful person who lived a Christian life" describes Elsie Louise Sondeen. Sondeen was the daughter of immigrants John Fredrik Sondeen, an inventor, and Blenda Fredrika Peterson Zehr, who were married on December 19, 1894, at the Swedish Lutheran Church. Miss Sondeen, a longtime employee of People's Savings Bank, served her church as a Sunday school teacher for more than 50 years. Photography, flowers, and baking Swedish pastries were her hobbies and, at the risk of some controversy, one of the authors feels that her *mandelkransar* have never been equaled.

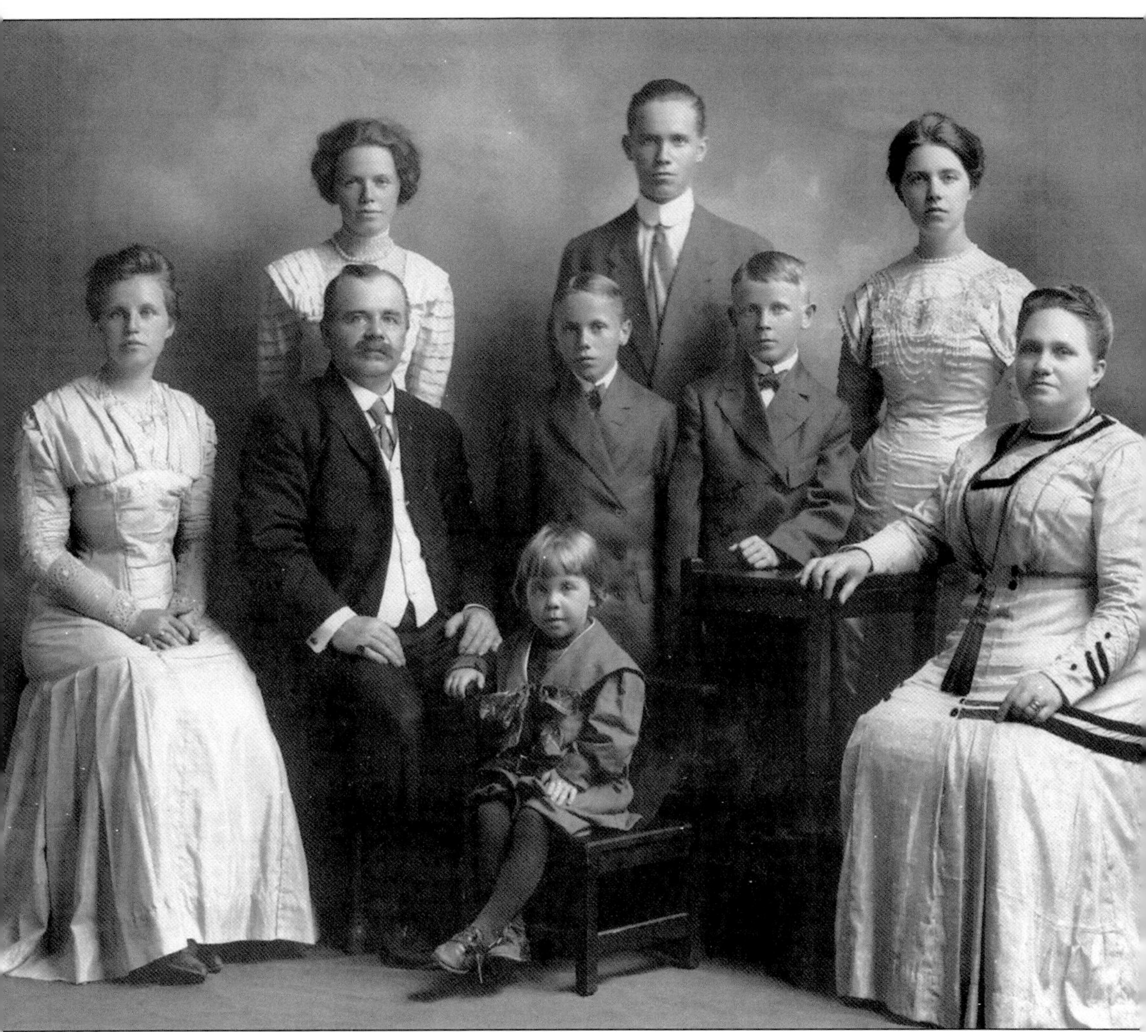

Johan Edward Lagerstedt, one of the Swedish pioneers, arrived in Brockton from his hometown of Nässjö in 1882 at age 20. He and wife, Hilda (Johnson), are surrounded by their seven children—Ebba (Bolinder), Nan (Churchill), Seth, Edward, Walter, Edythe (Thompson), and Kenneth. Once established in the shoemaking trade, he brought his father, Samuel Sebastian; his mother, Mathilda (Lundberg); his brothers Oskar, Elliot, Carl Philip, Per Wilhelm, and Alfred Gustav; and his sisters Nanny and Gerda to Brockton.

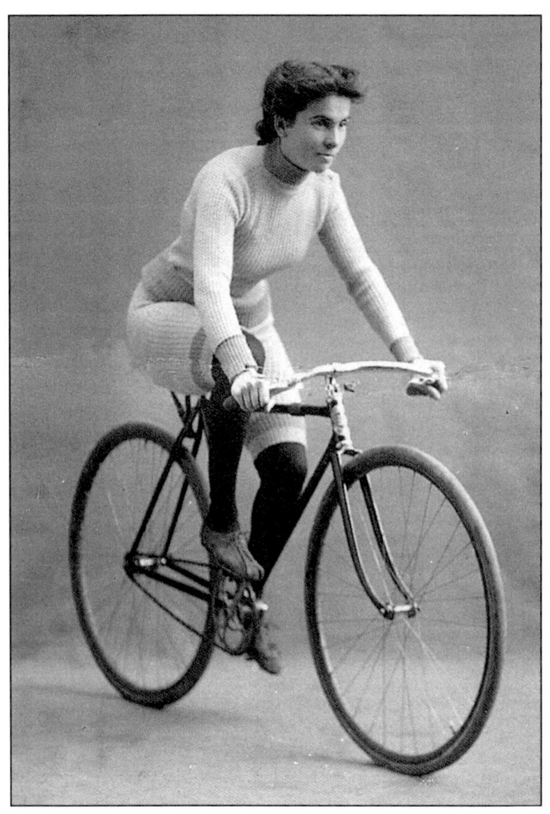

Margaret Knowlton Helander, a Passamaquoddy Indian and wife of Brockton alderman Charles Helander. In 1902, she and her sister Sadie undertook a 400-mile bicycle ride, which they completed in 33 hours and 49 minutes. For the first 100 miles, they were paced by Elwood Divine and W.H. Bussey of Brockton. Consider that there were no paved highways to traverse in 1902, mostly gravel country roads and those paved with cobblestones.

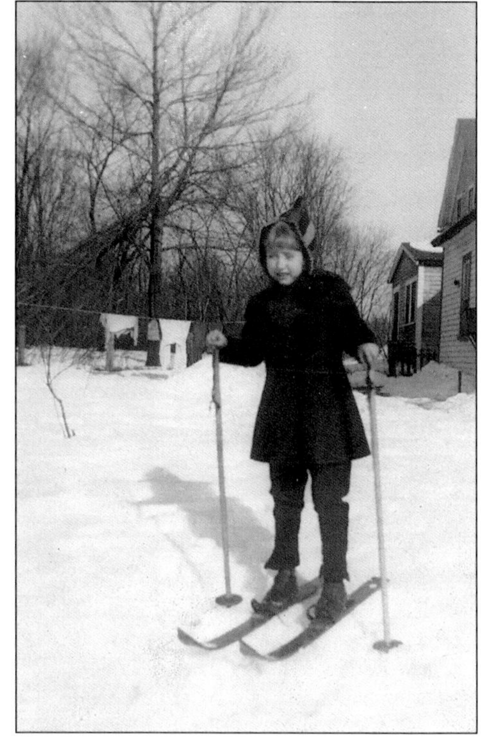

Joan (Hillstrom) DiMarzo was a frequent visitor to her uncle Peter Hillstrom's farm on Cary Hill in Brockton's Montello section. Apple orchards, pine groves, and open fields made it a year-round vacation spot within the city. Among the many other guests were Bror and Lily Gustafson of New Sweden, Maine, who regularly stayed with the Hillstroms while their son Carl Einar received treatments for cancer at Children's Hospital and the Dana-Farber Center in Boston. In May 1998, after 50 years of "anonymity," it was revealed to the public that Carl Einar was "Jimmy" of the Jimmy Fund, and he had survived.

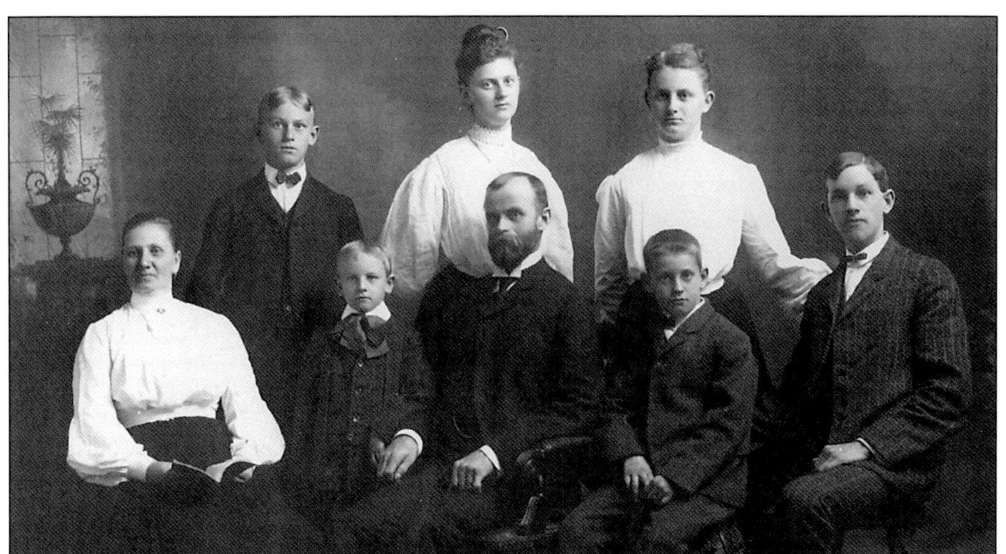

Family pride is exhibited in this *c.* 1923 portrait of Johanna Christine and Nils Peter Thompson with their six children. From left to right are the following: (front row) Johanna Christine, Henry, Nils Peter, Harold, and Edgar; (back row) Joel, Anna, and Edith. Nils Peter Thompson was sent to America at age 16 by his mother. He became a shoeworker and, as fortunes increased, became a corporator of Brockton Co-operative Boot & Shoe. Edgar and Joel followed their father into the shoe industry. Henry, the youngest, was employed by the C.V. Hultman Company. Harold, the first of the new generation to attend college, earned a degree in electrical engineering from the Worcester Polytechnic Institute. Daughter Anna married John Alden, a descendant of the famous Pilgrim cooper. In 2001, their great-great-granddaughter Johanna Christine Richardson graduated from Harvard University.

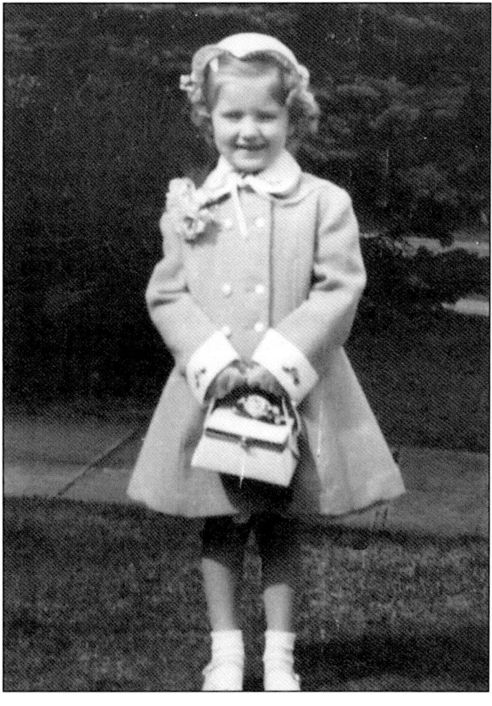

Shown here is great-granddaughter Maxine (Thompson) Richardson at age 5 in her Easter finery. A graduate of the University of Massachusetts at Amherst, she is a teacher at the Huntington School, the school attended by her parents, Lloyd and Martha Thompson, as well as her daughters Johanna and Jamie.

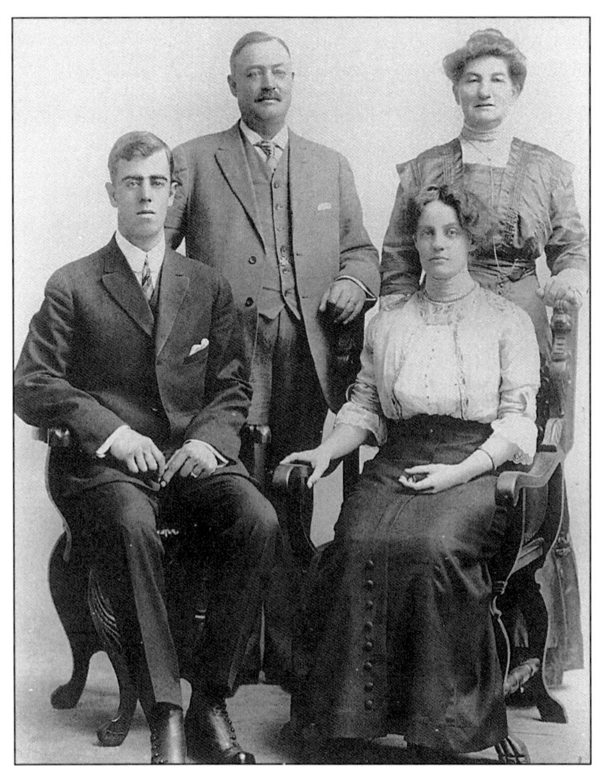

A mason, bricklayer, and builder, Charles Anderson arrived in Brockton from Skäne in 1885 and immediately entered the work force of the growing city. Two years later, he married Augusta Peterson. They are shown here with their two children, Martin and Esther. In the early 1900s, Mr. Anderson formed a mason-contracting business, Charles E. Anderson and Son, which operated until the mid-1950s. Among the many buildings to their credit were the Vasa Building, the William Cook Building, A.F. German Company, and numerous homes in Brockton.

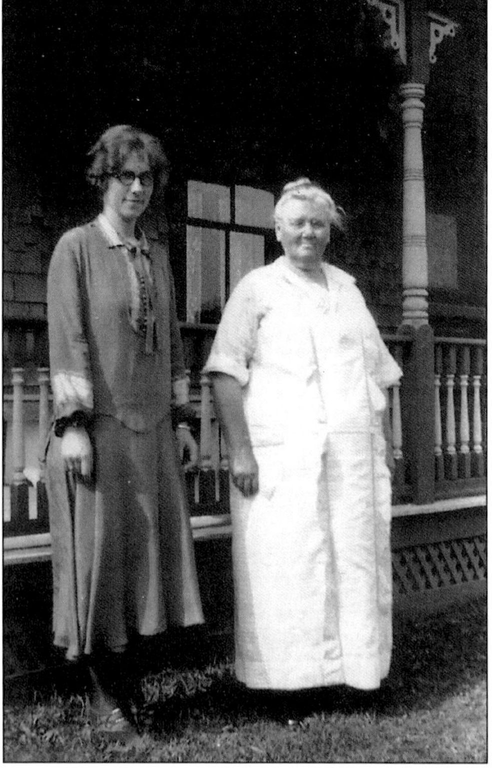

Known for their "fussiness," Swedish immigrants were sought after as domestics by the wealthy families of the area. Louisa Stahl, born in Smaland in 1859, settled in Brockton at age 18 and was soon employed by Mrs. George E. Keith. She worked in the Keith household for 17 years, married Piter Peterson in 1894, and raised five children—Mattie Marie, Arthur, Robert, Oscar, and Ebba. She is shown here with daughter Mattie.

Per Eric Bergstrom and his bride, Gerda Victoria Lundin, were married on November 6, 1917. Shortly after, he was drafted into the U.S. Army. Remaining stateside during the war, Mr. Bergstrom went to work for the Packard & Green Coal Company upon his discharge. In the late 1920s, he became a self-employed stonemason and landscaper. Gerda worked as a domestic for several prominent Brockton families, including the owners of the Thompson Shoe Company. The couple had four children—Helen, Harold, Elsie, and Gladys.

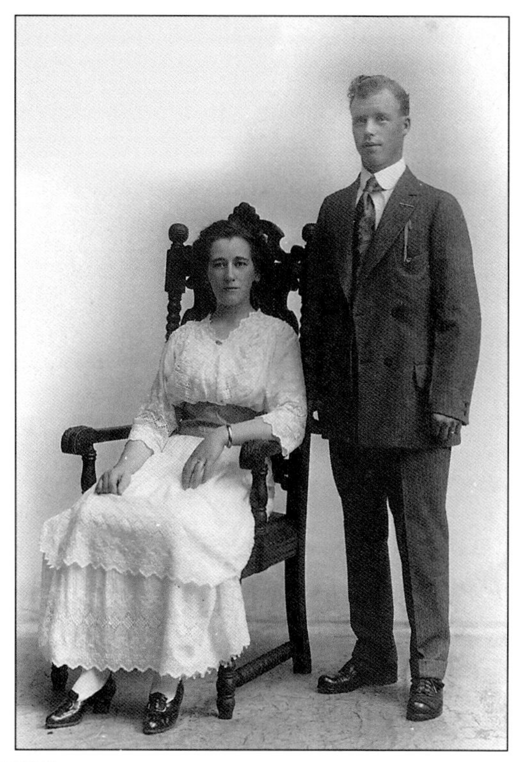

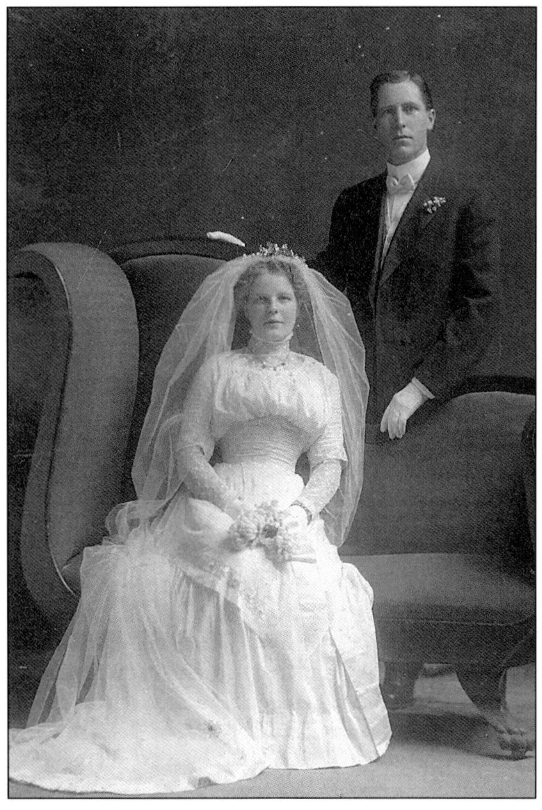

Frank and Agda (Landen) Johnson were just kids when they arrived in America. Johnson was 12 and Agda was 14. The couple was married at First Lutheran and raised a family of nine children—Lester, Herbert, Vincent, William, Roger, Corine, Constance, Madalyn, and Gerald. Johnson, highly respected for his craftsmanship, was an effective advocate among factory owners for Swedes needing employment.

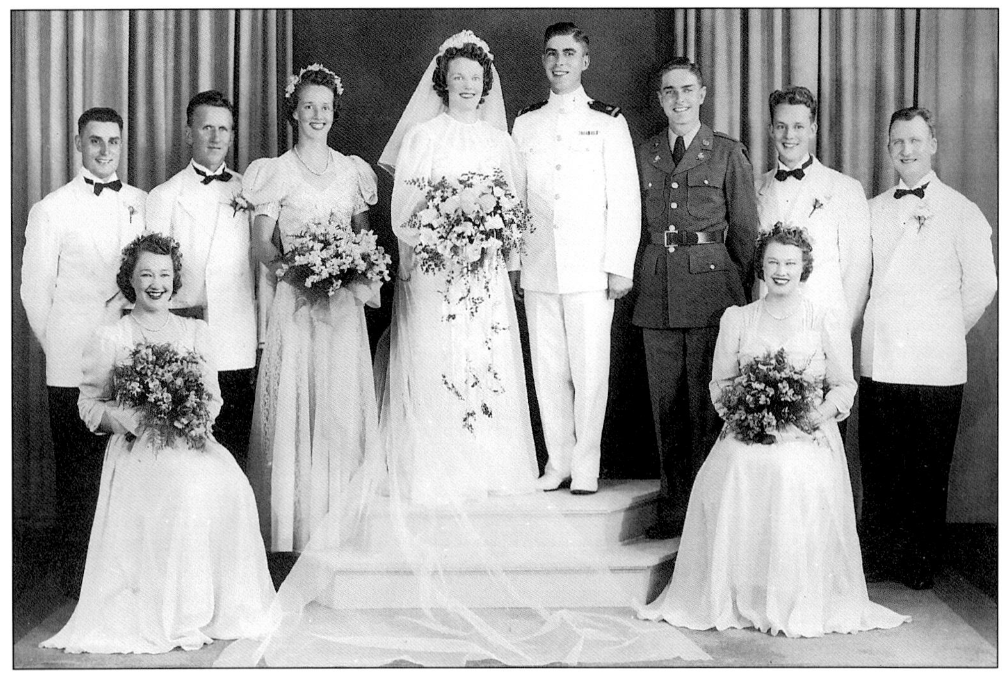

During the reception that followed the World War II wedding of Ens. Everett Johnson and Vera Ortendahl, July 21, 1943, the First Lutheran Church was thrown into a blackout. Although such alerts were common during the war, it took the wedding party and guests by complete surprise.

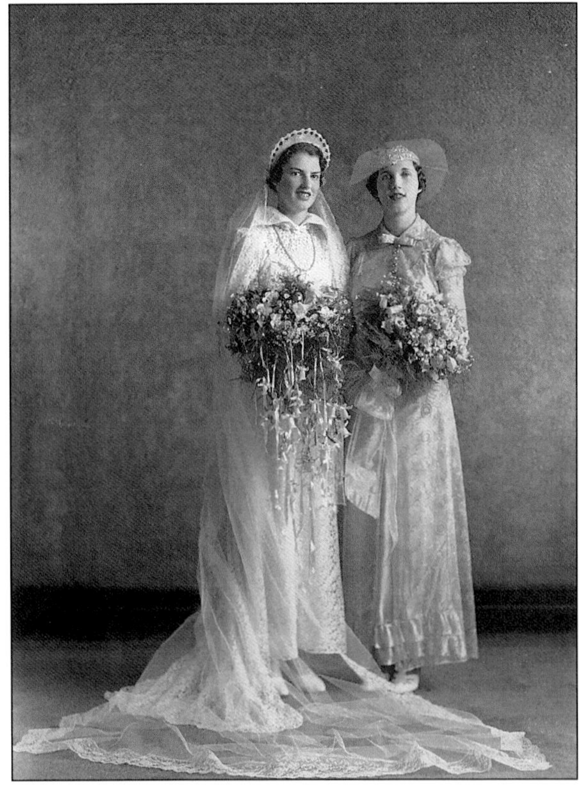

Stunning bride Martha (Erickson) Thompson and her matron of honor and lifelong friend Margaret (Nelson) Johnson take time from the wedding festivities for a formal portrait on June 27, 1937. Martha's wedding to florist Lloyd Thompson was an event long remembered in the Swedish community for the quantity and beauty of the floral arrangements, all creations of Thompson Florists. The Thompsons had two children—Lloyd, co-author of this book, and Maxine Martha (Thompson) Richardson.

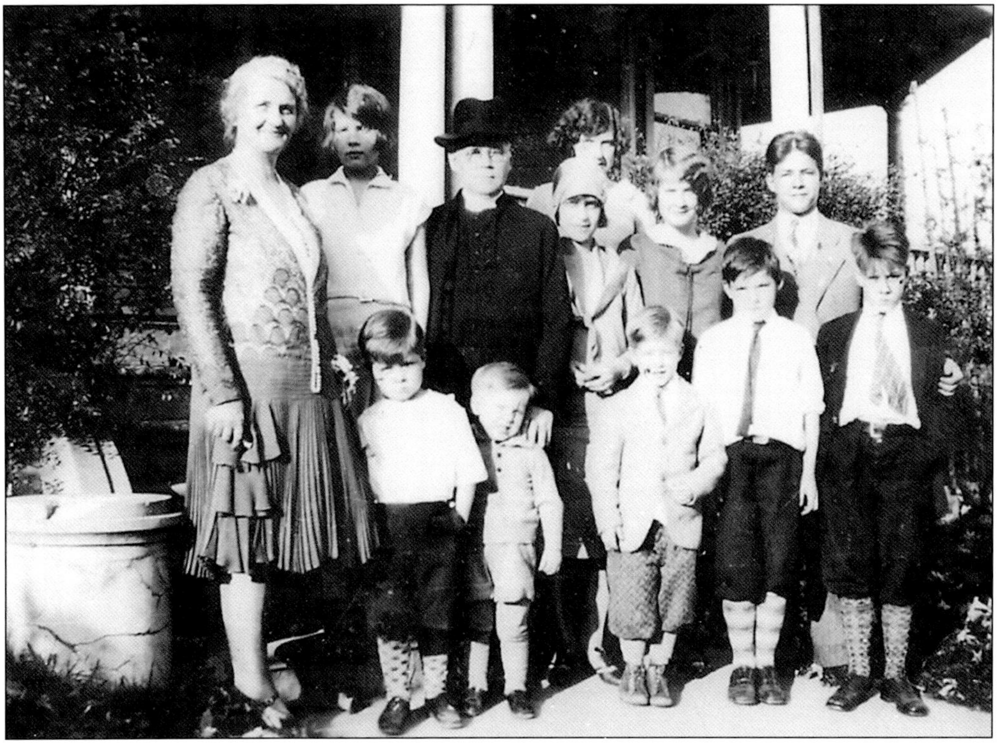

In 1920, the Martha and Dorcas Societies of the Swedish Lutheran Church purchased the home of Charles Hillberg, 81 Hillberg Avenue, for $8,000 to house the large family of Pastor Peter Froeberg. Imagine Sunday mornings with 10 children and their parents getting ready for church in a house with only one bathroom! All 10 of these children—Linnea, Margaret, Signe, Dorothy, Theodore, Joseph, Bertil, Kenneth, LeRoy, and Paul—were first-generation Americans and received college or technical degrees.

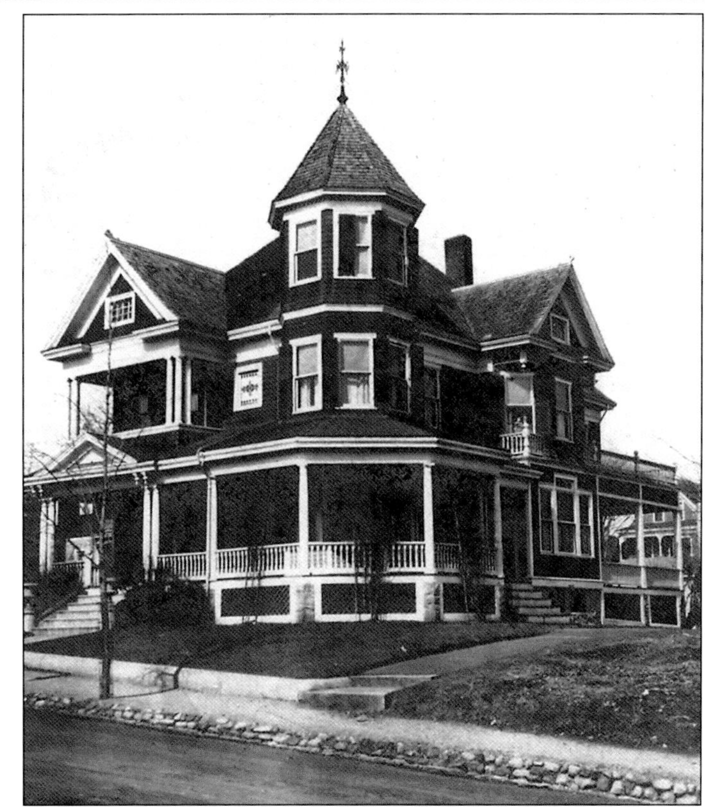

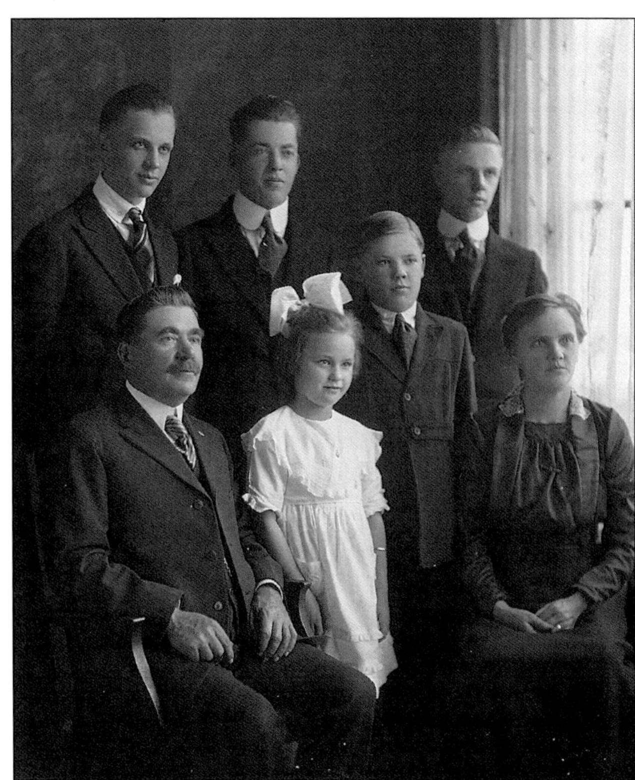

Residing at 20 Second Street, the family of Swante and Hilma Hollertz—Harold, Arthur, Vincent, Walter, and Edith—was a typical Swedish working-class family. Mr. Hollertz and his three eldest sons worked in the shoe factories. Arthur was well known locally as a vocalist. Walter operated an ice and oil business, and Vincent, a graduate of Upsala College, spent his career in the insurance business. Edith served for many years as organist at First Lutheran Church and at the First Baptist Church on West Elm Street.

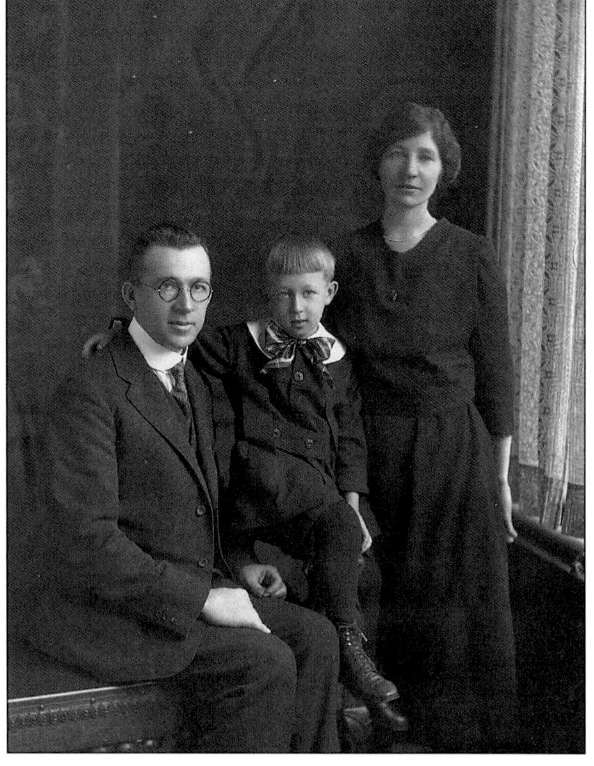

George Valentine Hollertz—shown here with his wife, Anna Carolina, and son George Verner—was a shoeworker for the W.L. Douglas Shoe Company, where his 1923 wages totaled $1,900. In the early 1920s, daughter Elsa was born and the family built a house in the Matfield section of West Bridgewater. Young George, a graduate of Howard High School and Bentley College, became treasurer of the Brockton Machine Company, served as treasurer of First Lutheran Church, and was a Town of West Bridgewater selectman from 1960 to 1972.

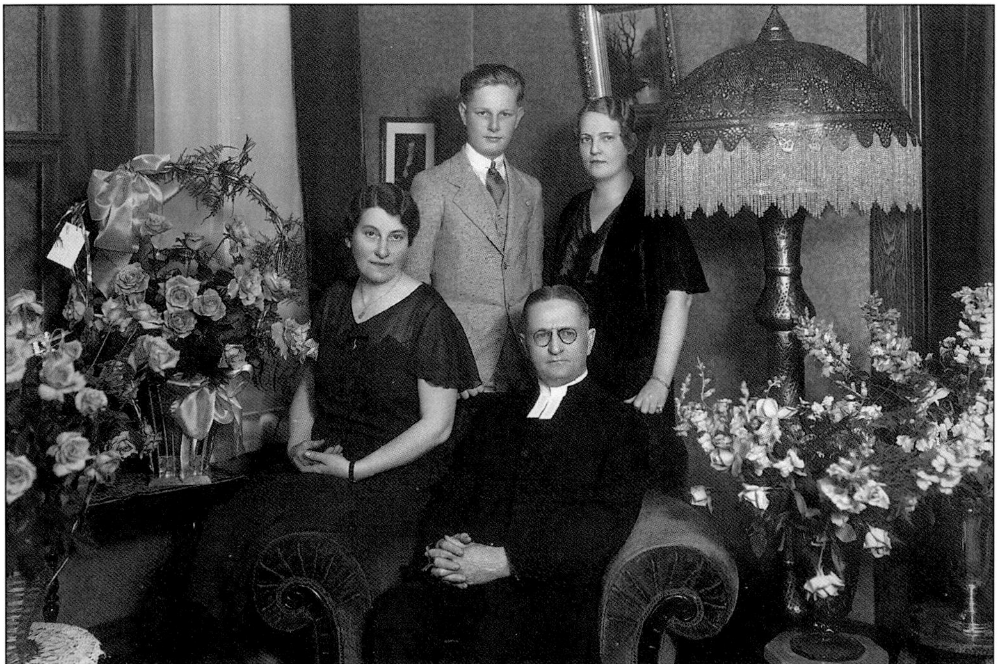

The Reverend Dr. Bror Julius Hulteen served First Lutheran from 1910 to 1917. Hulteen (shown with wife Olga and children Rupert and Ellen) introduced the tradition at First Lutheran in 1913 of presenting Bibles to children at Confirmation.

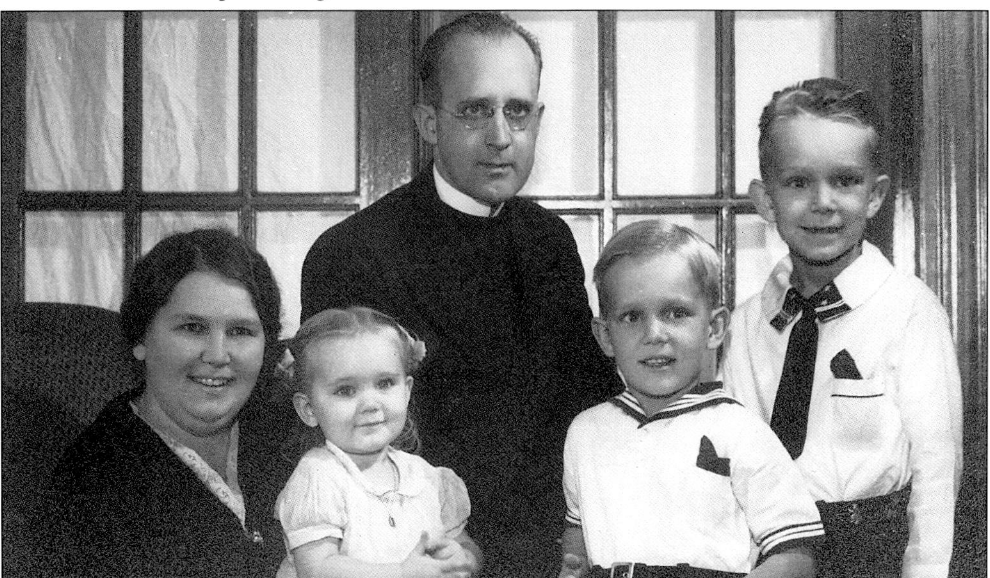

Rev. and Mrs. Harry Carlson are shown with daughter Ruth and sons David and Theodore. During his term as pastor of Gethsemane Lutheran Church, he was called to military service. Chaplain Carlson landed at Normandy on June 7, 1944, a day after the invasion. During the war, he made 40 Atlantic crossings, accompanying troops to Europe and comforting the wounded on the trip home. On these harrowing trips, he was presented with more than 100 crosses from the wounded men, clergymen, and even prisoners of war. During one Easter season, Elroy Ostlund displayed these crosses in the window of the Campello News Stand.

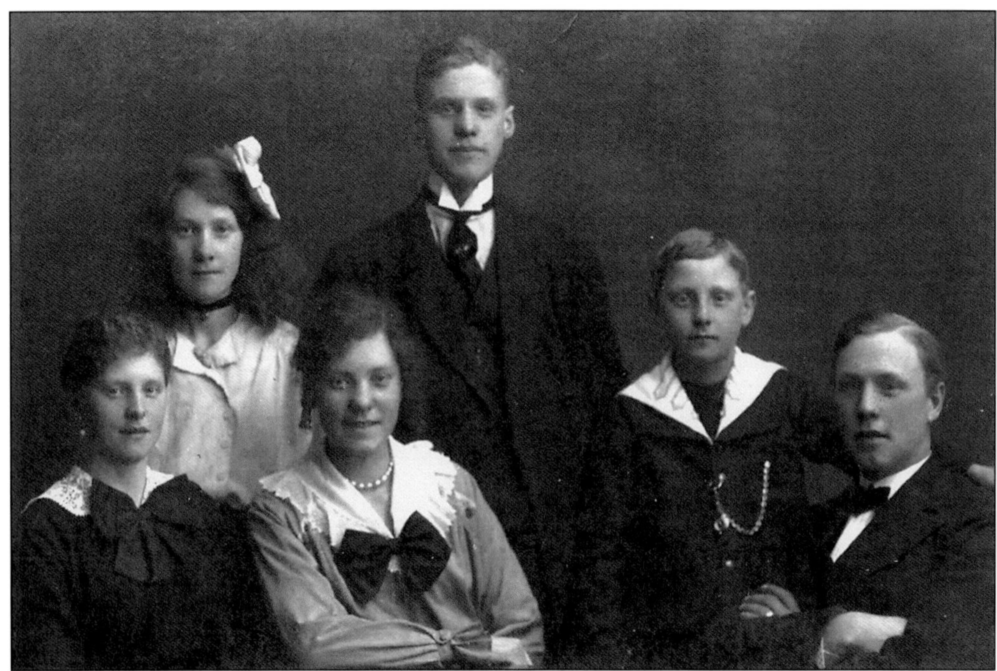

Gunnar Aaron Julius Peterson (center), a postal worker from Swedala in Skäne, "jumped ship" in Boston and headed for the home of his uncle Karl in Avon. Tragedy had struck his family when his mother, sister, and brother's fiancée fell victim to the Spanish flu. Alone in this new land, Gunnar was invited by Amelia Rabinius to spend his first Christmas in America at the Lutheran Children's Home. Gunnar was a stalwart citizen of Avon and a mainstay of the Republican party.

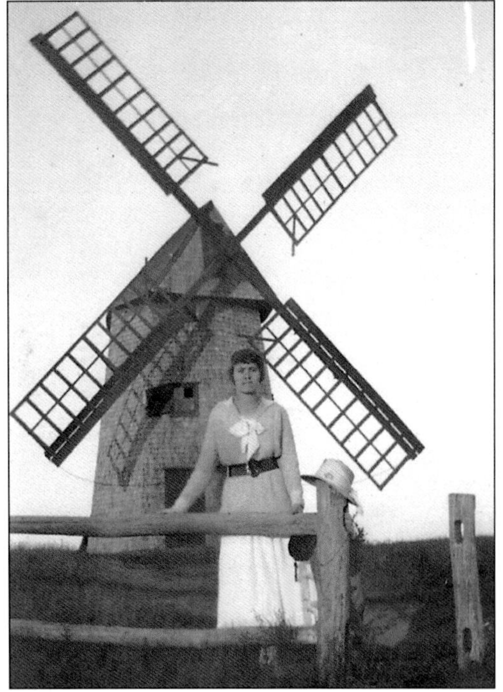

Betty (Karlsson) Peterson was employed by the Kingmans, a prominent banking family. Shown here on Nantucket, she received a bequest of $999 from the family, which was used as the down payment for the Peterson home in Avon.

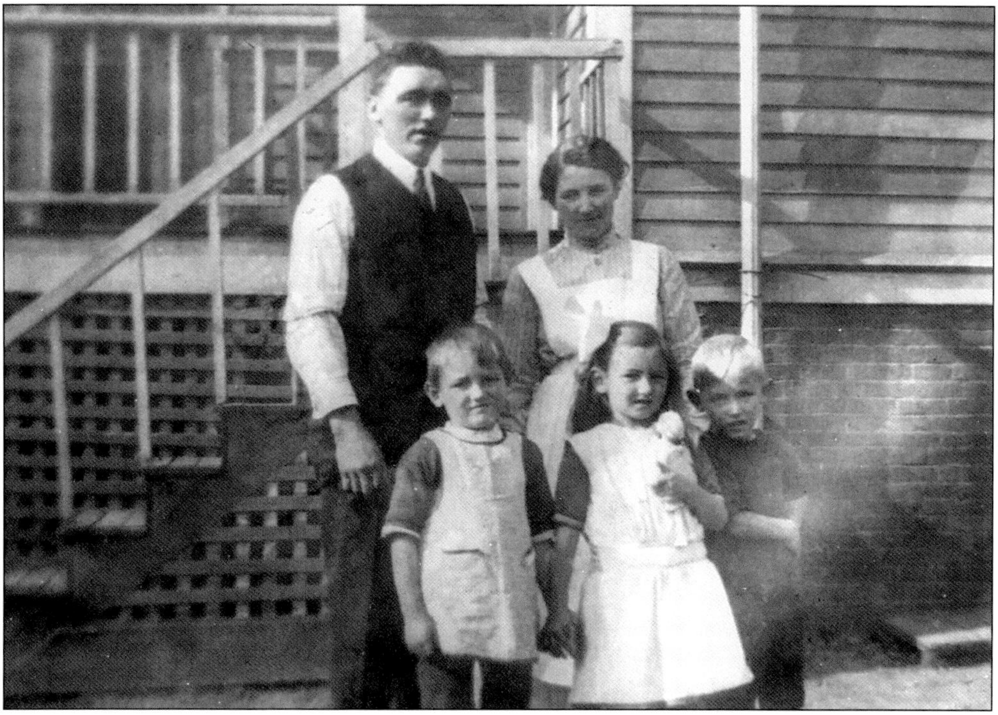

The Goransson family of Stoughton are shown *c.* 1916 on their very first Sunday in America. Axel and Hannah Goransson stand proudly with their children Arvid, Alva, and Lennart.

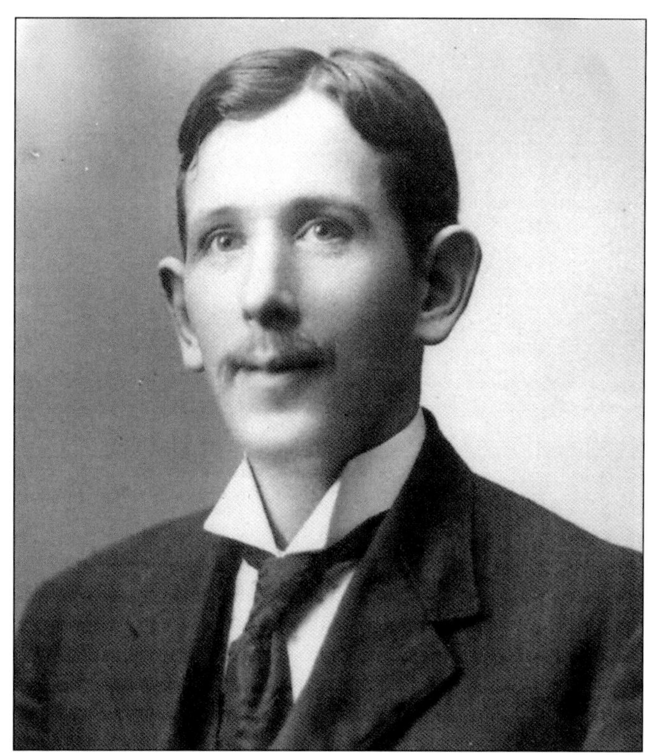

Gustaf Emil Johnson, one of seven children, came from Björstorp in 1903. He had an enormous capacity for labor and a tireless concern for his friends and neighbors. He worked first as a farmer. He then became a shoeworker and, later, a blacksmith. He and wife, Selma, raised four children—Signe, Ruth, Ejnar, and Ernest—in a loving and religious household. When he needed to buy a home but lacked the money, someone in church loaned him the funds on a "pay me back when you can" basis. Emil did, as he was a man of his word.

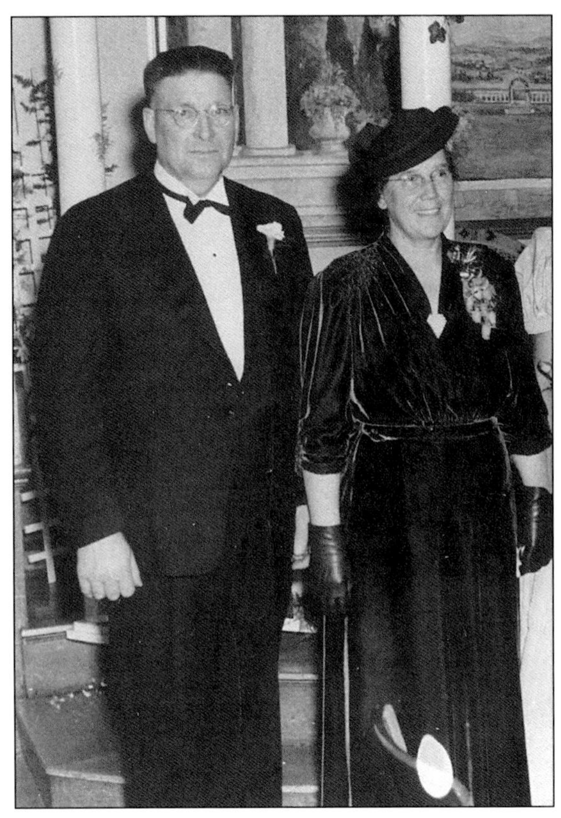

Arriving from Sweden in Liverpool, England, in March 1912, Karl Victor Anderson decided to take an available ship to America, foregoing the opportunity to book passage on the HMS *Titanic*. Making his way to Brockton later that year, he took residence at Mrs. Cook's Boarding House on French Avenue, which was the first American home to many Swedish immigrants. There he met and soon married Emma Otelia Rylander.

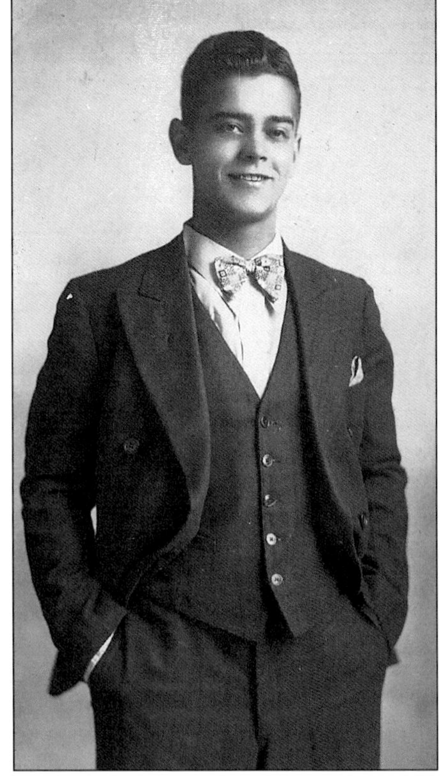

Albert "Gully" Gullbrantz was a popular neighborhood kid. He worked for Thayer Brothers and Johnny Leonard's store (later the Campello News Stand) and taught hand balancing, gymnastics, and judo at the Brockton YMCA. He served in the U.S. Army for five years during World War II and was in New Caledonia for three of them. After the war, he lived periodically in Sweden and, in 1966, became a Swedish citizen. He made more than 40 Atlantic crossings. His uncle Marcus, the janitor at the Keith School, died while accompanying Gully back from Sweden in 1934.

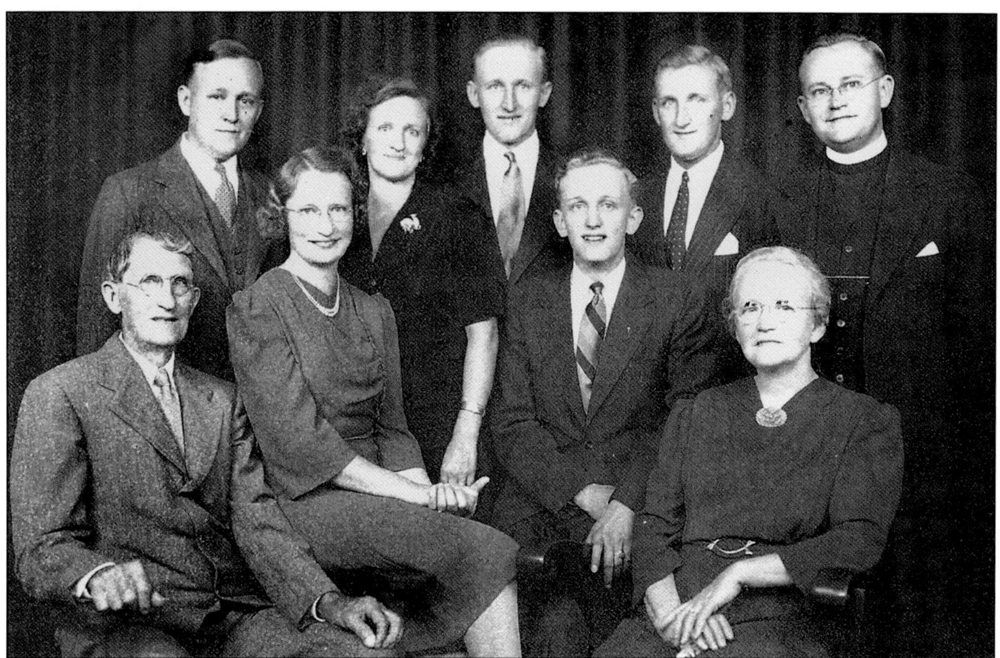

Shown here are members of the Anderson family of Campello and Matfield: C. Herman, Warren, Ruth, Evelyn, Loring, Robert, Roger, Agnes, and Howard. C. Herman, a farmer, was active in the Lutheran Church. Howard and Robert entered the Lutheran ministry. Loring operated the Cities Service station on Montello Street. Roger and Warren worked for Bird & Son.

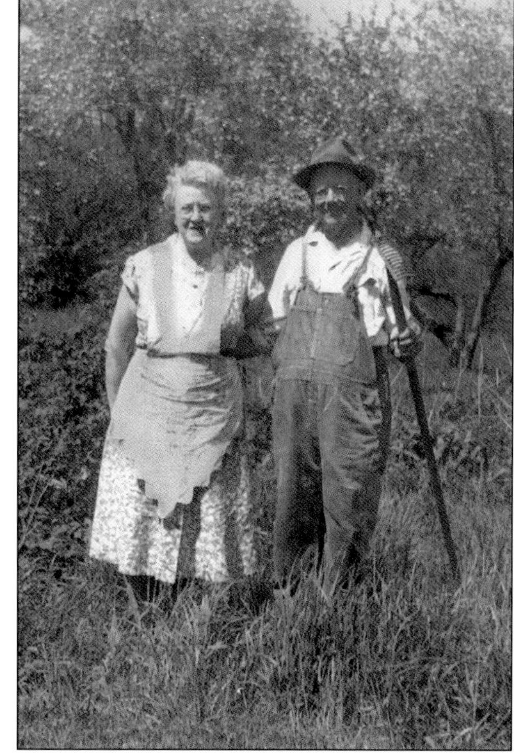

As a farmer and a "rough rounder" for several shoe manufacturers, Charles Johnson often arrived at home with a hearty appetite. Luckily, his wife, Elizabeth, enjoyed cooking. Her family's favorite dish was Swedish kalops, eagerly consumed at the old oak dinner table. In fact, the recipe was so good that it was featured as a "Recipe with a History" in the January 1997 issue of *Yankee* magazine.

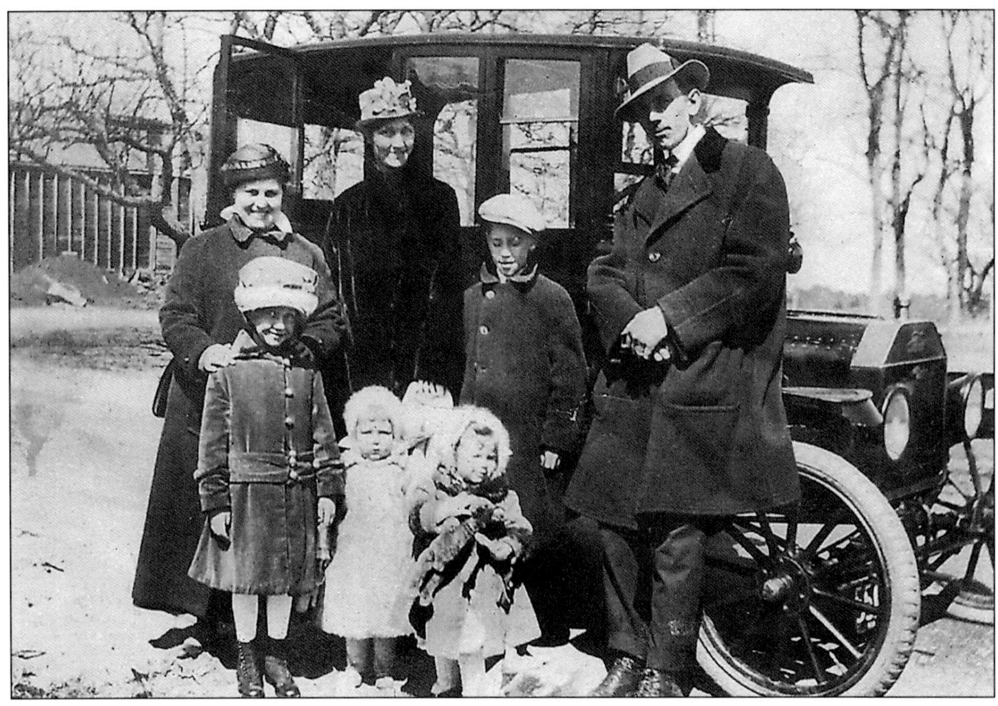

G. Fred Dahlborg and family pause during a Sunday afternoon drive in the country. The Dahlborgs lived in a well-landscaped home at 69 Echo Street (below). A few years after this *c.* 1920s photograph was taken, an enterprising neighbor, Carrie Hill, opened the Hill-Echo Kindergarten diagonally across from the Dahlborg home.

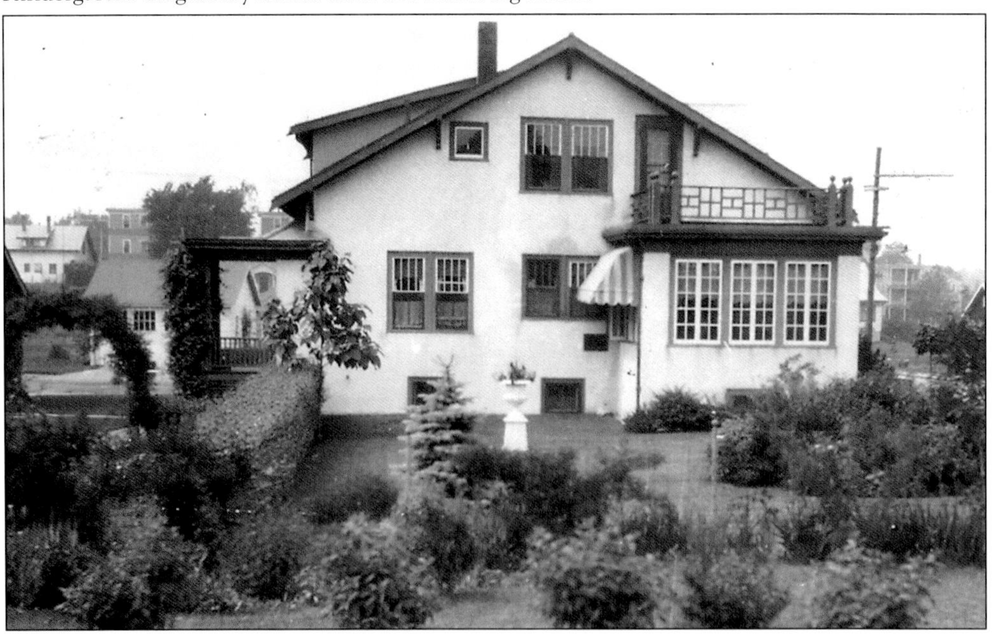

Joel F. Thompson and his wife, Edythe (Lagerstedt), take time out from the festivities of their daughter Merriel's wedding. The day was one of dual celebration, as it was also Mr. Thompson's 50th birthday. An edge trimmer, he was president of the Scandinavian Charitable Society and vice president of the Swedish Congregational Church.

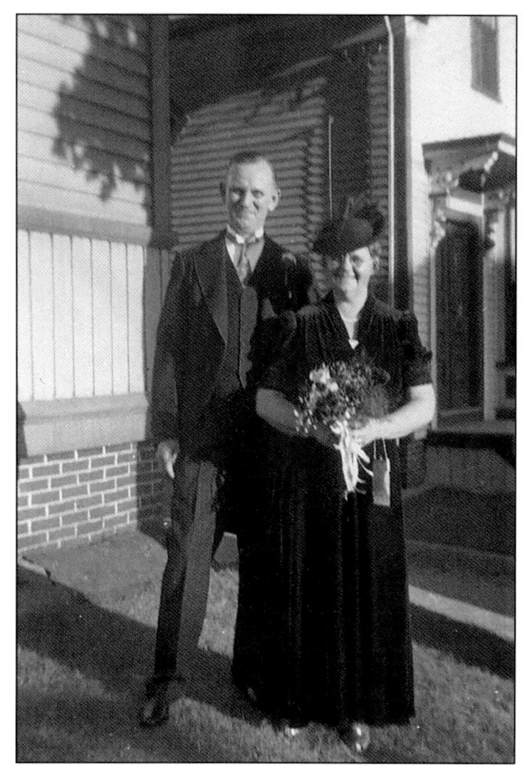

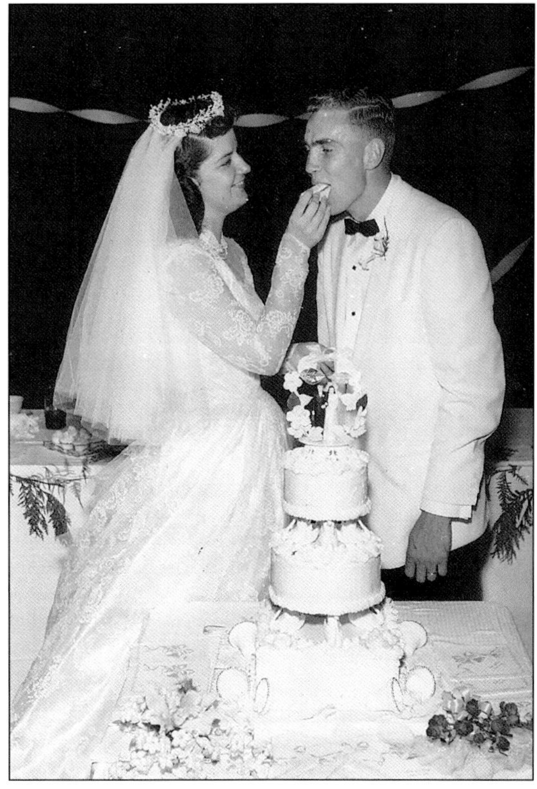

On August 12, 1956, Sven Erick Benson married his schooldays sweetheart, Leah Ann Soell. Erick, a graduate of Bridgewater State College, was the longest serving principal of West Bridgewater Jr.-Sr. High School, beginning his career there in 1971. Leah was a registered nurse and a graduate of the Brockton Hospital School of Nursing. Following her nursing career at Brockton Hospital, she became the school nurse at West Bridgewater High in 1970. In combined years, the Bensons served the West Bridgewater school system for half a century.

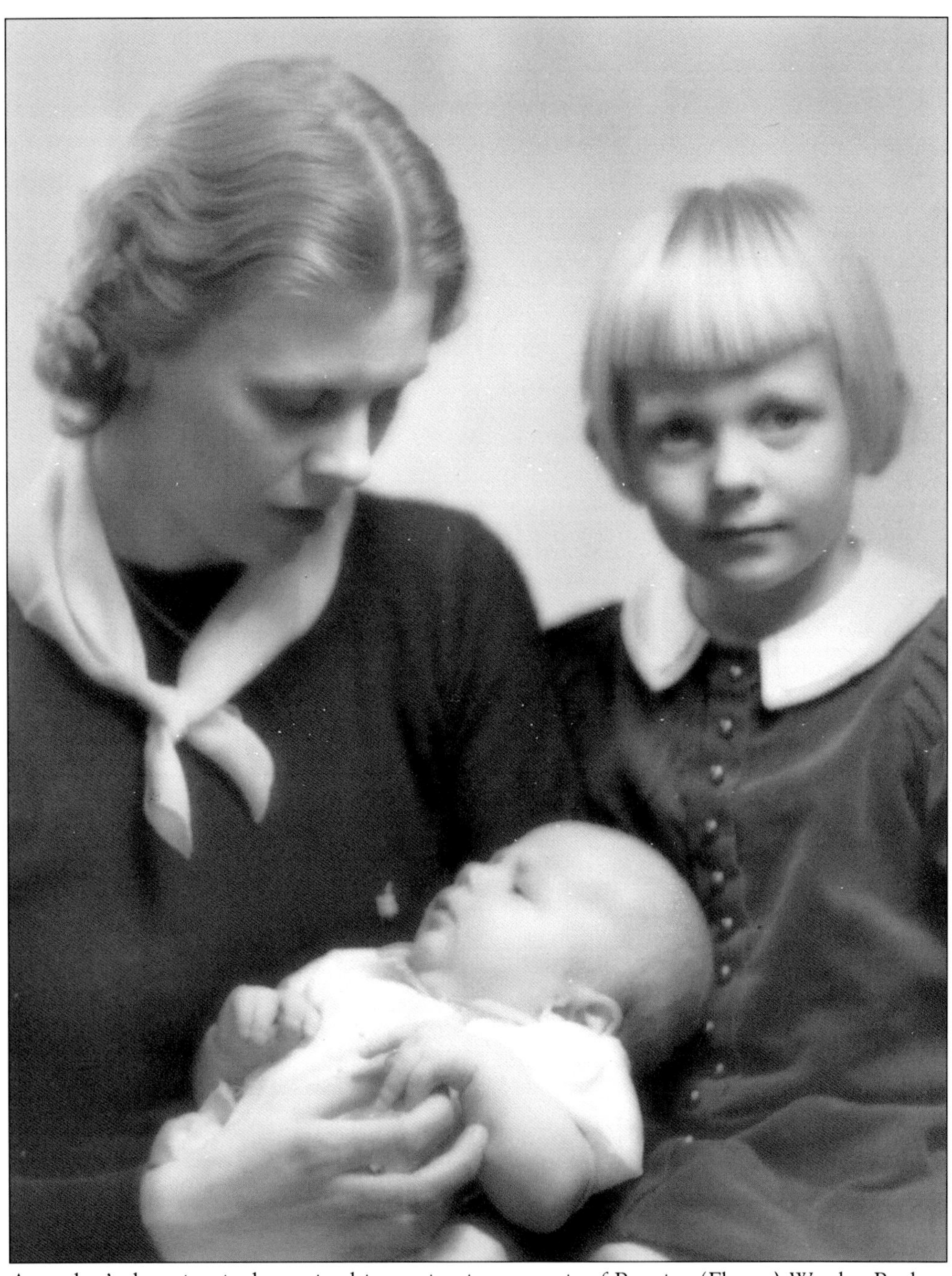

A mother's devotion is shown in this captivating portrait of Bernice (Floren) Wooley Becker, daughter Claire, and infant son Carl.

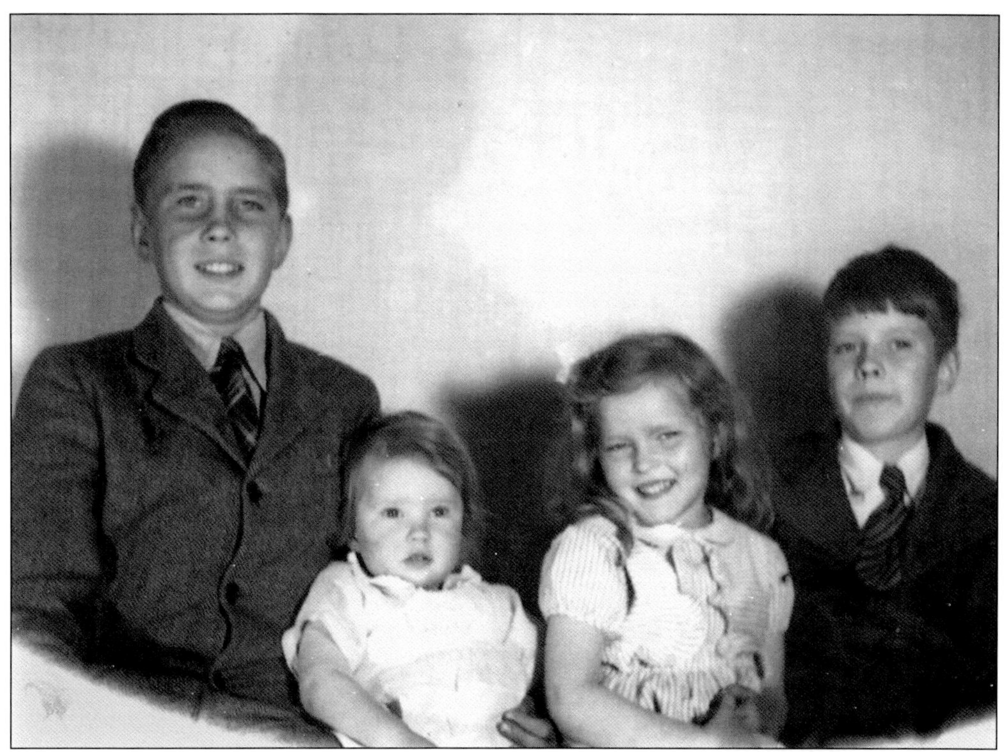

Cherubic Ellen Maria Gullbrantz (shown at right in 1907) would meet Bror Algot Benson at a Walk-Over Club dance in the 1920s and marry him in 1932. They were the proud parents of Sven Erick, Vera Ellen, Betty Anna, and Bertil Alfrid (pictured above). For many years, Ellen was employed as a domestic by Mr. and Mrs. James B. Fraser, owners of Fraser's Dry Goods. Well known throughout the area, she was active in the Star of Liberty Lodge and the West Bridgewater Baptist Church.

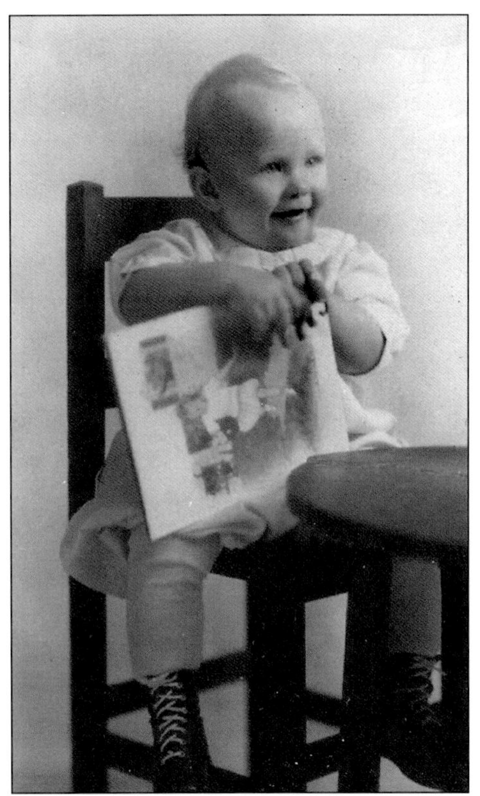

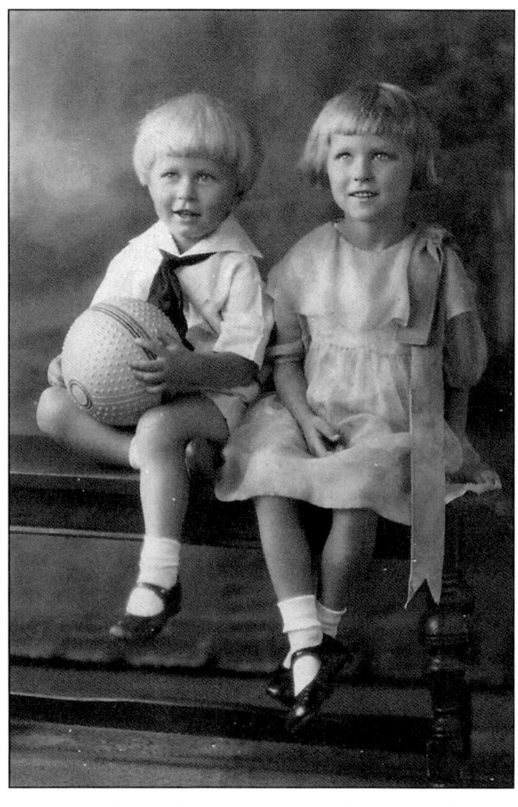

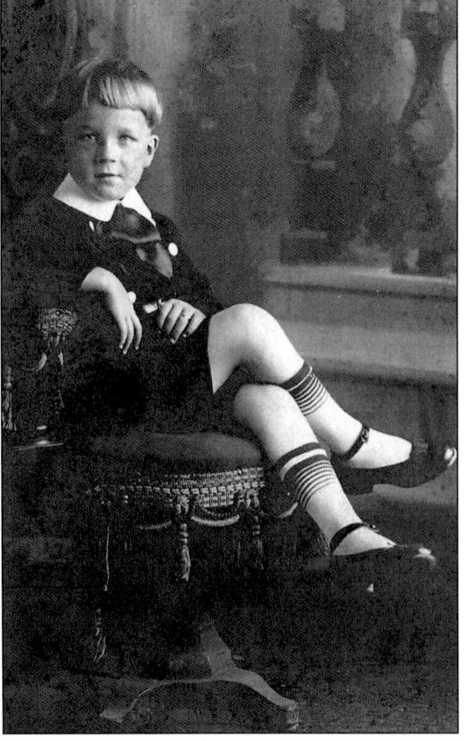

*Gud som haver barnen kär, Se till mig som liten är. Vart jag mig i världen vänder, Står min lycka i Guds händer. Lyckan kommer, lyckan går, Den Gud älskar lyckan får.* "God has many dear children of which I am the smallest." It is certain that Winston Bolinder (top left), Martin and Virginia Johnson (top right), and Everett Lundin were each taught this familiar Swedish bedtime prayer by their parents.

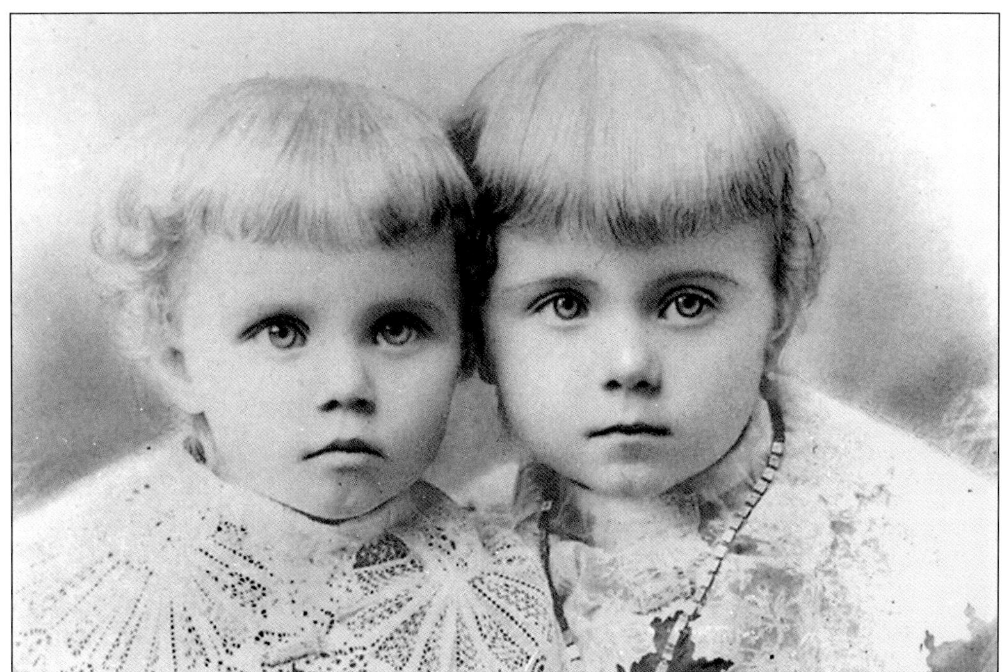

Eyes fixed on the camera, three-year-old Ebba and four-year-old Edythe Lagerstedt pose in their finest crocheted lace collars. These first-generation American daughters of John Edward and Hildur Lagerstedt remained lifelong residents of Brockton. In later life, Ebba was famous for her delectable Swedish cooking. Edythe was well-known for her hobby of making paper flowers and was featured in the February 1973 edition of *Yankee* magazine.

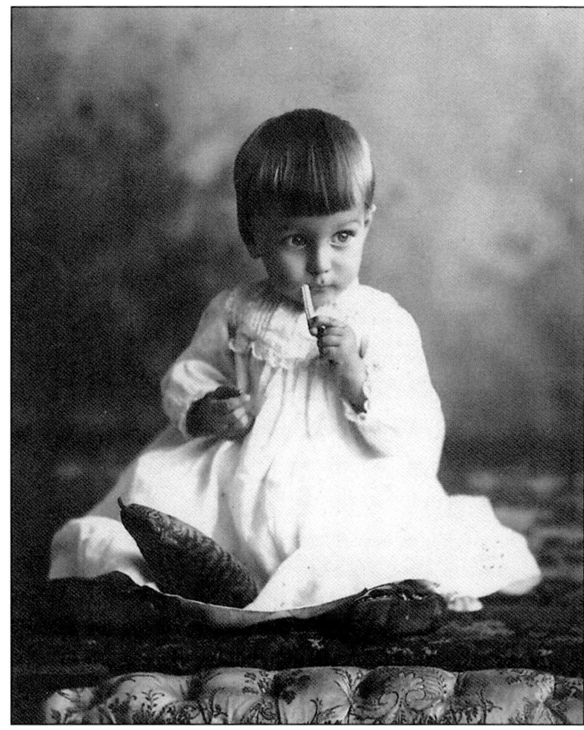

Candy in hand and elegantly dressed, a young Arabam Lagerquist poses for the camera. Son of Edward and Maria Lagerquist (his father a partner in the painting firm of Lagerquist and Johnson), he lived at 23 Custer Street and was a founding partner in the Brockton Machine Company.

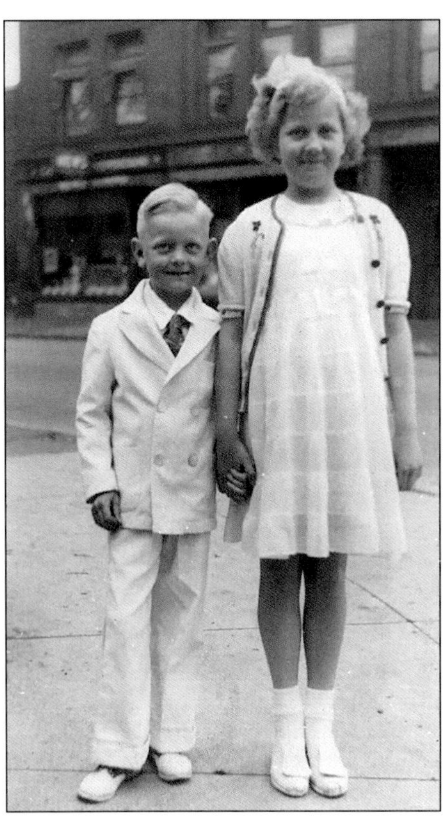

On their way to the 1942 Huntington School Memorial Day Parade, Ruth and Arnold Thorell pause for a picture in their best clothes at the corner of Main and South Streets.

Holding little brother Carl securely, Eleanor (Sondeen) Morlino (children of Carl and Irene Sondeen) enjoys the summer sunshine in the yard of their Menlo Street home. Eleanor became a schoolteacher and, later, a telecommunications specialist. Carl, a graduate of Northeastern University, serves as business manager of a church in New Jersey.

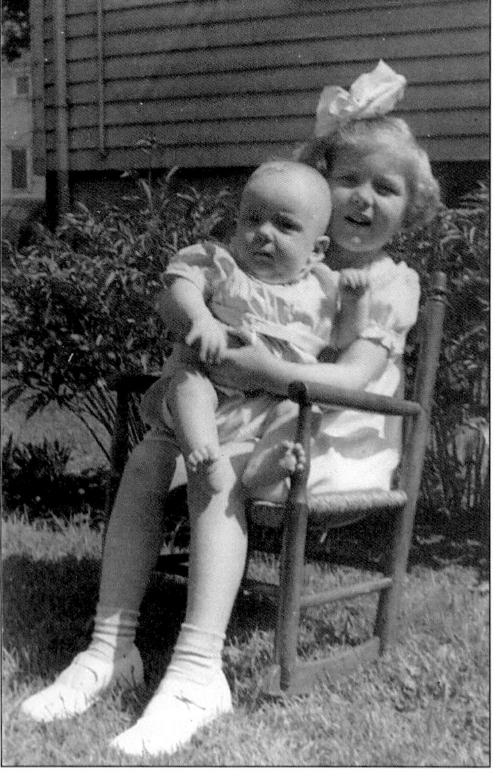

Mirror twins David and Donald Seablom are seen here with their 1929 Indian Scout motorcycle. David is astride the motorcycle, and Donald is resting on the rear carrier. With money being tight at the time, the wearing of the "Indian" sweatshirt was shared by the boys, as were most activities throughout their lives.

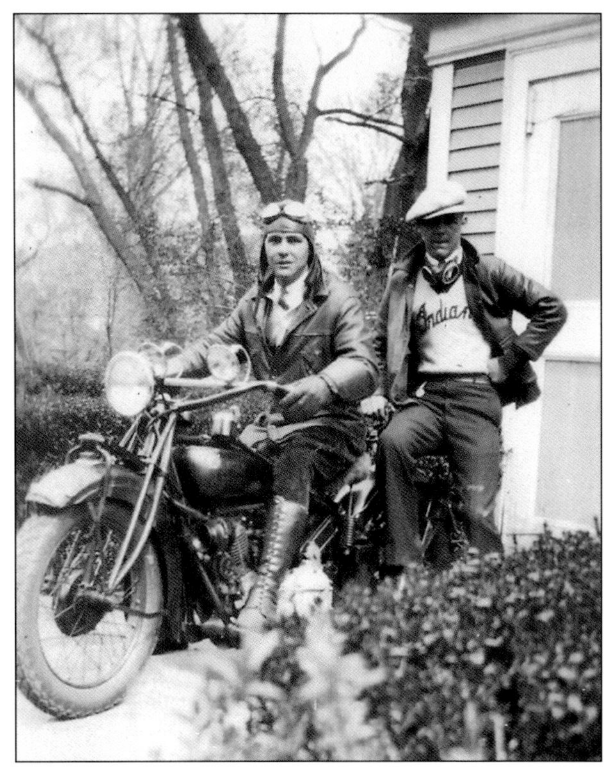


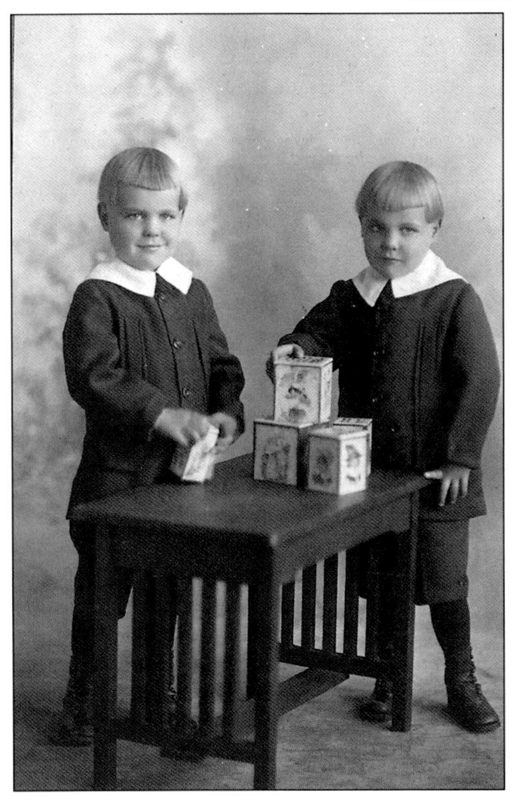

Prophetically posed with building blocks, the Seablom twins were to become highly skilled finish carpenters, their lifelong trade.

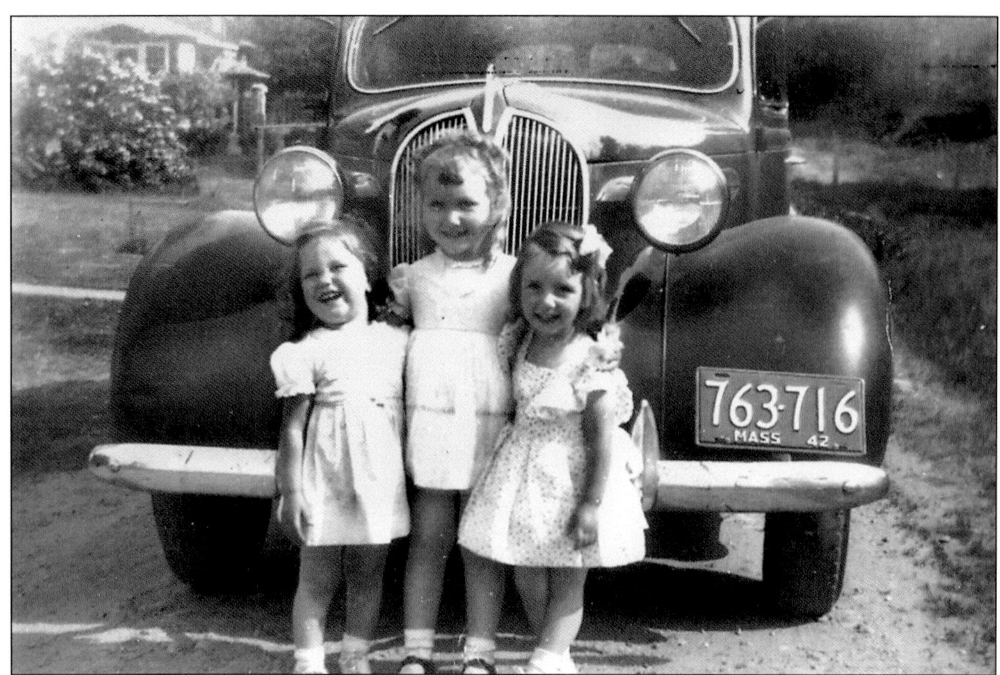


As the song says, "thank heaven for little girls, they grow up in the most delightful ways." All three of these girls later became college graduates. Judy Goransson (left) went on to an important position in computer operations with John Hancock Life Insurance Company. Jean (Goranson) Muncy (center) became president of the Hull Credit Union. Ruth (Parent) Fitzpatrick (right) taught at the Laboratory School at Bridgewater State College.

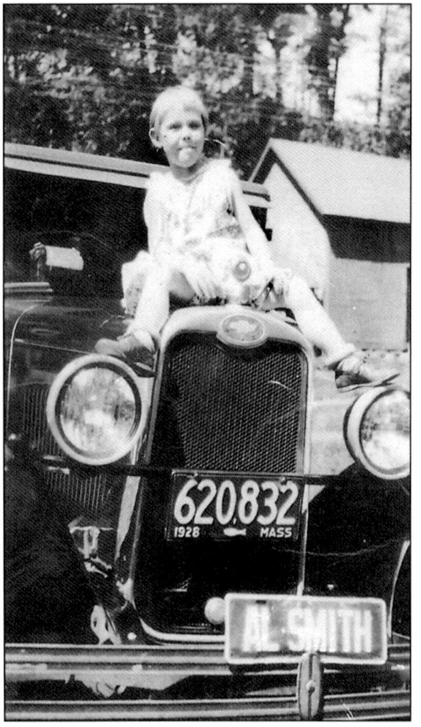


Although Al Smith's political career was brief, Ruth (Holmberg) Emberg Johnson possesses a long and eclectic resume. Throughout World War II, she worked as an electrician aboard LSTs and destroyer escorts at the Hingham Shipyard. When peacetime finally arrived, she married druggist Richard Emberg and, in 1956, entered the New England College of Pharmacy. A registered pharmacist, Ruth was behind the counter at Emberg's until her retirement.

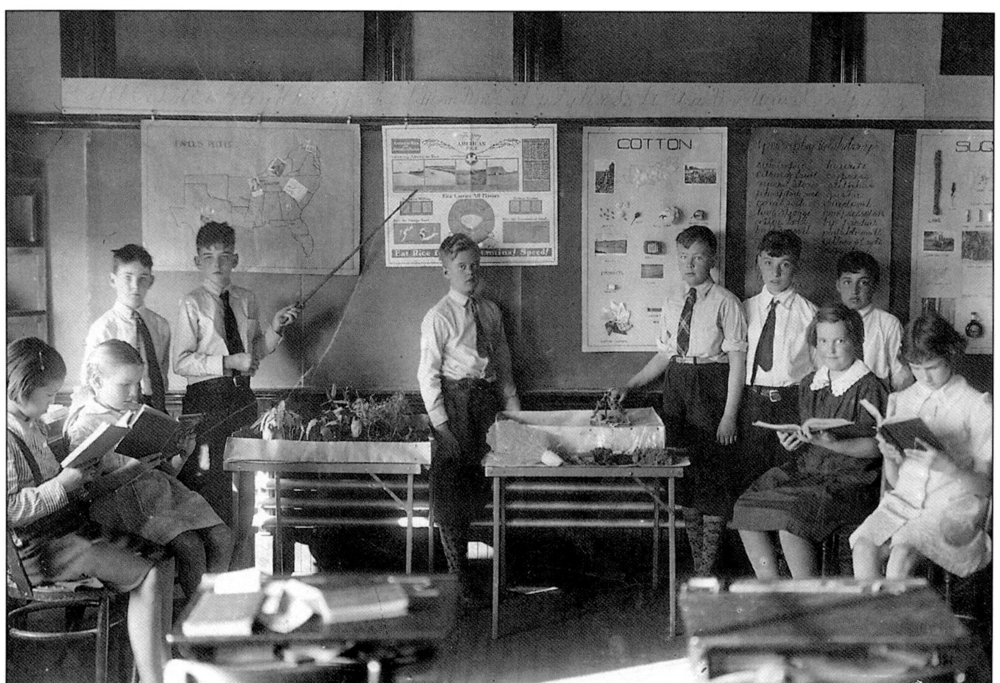


Precious memories of Keith School are preserved in this 1935 scene of Elsie Lawson's fifth-grade class. The children presenting their agricultural experiments are, from left to right, Rose Gabriel, Jeanette Johnson, John Lehan, Andrew Ward, Alton Nelson, Gordon Benson, Lawrence Emerald, Danny Ferrole, Charlotte Chute, and Elaine Butler.

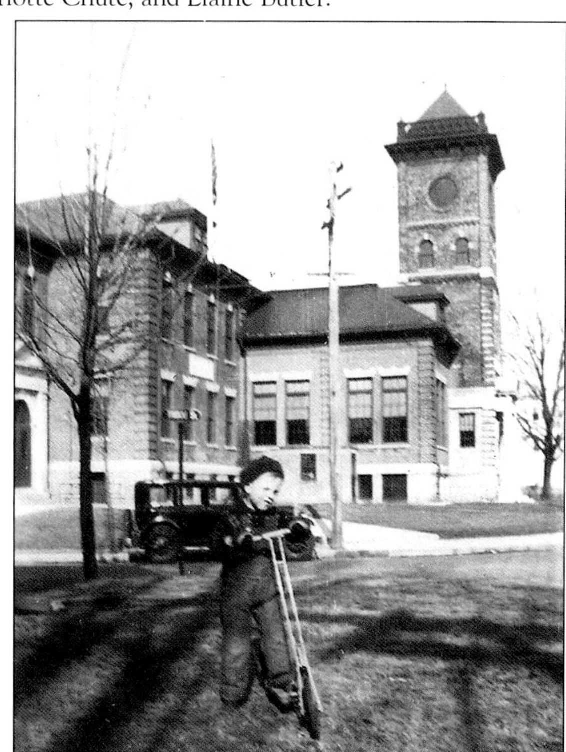

An impatient Richard Ostlund gets ready to zip away on his new scooter. Behind him is the Keith School.

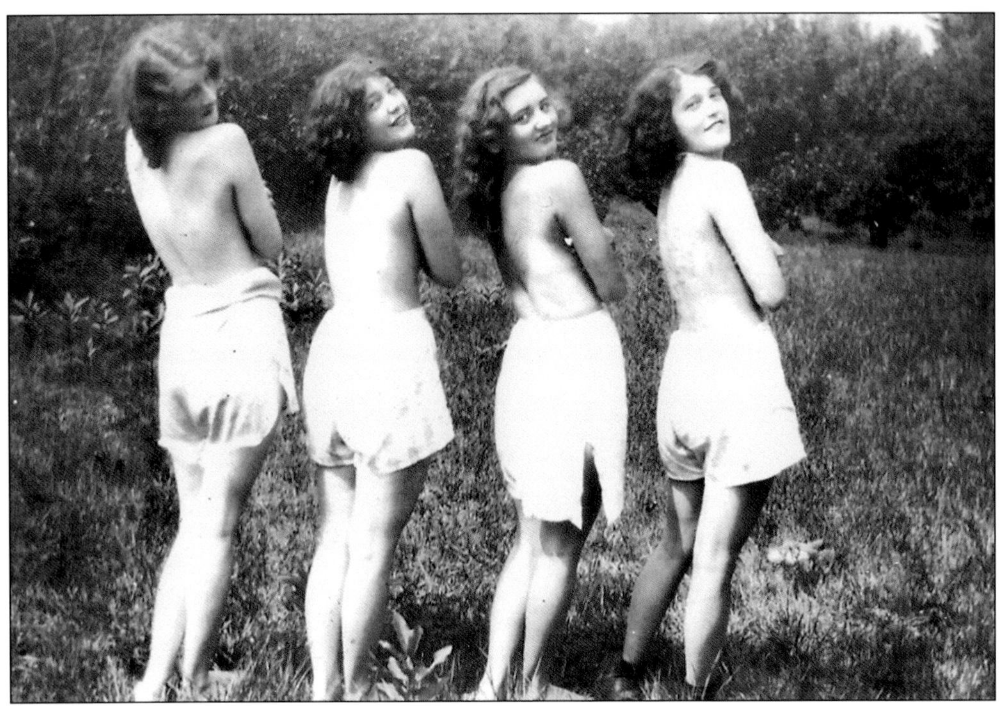

The girls of summer—Ruth McBride, Myrtle, Alva Goranson, and Elvira Ayres—pose playfully in a New Hampshire field.

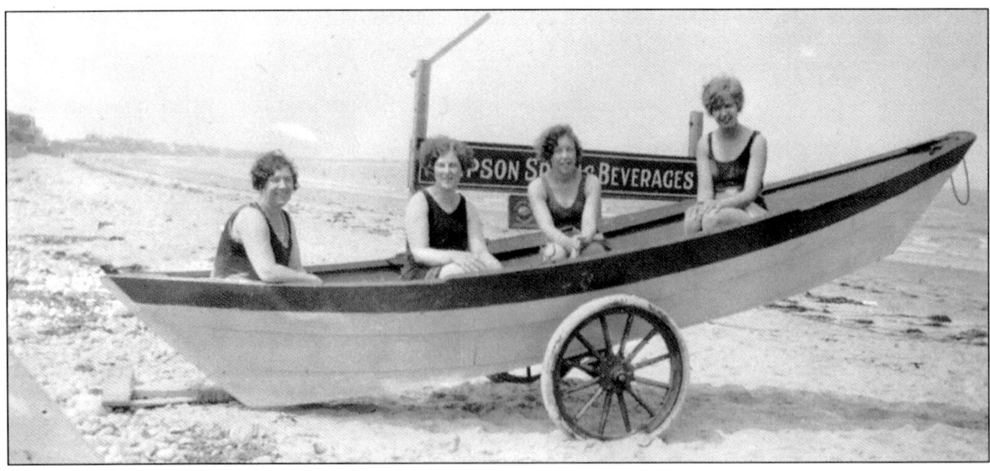


Green Harbor, June 22, 1929, is the seaside setting for Esther Ornval, Bernice Arvidson, Doris Ornval, and an unidentified companion in their high and dry dory.

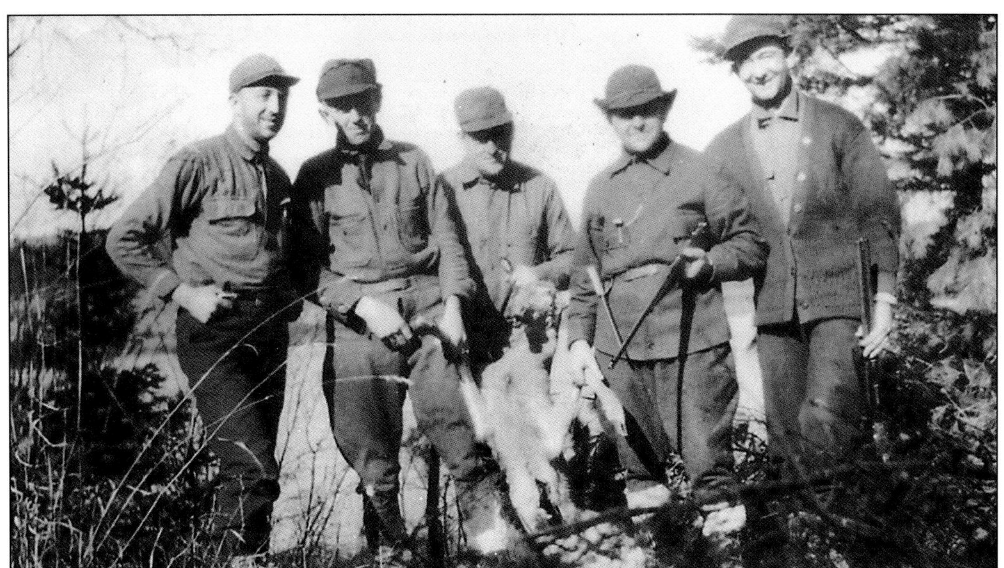

One of the great tragedies to befall Brockton was the loss of nine of its prominent citizens in a boating accident on Moosehead Lake in Maine. On May 13, 1928, the boat *Mac II* set out from Sawyer's Wharf in Greenville, Maine, headed for R.F. Spinney's camp at Tomhegan. The destination was never reached, as the boat sank in the icy waters off Sandy Point. Aboard were G. Fred Dahlborg, Dr. Frank Moberg, John Sandberg, Knute Salander, Dr. Arthur F. Peterson, Dr. David Bridgwood, William F. Daley (Brockton fire chief), Harry G. Howard, Samuel Budden (guide), and James E. Lays (police captain), the sole survivor. In the above photograph, taken three years prior during their annual trek to Maine, are, from left to right, Dr. David Bridgwood, G. Fred Dahlborg, two unidentified men, and Dr. Frank Moberg.

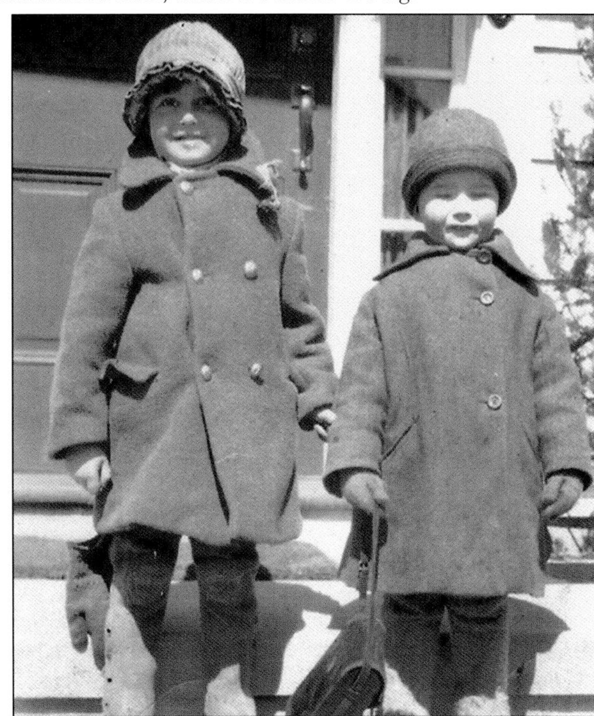

Five-year-old Dorothy (Dahlborg) Kendrew lost her father, G. Fred Dahlborg, in the tragic accident. Posing with her is a young friend, John Alden.

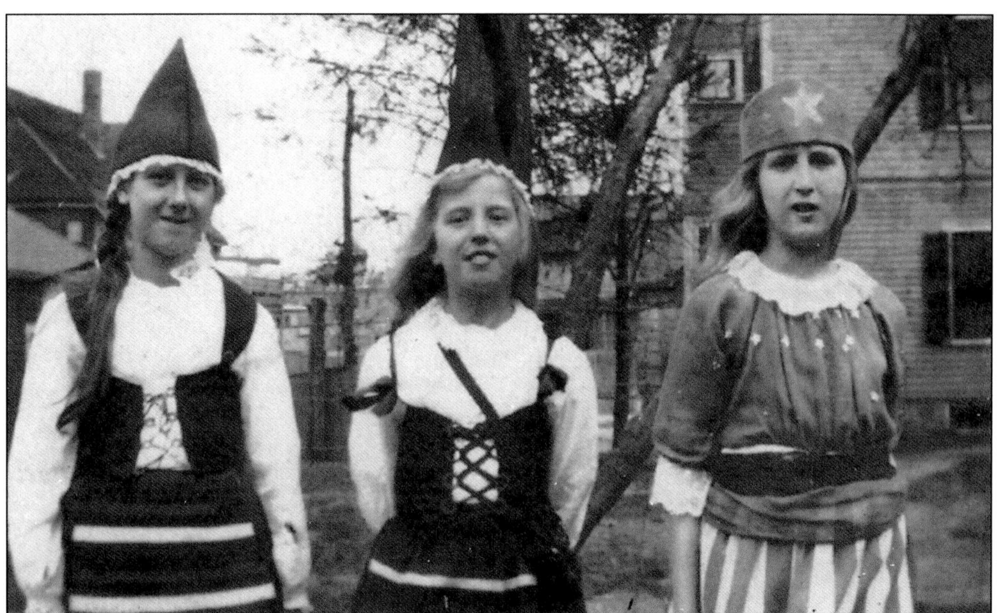

Anna and Edith Max, dressed in Swedish costumes, and sister Helen, dressed in patriotic attire, are ready to perform at a Liberty Lodge function. They are the daughters of the venerable Abel Max, known as "Mr. Swedish Lodge" for his numerous contributions to fraternal organizations.

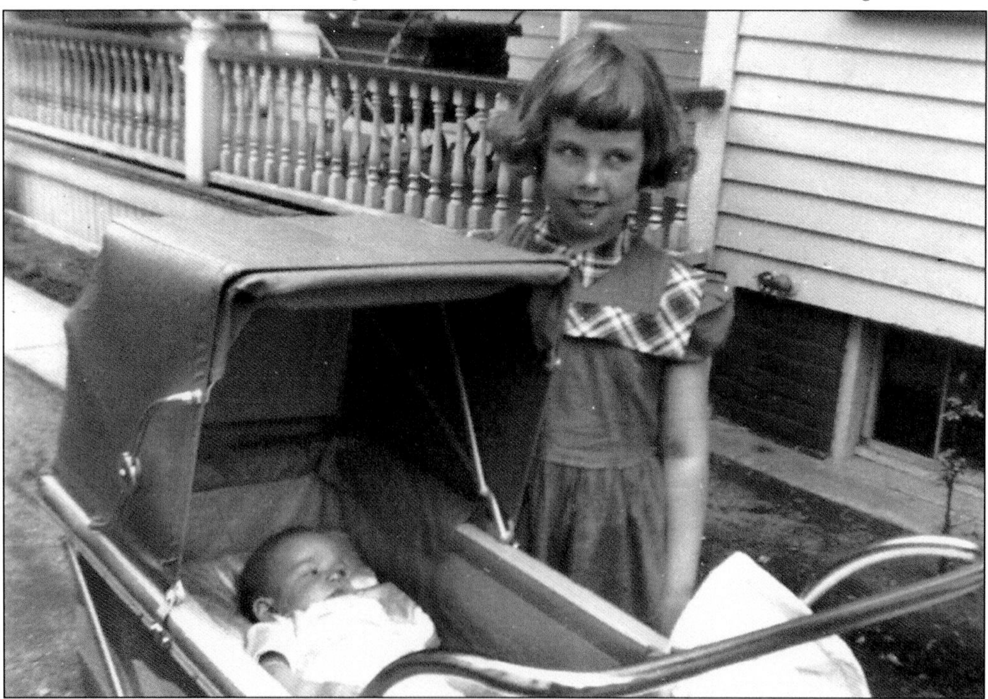

Marie Syverson stands proudly beside her charge Russell Edward Perkins, great-grandson of John Edward Lagerstedt. Miss Syverson, a graduate of the Brockton Hospital School of Nursing and Curry College, has served for 25 years as an ambulatory surgical nurse at New England Medical Center. Mr. Perkins, who served aboard the carrier USS *Independence*, became a banker and real estate appraiser.

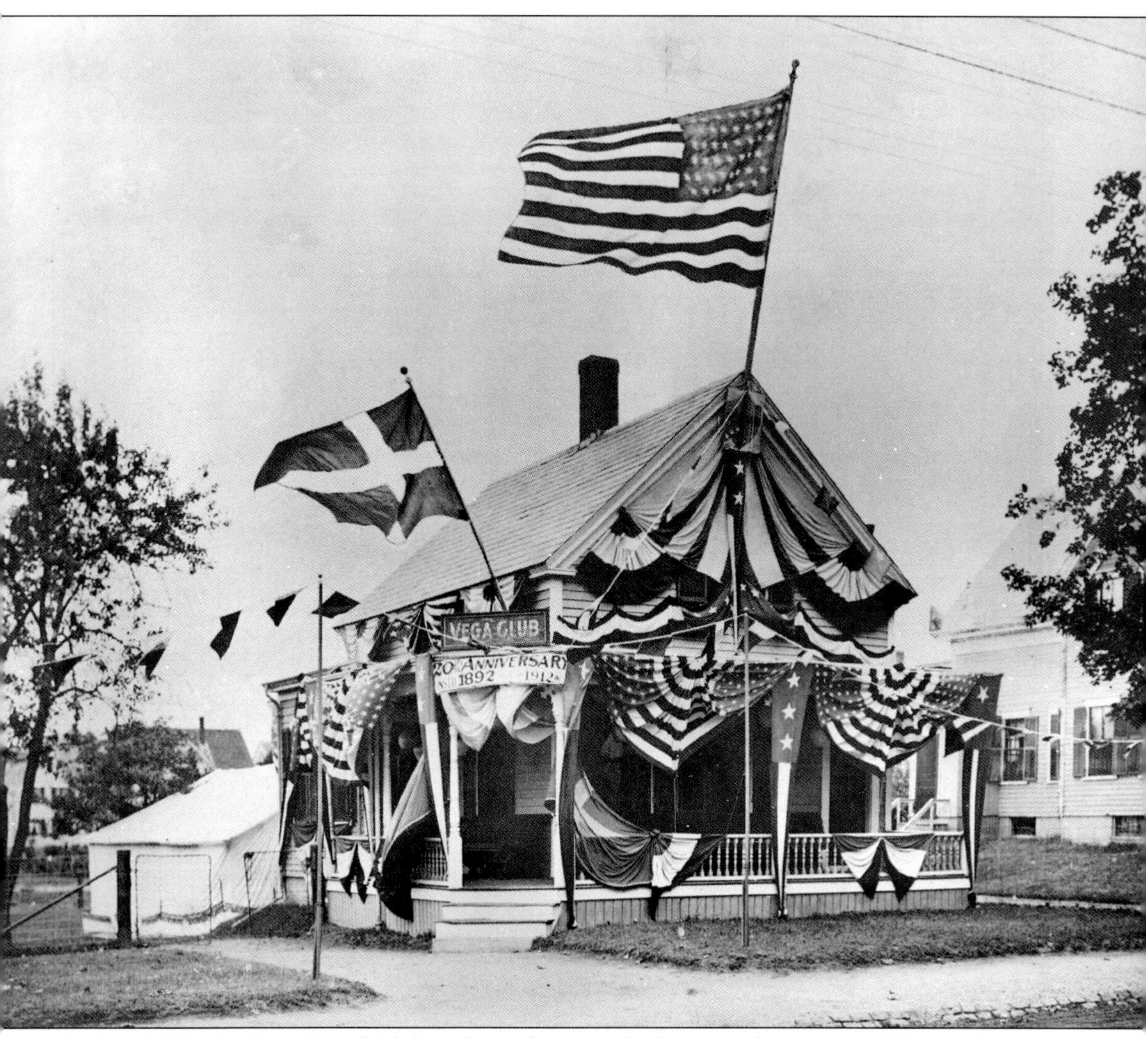


In June 1902, the Vega Social Club took residence in this house at the corner of Warren Avenue and Nilsson Streets for an annual rental fee of $200. The elaborate decorations are to celebrate their 20th anniversary. The Vega Social Club came into being on September 11, 1892, for the express purpose of "Profit and Pleasure." The club was named for the famous Swedish ship *Vega*, which, under the command of Capt. A.E. Nordenskold, was the first to complete the Northeast Passage. The Vega Social Club remains an active organization in 2001.

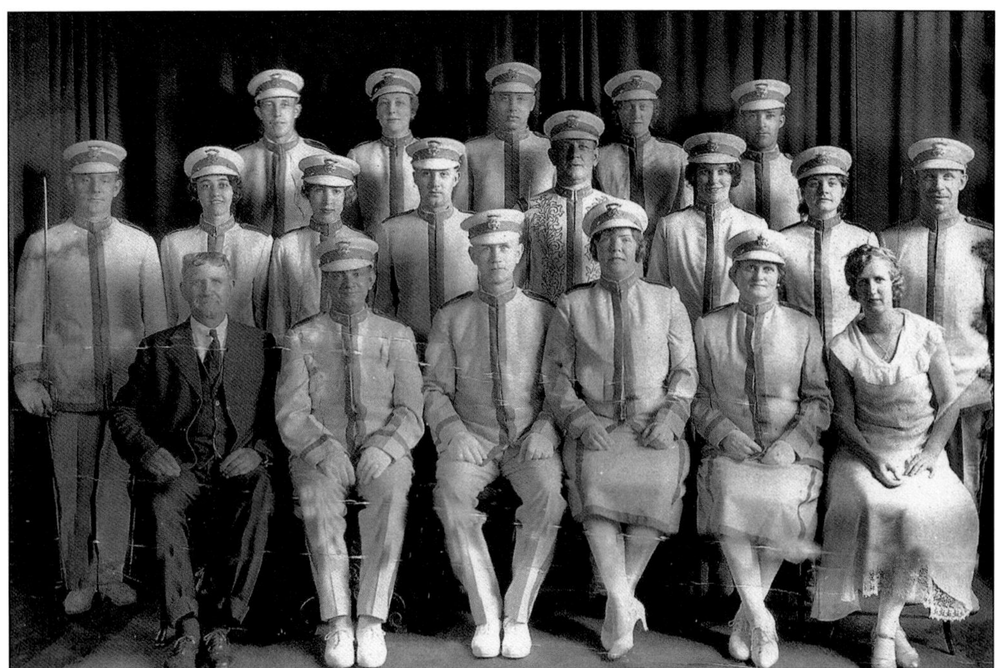

This rare photograph of a Vasa "Degree Team" presents the seriousness of purpose and formal preparation required for this recognition. In the front row on the far left is Abel Max. The woman sitting fourth from the left is Walborg Johnson, the only woman farm owner in the region. At the far right in the front row is the piano player for the group, Helen Max, who was trained by Hannah Rosendahl.

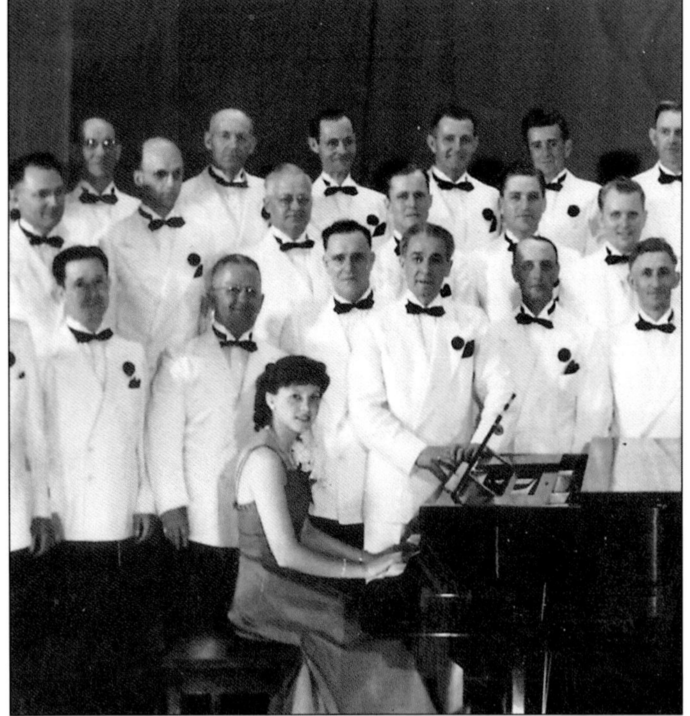

Shown here surrounded by the American Legion Male Chorus, beautiful pianist Laverne (Gustafson) Ekberg and conductor Herbert Otterberg (with his hands on the piano) performed throughout the region for more than 15 years. A sought-after piano teacher, Laverne began her teaching career at age 13 and has shared her musical gift with hundreds of eager students.

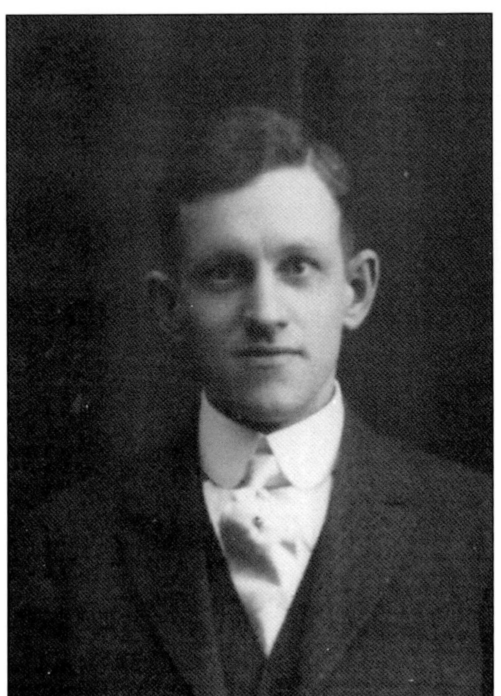

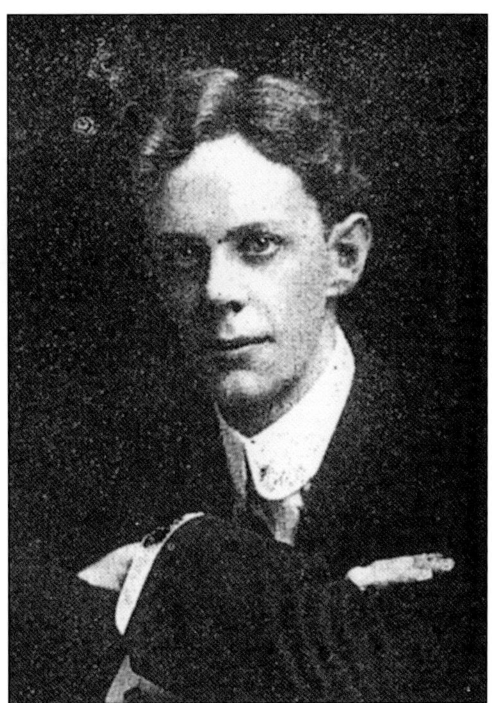

"It is an honor to serve," Edgar Thompson (above left) would often say when commenting on the political shenanigans of more recent times. This same duty-bound approach to public service was taken by Edward Dahlborg (above right) and Charles Helander in their many years in office. Mr. Thompson was an alderman in 1919. Mr. Dalhborg served as a member of Brockton City Council in 1912; as a member of the state House of Representatives in 1913, 1914, and 1916; and as a member of the state Senate from 1917 to 1920. Mr. Helander, shown below with his grandson Carl and several pond yachts he built, was an alderman in the 1920s and 1930s.

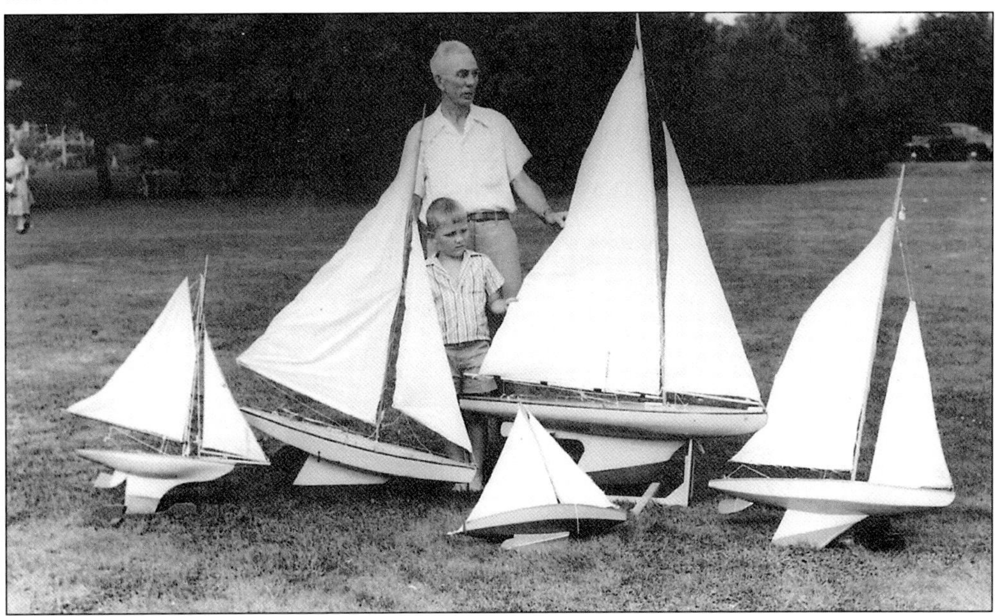

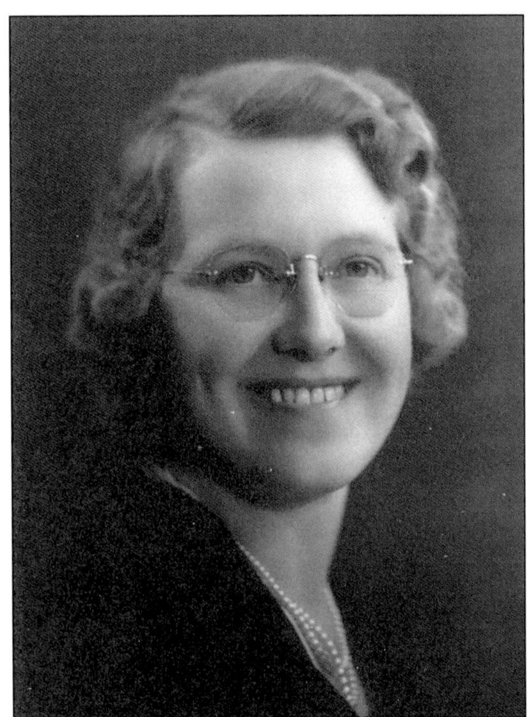

Brockton's First Lady from 1926 to 1931 was Elva Ahlstrom Bent, wife of Harold Dexter Bent, mayor and local businessman. It is noted in a 1928 history of Plymouth, Norfolk, and Barnstable Counties that he "is devoting his energy and enthusiasm to the improvement of the city which has thus honored him." Elva, a solid political figure in her own right, carried that same dedication to her position as a Plymouth County commissioner, an office she held from February 15, 1938, to January 1, 1964.

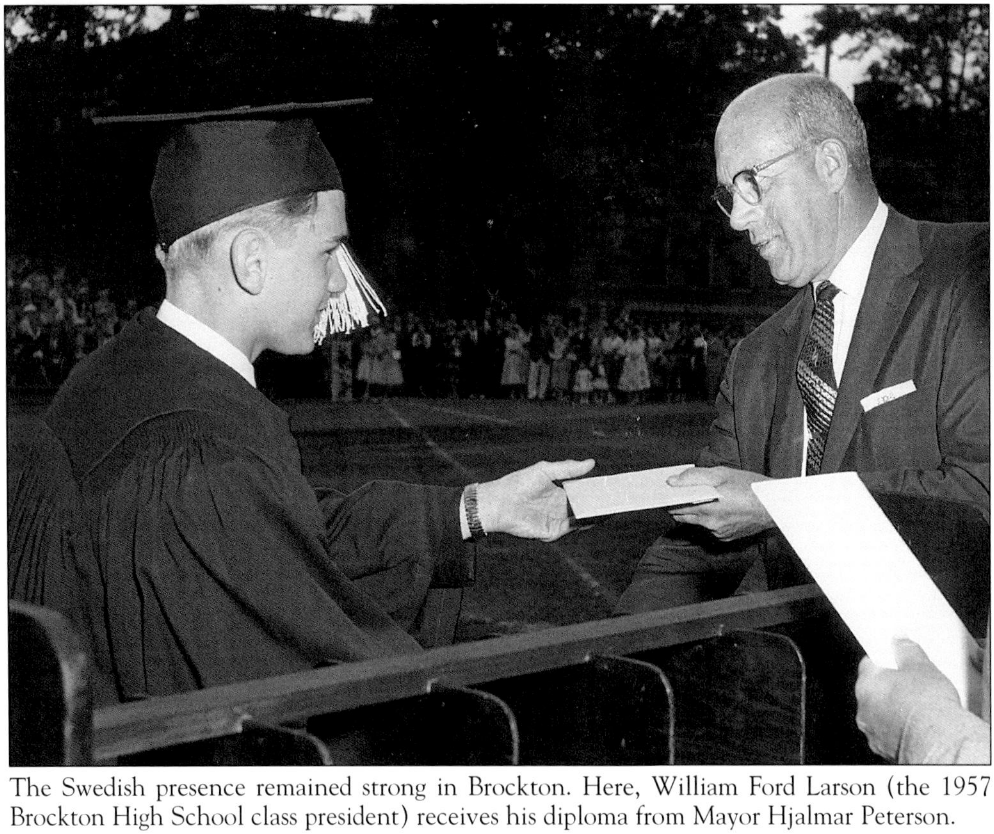

The Swedish presence remained strong in Brockton. Here, William Ford Larson (the 1957 Brockton High School class president) receives his diploma from Mayor Hjalmar Peterson.

# Four

# OCCUPATIONS

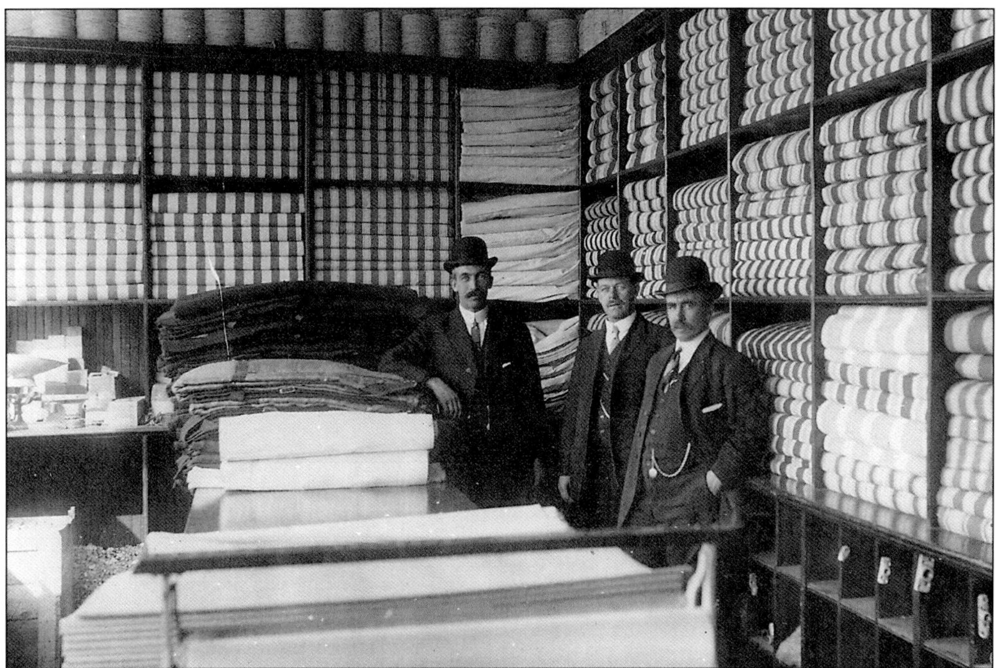

A handful of humility, a cup of determination, two measures of honesty, and a pinch of good old-fashioned stubbornness was the Swedish recipe for success in their new land, and succeed they did. By the 1900s, Swedish-owned businesses dotted the urban landscape. There were bakeries, cobbler and tailor shops, florists, pharmacies, ice-cream parlors, and grocery, paint, and hardware stores. The Swedes sold ice, coal, and oil. They also sold milk, grain, and hay. The Swedes, too, were carpenters, cabinetmakers, masons, and machinists. Enterprising Swedes formed Brockton Co-operative Boot & Shoe, Campello Nail-Less Heel, and the Brockton Machine Company. H.M. Christenson founded a razor-manufacturing business, while the firm of Olson & Arvidson manufactured cigars.

The Swedes also filled the ranks of the medical and legal professions. Dr. J.M. Morin, a graduate of Malmö Higher University of Medicine, was Brockton's first Swedish doctor. Raymond Johnson and Richard Lagerstedt practiced dentistry in Campello. Warren Lindberg was a long-practicing attorney of excellent reputation.

The first Swedish-born resident to serve in city government was A.F. Nordbeck, a building contractor who was elected alderman in 1901. Adolph Johnson gave Brockton a quarter century of distinguished service in the Great and General Court of Massachusetts.

Sigrid Lindstrom operated a successful millinery shop. Tekla (Lawson) Fhyr operated a long-remembered dry goods store. Hannah Seablom and Selma Brogren were grocers. These pioneer women merchants made their mark before the World War II era.

Swedish self-reliance and integrity in business and personal affairs earned the respect of the total community. That legacy remains.

**F. L. BRACONIER,**

REGISTRERAD APOTEKARE.

SVENSKT APOTEK.

ALLTID PÅ LAGER ETT STORT SORTERING AF

**SVENSKA MEDICINER.**

Receipt expediering en Specialitet.

---

**EDW. A. ROSENDAHL,**

**839 South Main St., Brockton, Mass.**

FÖRSÄLJER

**Rökt och färskt kött,**

**Fläsk, Lam och Fogel, m. m.**

TYSK KORF EN SPECIALITET.

EDW. A. ROSENDAHL,

839 SOUTH MAIN STREET, BROCKTON, MASS.

BROCKTON

Co-operative Boot & Shoe Co.,

CAMPELLO, MASS.

*Inkorporeradt 1886.*

ANDREW SWANSON, Superintendent.

Fabrikanter af

**Skodon**

**För män och Kvinnor.**

**Vi tillverka de välkända och berömda ELITE SKODONEN.**

Till hrr skohandlare vilja vi särskildt rekommendera våra skosorter och til den svenska ailmänheten endast säga: **uppmuntra svensk företagsamhet** och köp skodon hos de handlande som innehafva våra tillverkningar.

Brockton Boot & Shoe Co.,

Campello, Mass.

Shown here are advertisements from the 1903 *Swedish-American Affairs Calendar and Almanac.* (*Svensk-Amerikansk Affärskalender och Almanack för är 1903.*)

**CARL MOGREN,**

**Fredsdomare,**

**810 MAIN ST., BROCKTON, MASS.**

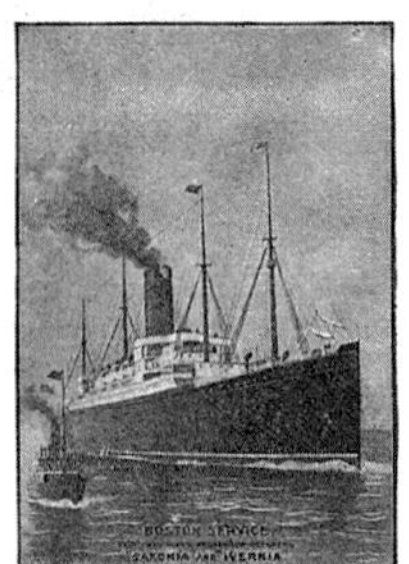

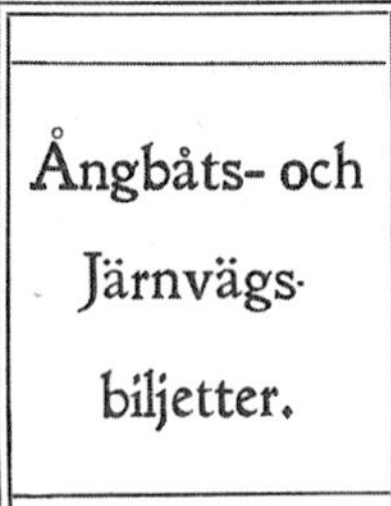


Böcker, Skrifmaterialer och Tidningar.

Lånbibliotek, Svenska och Engelska böcker.

Toalettartiklar, Klockor, Fickur och Kedjor.

LEKSAKER FÖR BARN.

Soda, Candy och Cigarrer.

*U. S. Post Office—Substation No. 2.*

**CARL MOGREN,** 810 MAIN STREET, BROCKTON, MASS.

**ALBIN F. NORDBECK**

**57 MENLO STREET, BROCKTON, MASS.**

Assistance given in placing Loans. Plans and Specifications furnished.

**Contractor and Builder.**

All kinds of orders in the Building Line promptly attended to.

**ALBIN F. NORDBECK**

**57 MENLO STREET, BROCKTON, MASS.**

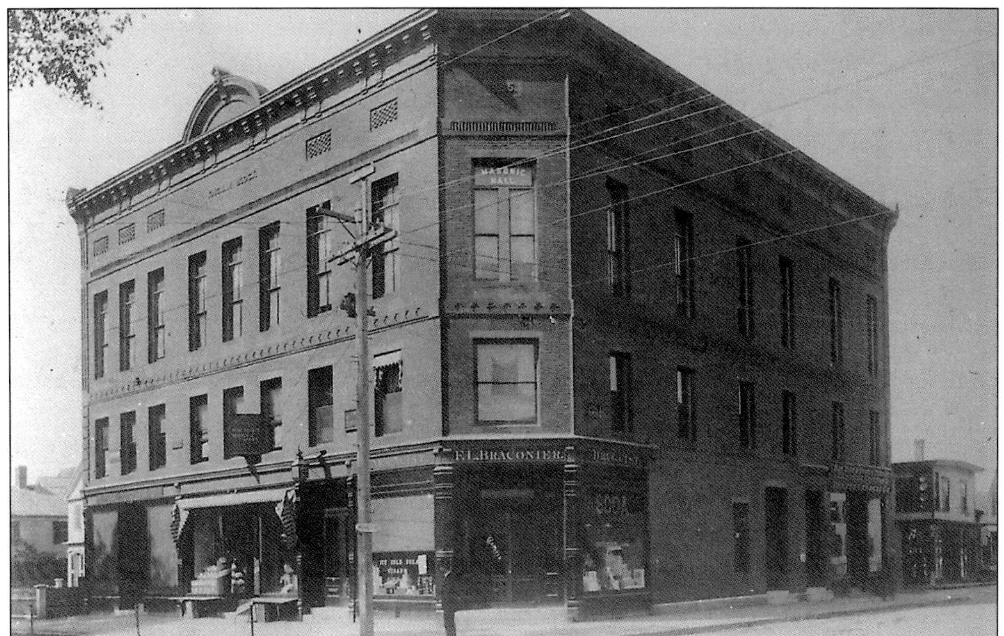


One of the first Swedish businesses in Brockton was Braconier's Pharmacy, established in 1880 by Frans L. Braconier and located in the Kingman Block at Market and Main Streets. Braconier studied at Lund University in Sweden, where his uncle was a professor. He had previously opened apothecary shops in Boston and Lowell.

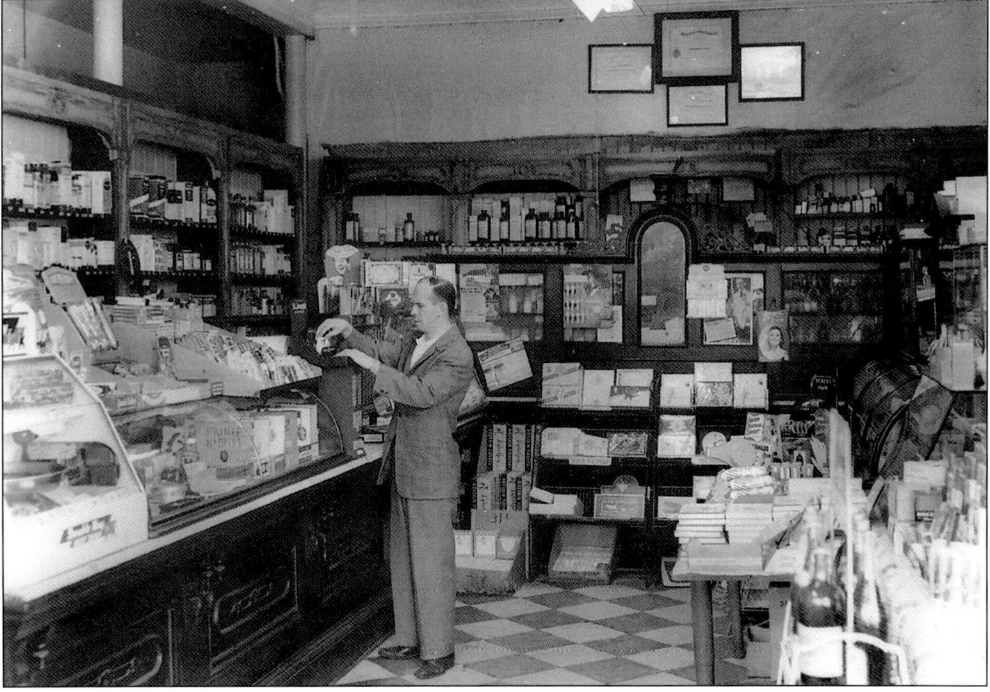

The successor to Braconier's was Campello Pharmacy, the interior of which is shown in this 1948 photograph. The shelves, display cases, and stamped tin ceiling were, more than likely, original to the store. (Stanley Bauman photograph.)

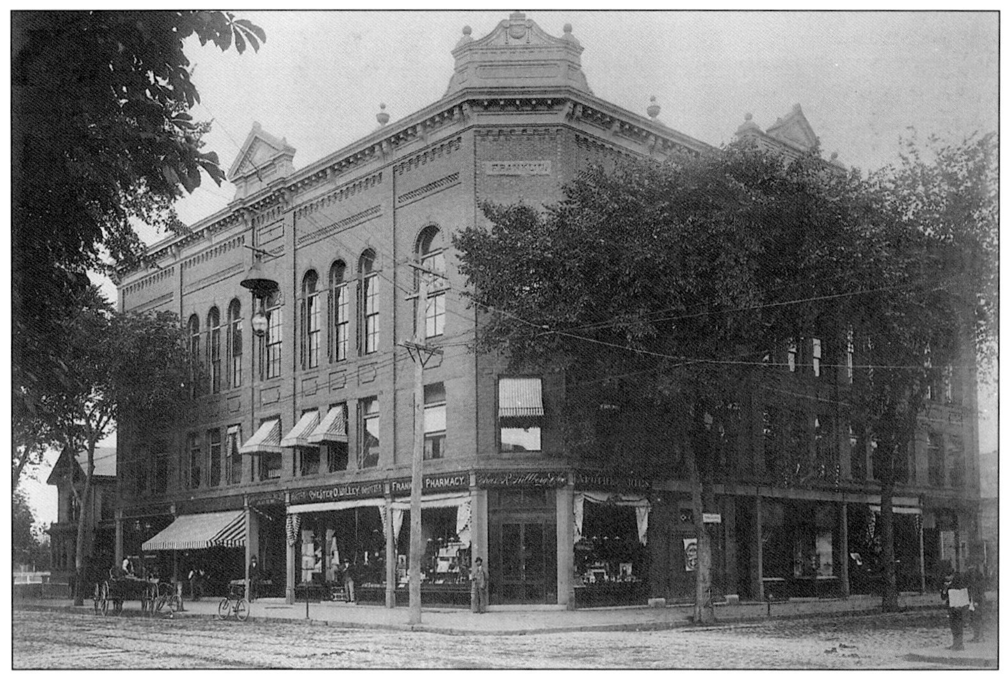


A native of Jönköping, Charles R. Hillberg was educated in the apothecary business in Lungby, Smaland. Arriving here in 1881, he purchased a pharmacy on Center Street and, in 1893, opened a store, eventually known as the Franklin Pharmacy, in the Franklin Building at the corner of Main Street and Perkins Avenue. Hillberg could stand in the front door and look south on Main Street into the front door of his largest competitor, Braconier's.

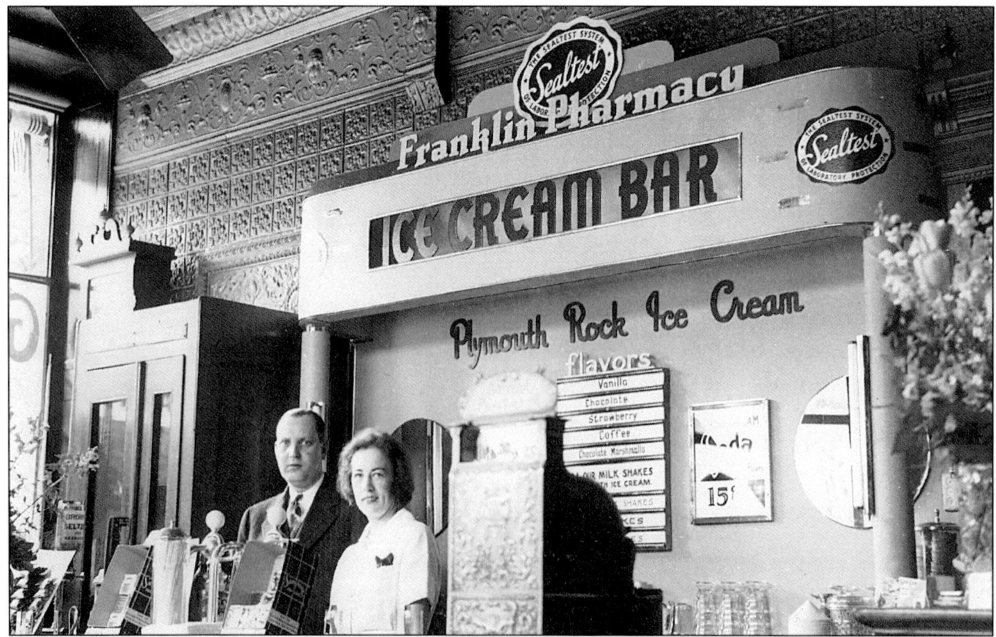


Acquiring the Franklin Pharmacy from Charles Hillberg, Mr. and Mrs. Roy Franzen Sr. celebrated the grand opening of Franzen's Pharmacy on May 21, 1938. Ice cream and the biggest soda fountain in Campello became a mainstay of the business.

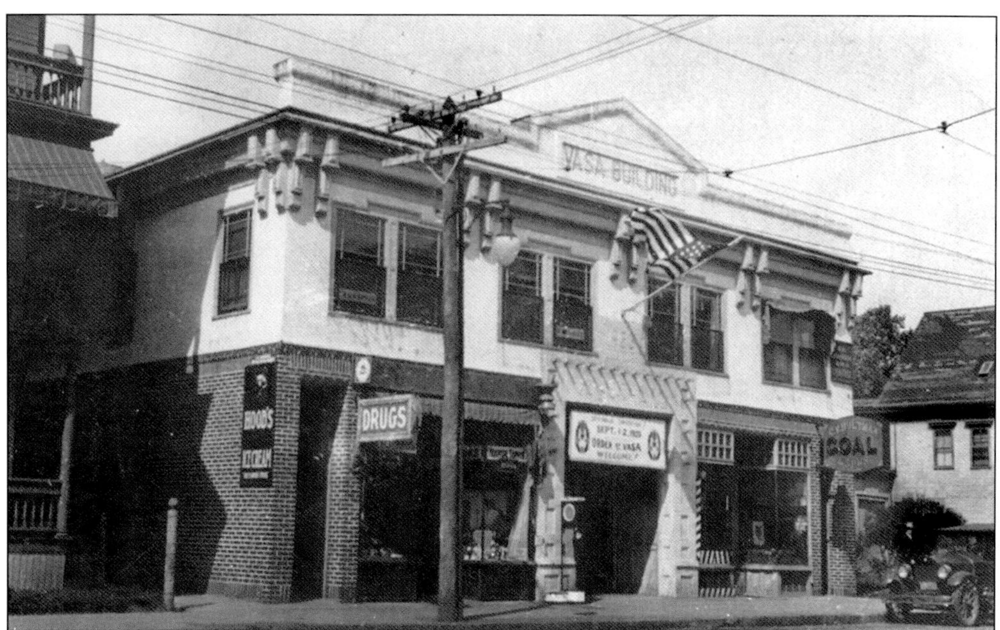


Vasa Hall was home to a number of Swedish-owned businesses and professional offices: Emberg's Pharmacy; C.V. Hultman Coal and Oil; Dr. Raymond Johnson, dentist; Dr. Rudolph Kruger, M.D.; and the Elizabeth (Lindberg) Ford Beauty Parlor. The building also housed a bowling alley, a large auditorium for dances and other events, and a well-patronized neighborhood establishment.

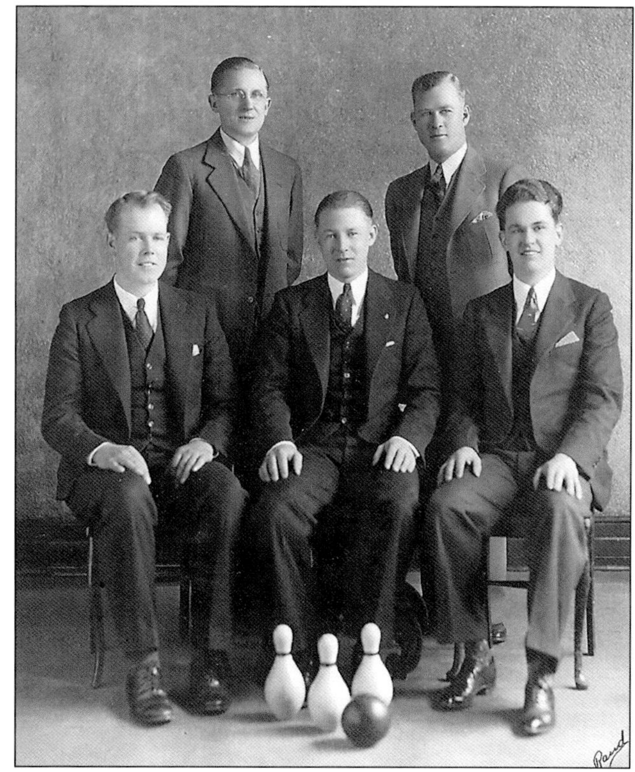

Shown from left to right are the 1935–1936 Vasa Bowling League Champions: (front row) Richard Seaquist, Herbert Peterson, and Edward Larson; (back row) Sigurd "Sig" Ryberg and an unidentified gentleman. Edward Larson, a Hires Root Beer salesman, was the father of William F. Larson, who in 1957 served as BHS class president. Sig Ryberg, a barber, had his shop on the ground floor of Vasa Hall.

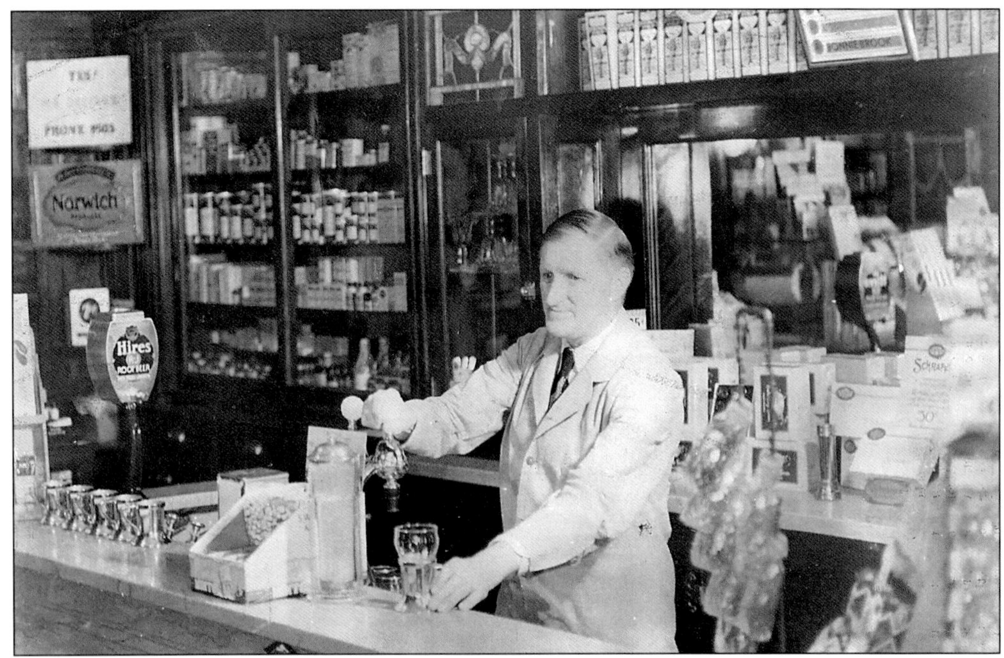


If you wanted a great ice-cream soda, a malted frappe, or a cold glass of his orange slush, you headed for Emberg's Pharmacy. Frank Emberg had emigrated from Karlskröna and, on arrival in Brockton, joined the ranks of the Swedish shoeworkers. However, an early interest in science caused him to attend the Meriano School of Pharmacy in Boston, where he learned both English and Latin. In the mid-1920s, now a registered pharmacist, he founded two drugstores: Emberg's in Campello and Ames Drugs in Montello.

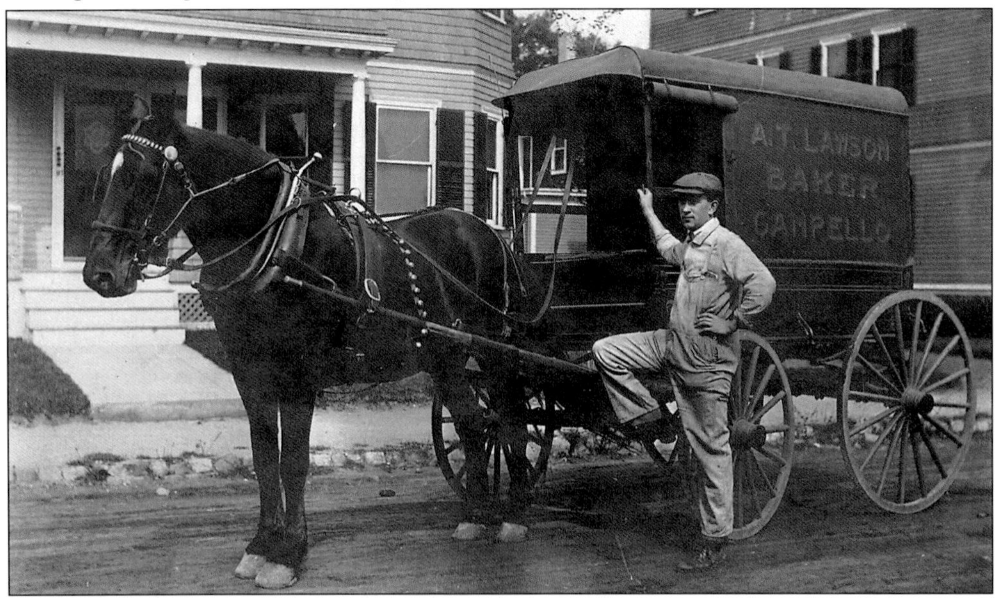


Like other neighborhood bakers, A.T. Lawson offered home delivery of rye breads, pastries, cookies, and pies. Shown in this c. 1920 photograph is Ernest S. Lindgren, one of Lawson's deliverymen. In 1923, Ernest and his wife, Bertha, opened a variety store at 352 North Elm Street in West Bridgewater, appropriately called Lindgren's Store.

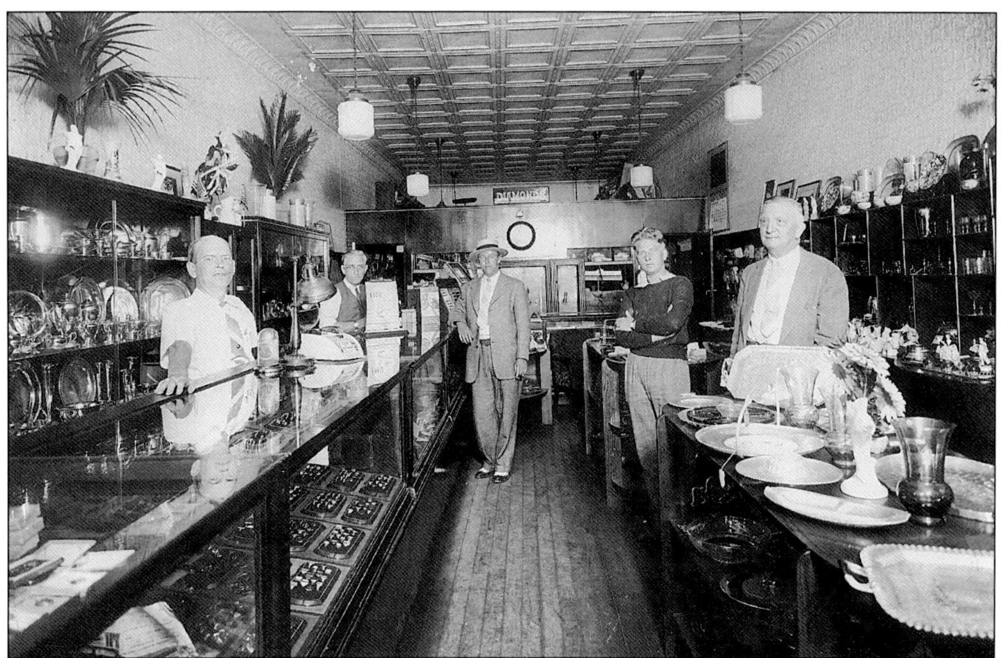

The precision required to be a jeweler was demonstrated in the accurate and detailed records left by Helmer Bystrom of Taft's Jewelers. In the photograph, from left to right, are Earl Hastings, clerk; A.H. Bystrom, owner; Harold Peterson, a customer; Bill Bystrom, an apprentice recently graduated from high school; and Bill Mantz, a jewelry salesman from New York City. The photograph was taken using flash powder.

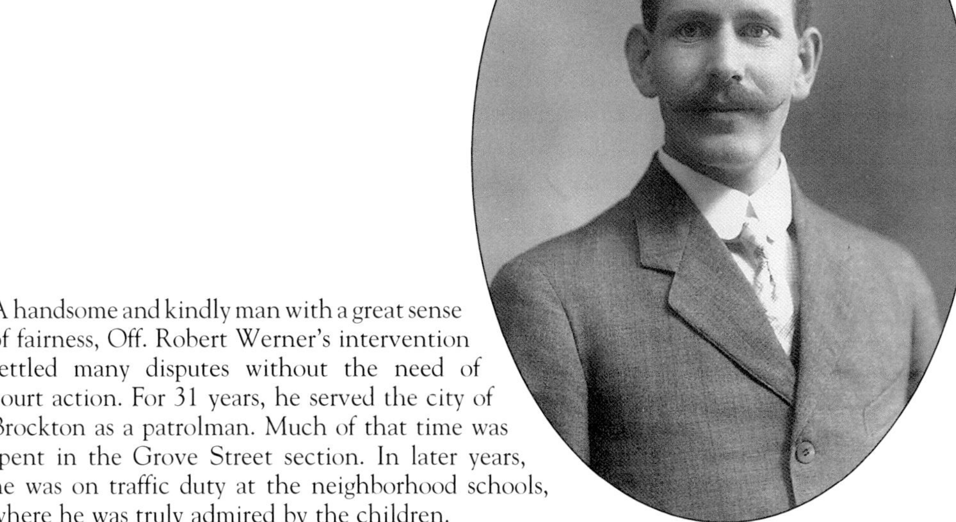

A handsome and kindly man with a great sense of fairness, Off. Robert Werner's intervention settled many disputes without the need of court action. For 31 years, he served the city of Brockton as a patrolman. Much of that time was spent in the Grove Street section. In later years, he was on traffic duty at the neighborhood schools, where he was truly admired by the children.

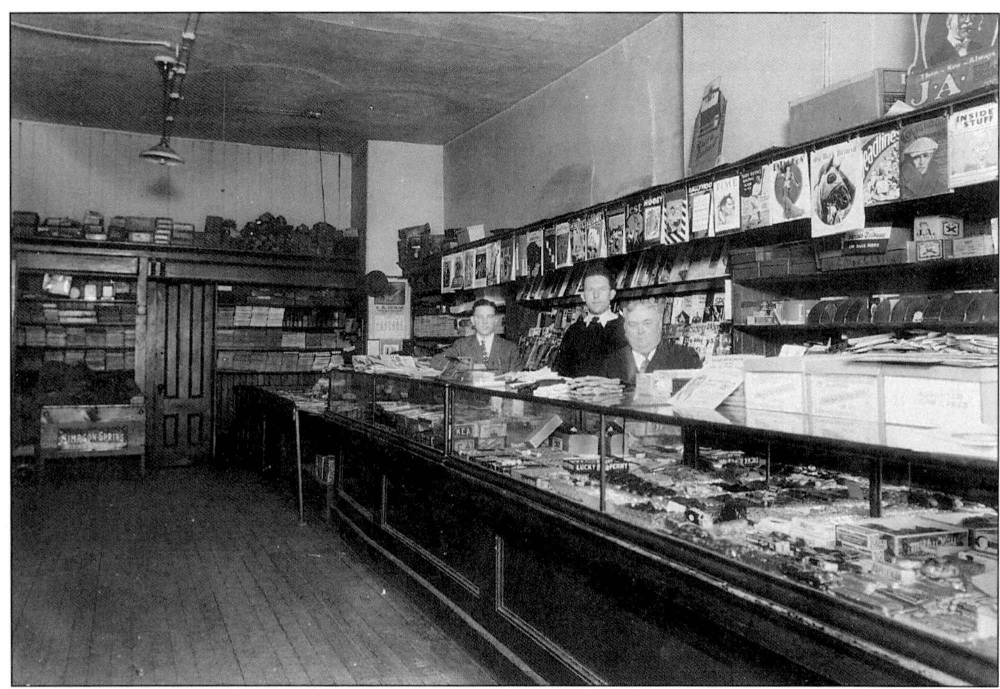


Another one of those great neighborhood institutions was the Campello News Stand, originally owned by John Leonard, who is pictured above with John Hallinan and Elroy Ostlund. On Saturday afternoons, the back room was frantic with activity as newsboys assembled the sections of thousands of Sunday papers and readied them for delivery. In addition to newspapers from all over, the Campello News Stand sold candy, soda, greeting cards, paper, writing supplies, and games. Elroy Ostlund, shown below with his characteristic welcoming smile, was often referred to as "the Mayor of Campello."

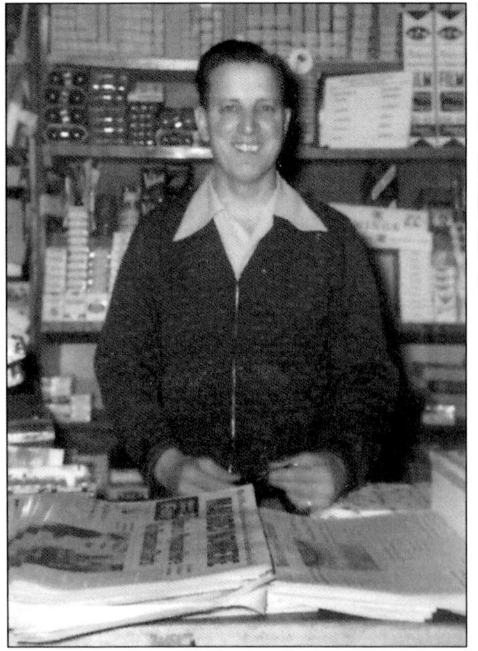

BUS. TEL. 2782

**ALBERT E. (GULLY) GULLBRANTS**

CHIEF LITERATURE DISPENSER
FOR THE
MAYOR OF CAMPELLO.

14 VAUGHAN CT.. CAMPELLO. MASS.

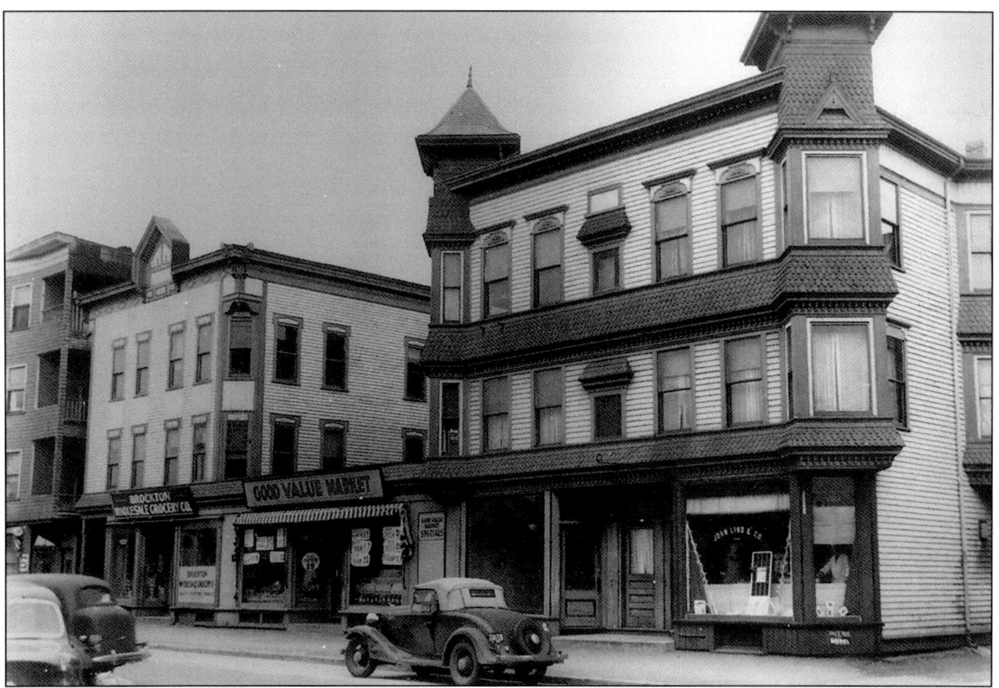


John Lind's was possibly the most popular ice-cream parlor in Campello. Located on Main Street, Lind's served frappes, ice-cream sodas, fountain drinks of all kinds, sundaes, and, of course, a 5¢ ice-cream cone complete with sprinkles. In the mid-1940s, Mike Sheehan, Lind's partner, took over the business and carried on the tradition of making and serving the best ice cream anywhere. (Stanley Bauman photograph.)

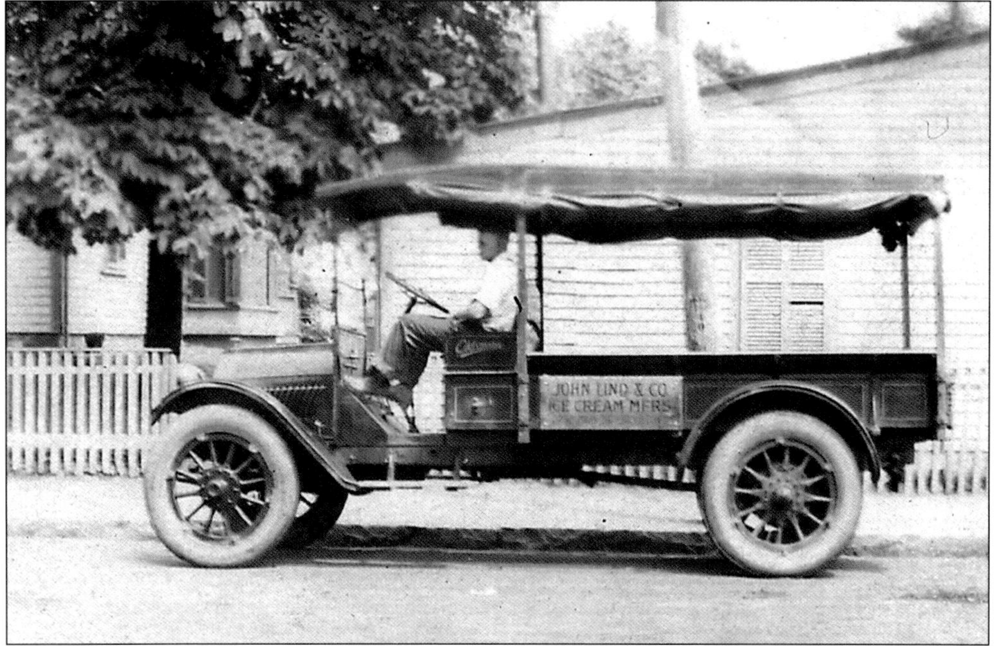


John Lind's delivery truck, being driven here by Harry Gustafson, was a welcomed sight in the neighborhoods. The question remains—how did he keep the ice cream from melting?

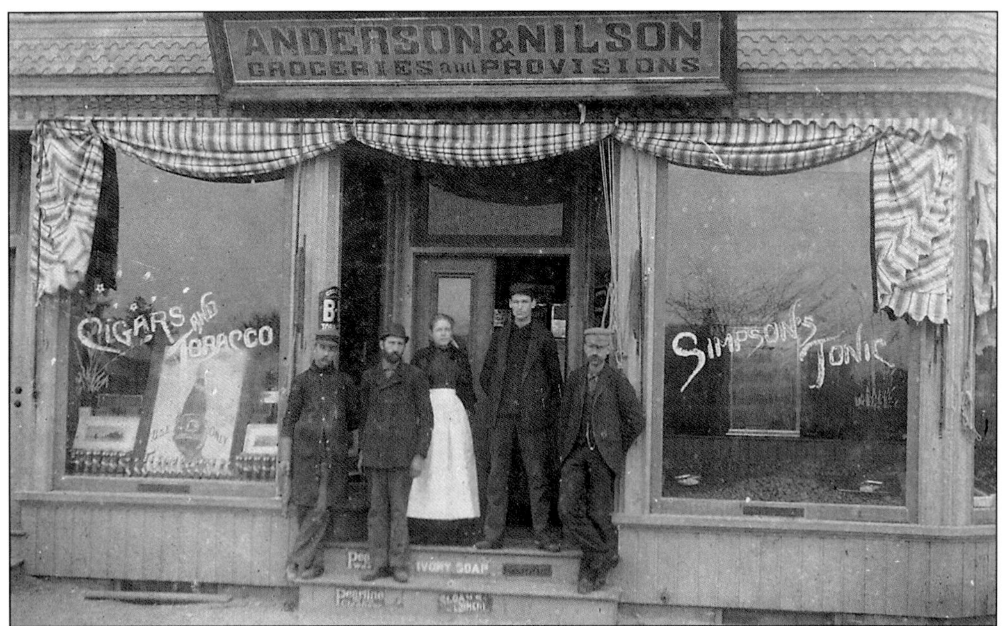


With two locations and 15 employees, Anderson & Nilson was the largest Swedish grocery in Greater Brockton during the early 1900s. Monday through Saturday, eight horse-drawn delivery wagons carried goods to customers throughout the city. The business, known for its quality and honest prices, was owned and operated by Erik Anderson, Swante Anderson, Alfred Nelson, Andrew Nelson, and Patrick Nelson.

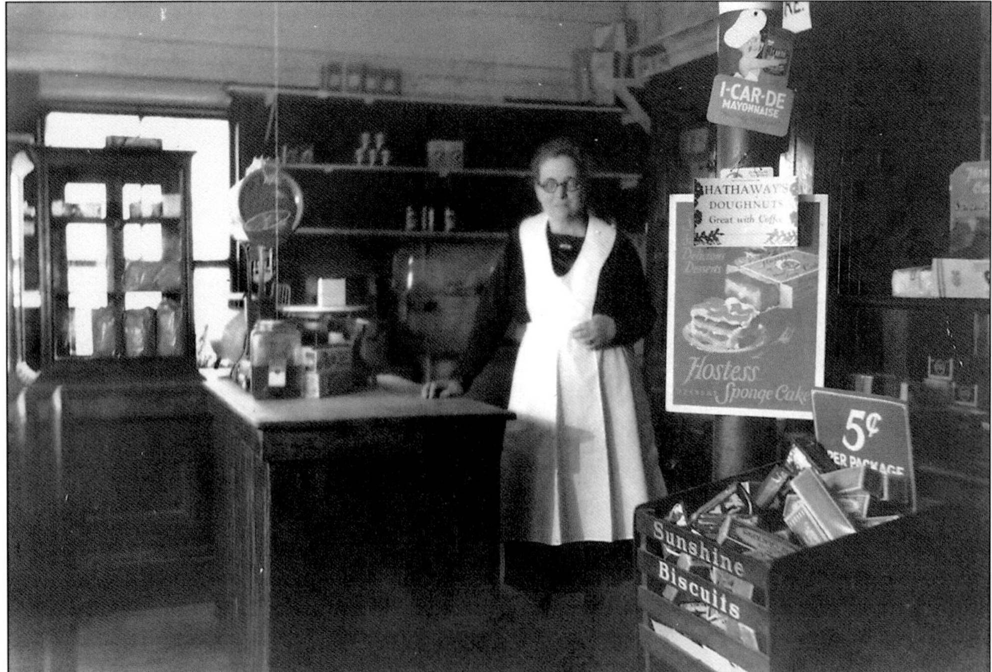


Selma Brogren was one of a handful of women who operated grocery strores in the city during the early 1900s. She is shown here in her place of business on Hovendon Avenue in Brockton's North End.

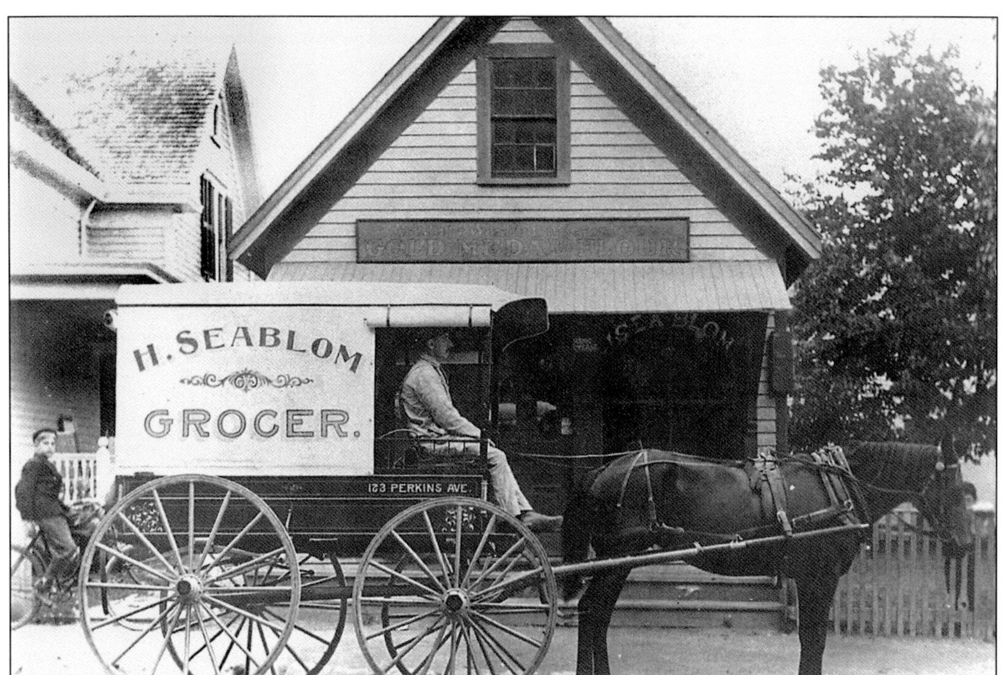


Hannah Anderson Seablom (Sjöblom) managed the firm of H. Seablom Grocer from the early 1900s to 1930. An enterprising woman, Hannah sold a wide variety of goods from her store on Perkins Avenue. Customers were encouraged to phone in their orders, which kept her driver and her horse, Ted, pretty busy.

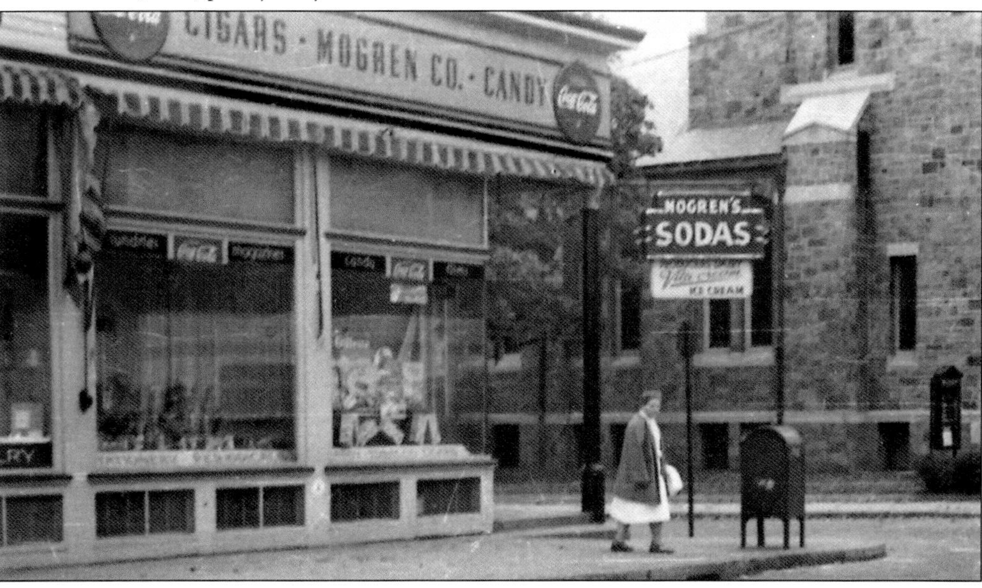


Without doubt, in the early 1900s, the city's most popular businessman was Carl Mogren. Daily visits to his shop numbered in the hundreds. A postmaster of Station No. 2, a justice of the peace, and an agent for the world's largest steamship lines, Mogren also ran the Swedish Lending Library. Among the many goods he sold was Dr. Peter's Kuriko for constipation and poor digestion. In later years, the store was known as Nilsson Variety under the ownership of Gus Johnson.

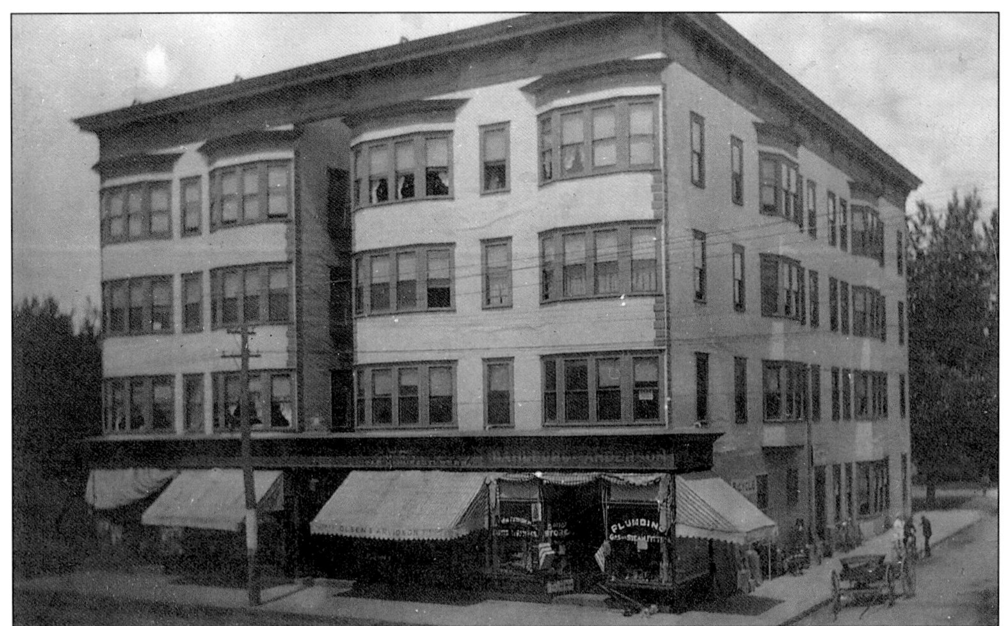


At the corner of Grove and Main Streets loomed this large structure known as the New York Apartments. Home to numerous Swedish families c. 1900, it also housed Dahlborg & Anderson Plumbing, a five-and-dime store, Olson & Arvidson cigar manufacturers, a bicycle repair shop, and a barbershop. In 1928, Dahlborg & Anderson gave way to O'Connor's Pharmacy. The building was later renamed the Grove Apartments.

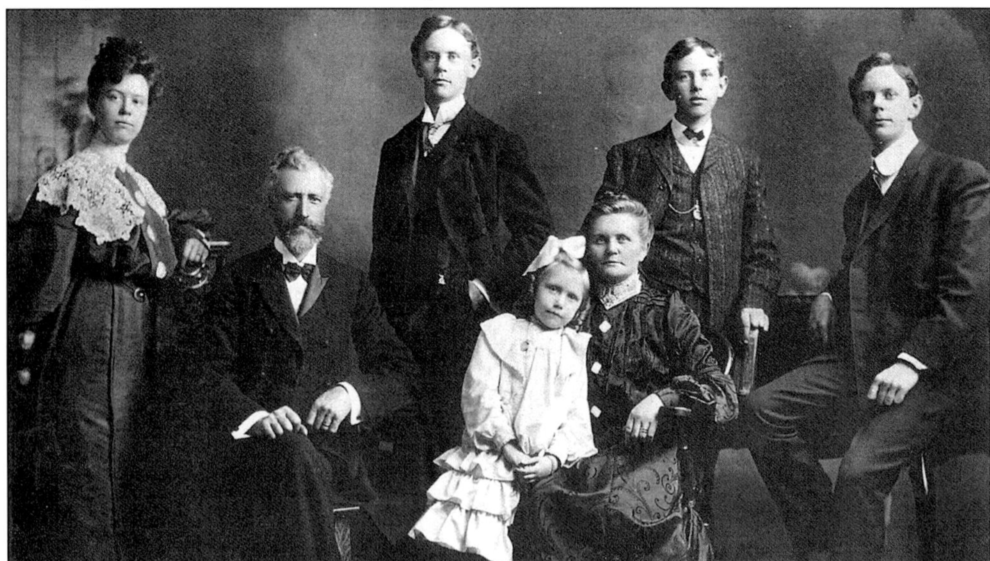

Prominent among the Swedish business families was that of Charles F. Dahlborg. Arriving in America in 1874, Dahlborg opened a hardware, plumbing, heating, and roofing firm on Main Street in 1885. In 1902, he started an undertaking business, known today as Dahlborg-MacNevin. Active in politics, he was a member of the Brockton City Council. In this family photograph are, from left to right, Ida, Charles F., Carl Emil, Lillian, Laura, G. Fred, and Edward. Emil entered the funeral business. G. Fred died in the Moosehead Lake tragedy in 1928. Edward was a prominent attorney and politician.

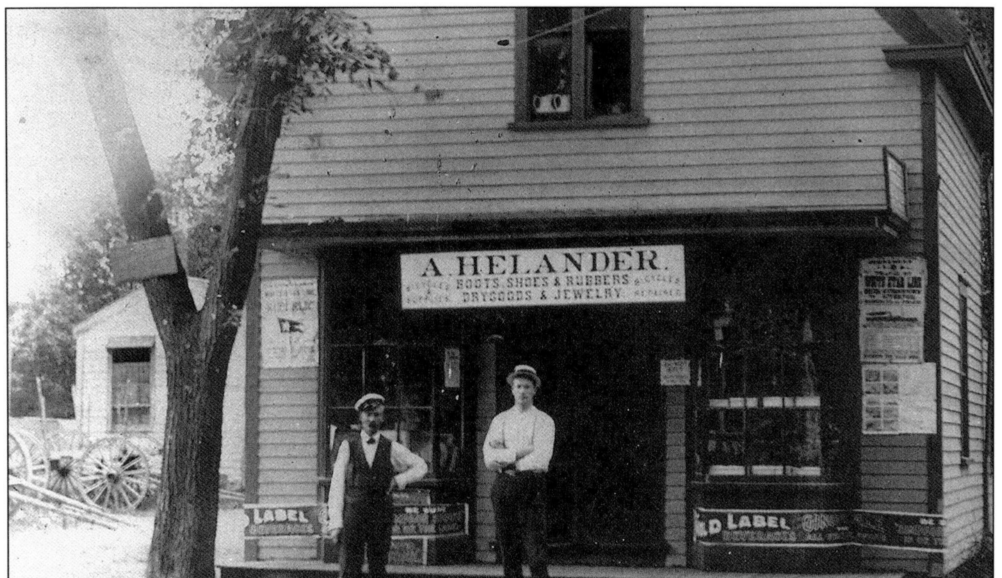


Anders Magnus Helander, pictured above with son Victor, arrived with his family in Boston on November 21, 1892, aboard the steamship *Catalonia*. A small ship, it listed only 375 people on the manifest. Of those, 216 were in steerage and were assumed to be immigrants. Anders and his wife, Charlotta, settled in North Easton with their children Victor, Charles, Lena, and Tekla Serafia. Their eldest daughter, Hilma, had immigrated sometime before them. Pictured below are daughters Hilma and Tekla. Daughter Lena later became the grandmother of Brockton mayor Winthrop Farwell. Helander opened a general merchandise store on Center Street.

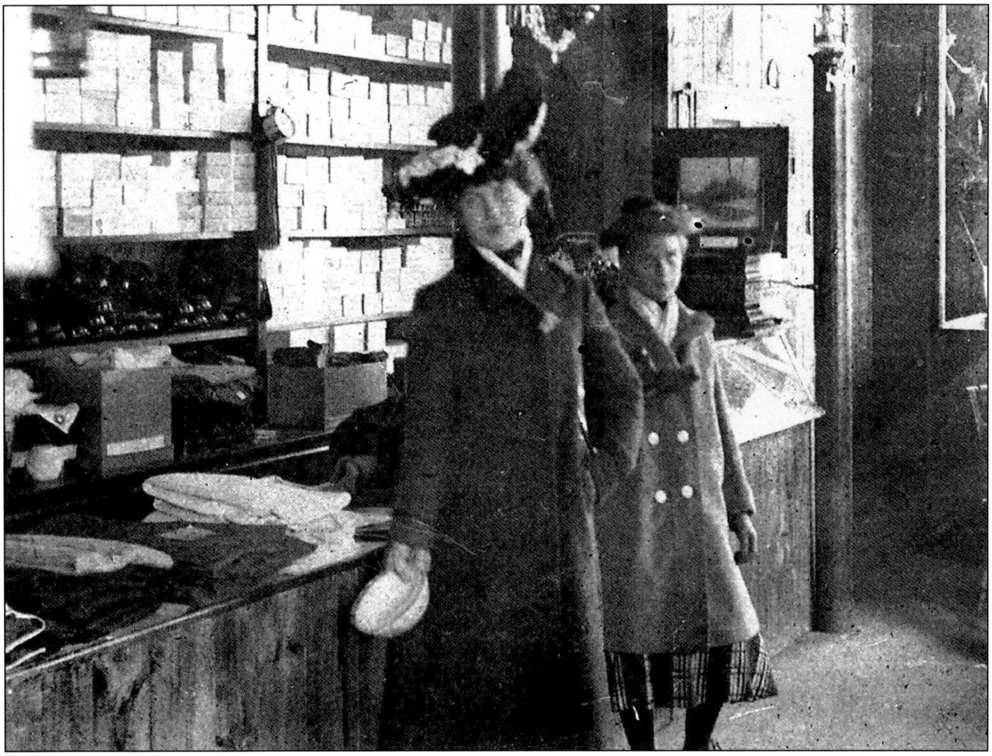

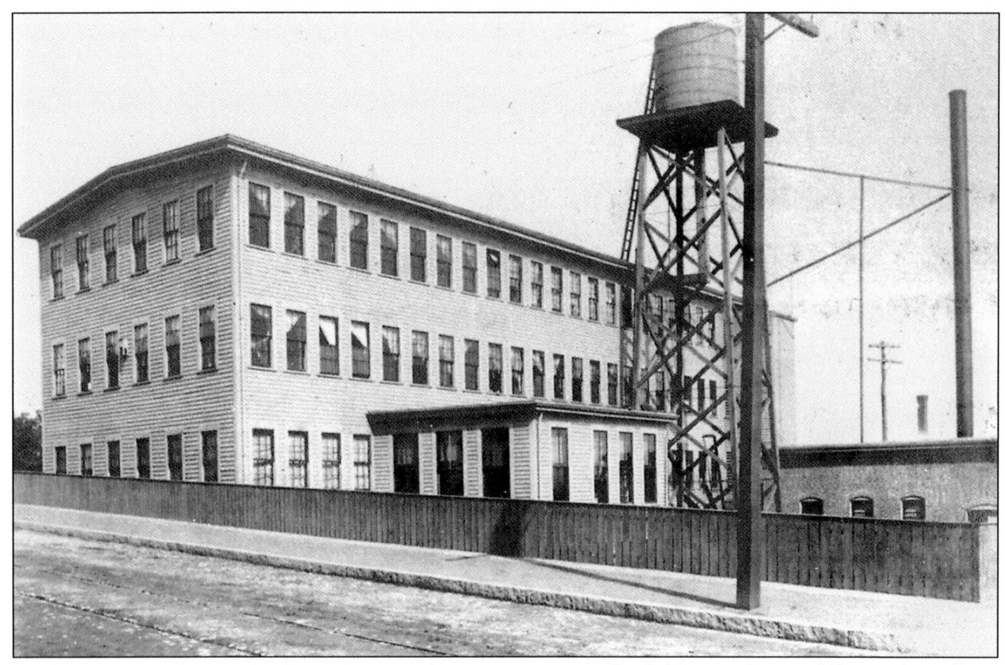

Seeking to produce a high-quality product at a price affordable to the middle and working classes, a group of entrepreneurial Swedish immigrants organized a shoe factory under the name of Brockton Co-operative Boot & Shoe. On November 26, 1886, this group of 22—led by Olaf Johnson, Andrew Swanson, Charles Carlson, Peter Nelson, and Olaus Johnson—incorporated under the laws of Massachusetts. Originally financed with capital stock valued at $10,000, the enterprise operated for 83 years.

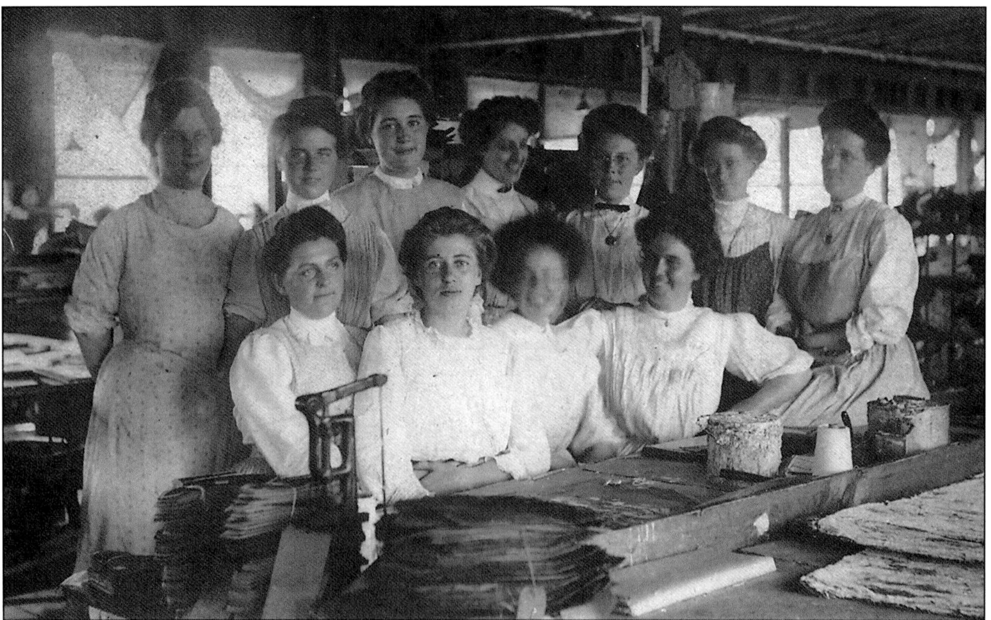

Enjoying a moment of relaxation in the Brockton Co-operative Boot & Shoe cutting room, this group worked long, hard hours to produce the quality product for which the company was known. Sleeves rolled up and portraying a great show of humor is Signe (Pearson) Peterson.

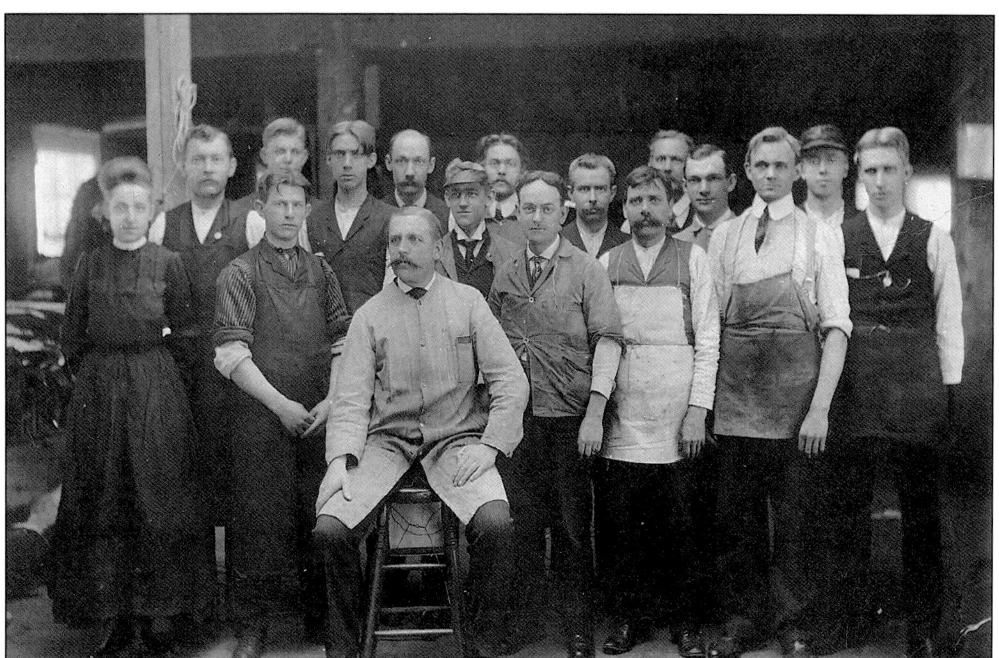

Lars Peterson (seated) was the superintendent of Brockton Co-operative Boot & Shoe and eventually became the treasurer and general manager of the company. Upon the death of his wife, Beata, he donated a share of company stock in her name to the First Lutheran Church, the income from which shoes were to be bought for needy children. Standing third from the right is August Anderson, father of insurance agency owner Esther Lundin.

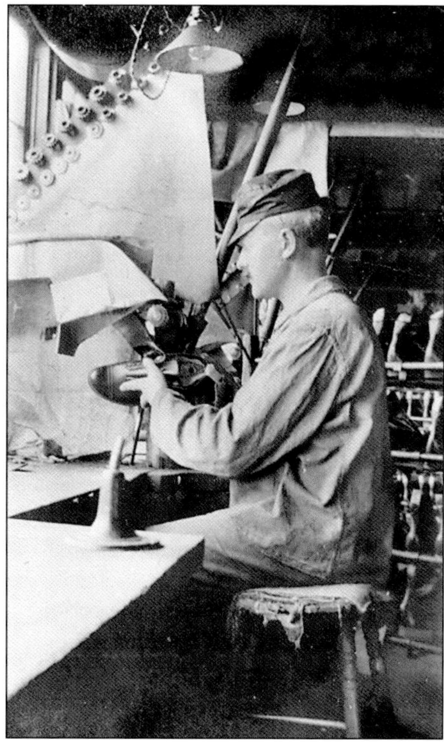

Skilled craftsmen played a key role in the growth and excellent reputation of Brockton's shoe industry. Carl Victor Erickson (born in Lungsund, Varmland, Sweden) arrived in Brockton in 1905 and worked as an edge trimmer at the Diamond Shoe Company, Packard Shoe Company, and George E. Keith Company (makers of the famous "Walk-Over" shoe). During the late 1930s, he earned as much as $55 per week, underscoring Brockton's claim that the labor force in its shoe factories was among the highest paid in the United States.

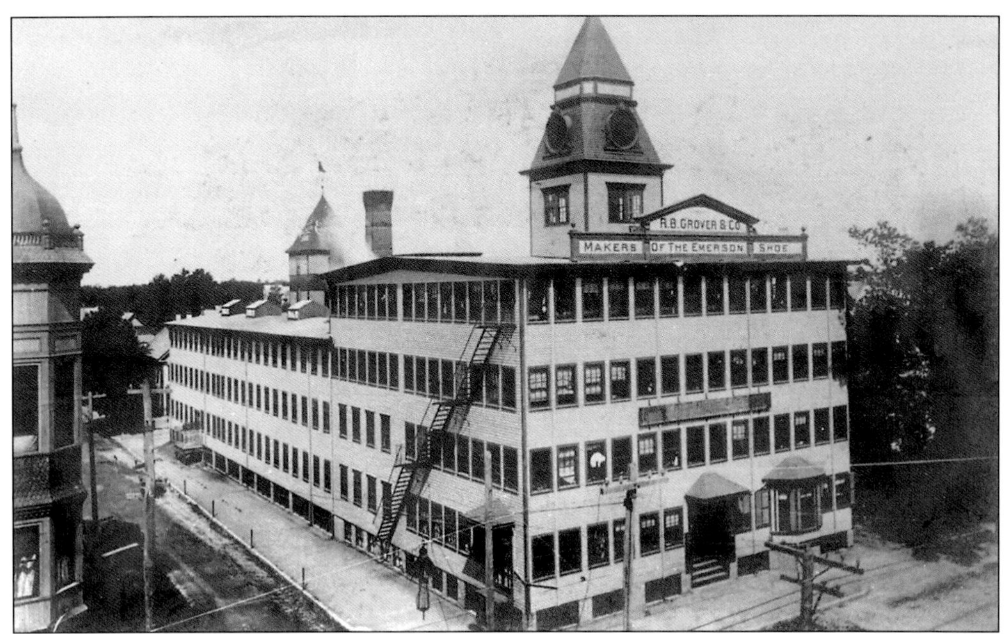


The R.B. Grover & Company factory was the scene of Brockton's great disaster when, on the morning of March 20, 1905, a boiler explosion and ensuing fire caused the death of 58 employees and injuries to 150 others. The building was a complete loss, and the business closed. People from Brockton and throughout the country spontaneously contributed to a fund for the widows and orphans of the fire. More than $104,000 was raised.

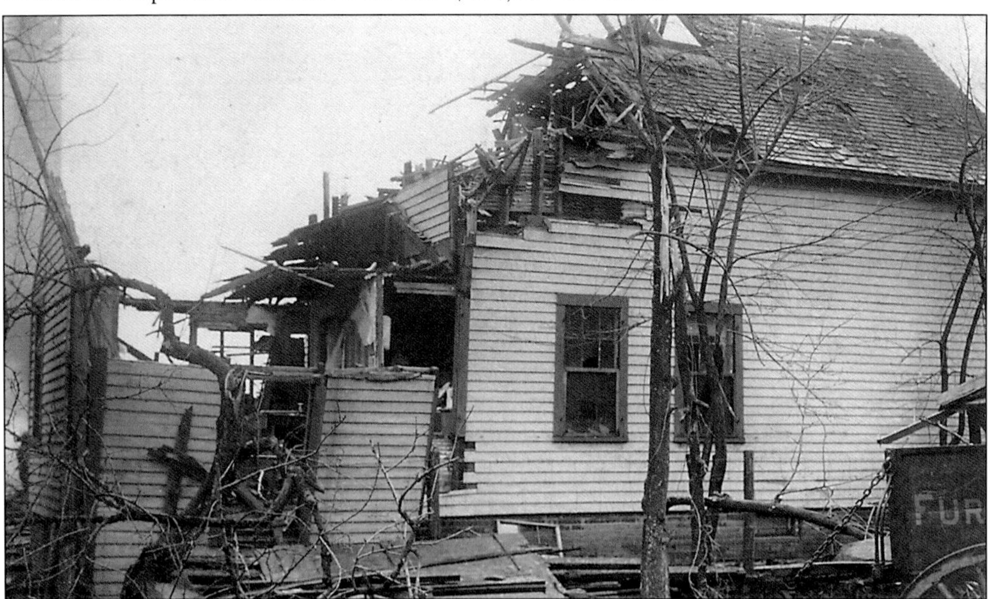

The exploding factory boiler flew some 100 yards, leaving a path of destruction along neighboring Denton Street. The vessel crashed through the roof of the home of plant engineer Donald Rockwell and came to rest in the adjacent home of Mary Pratt. Rockwell headed to work 30 minutes before the blast and was likely in the boiler room at the time of the explosion. As the boiler passed through his home, his wife and children were not injured. Ironically, he had commented to his wife on the potential hazard of the antiquated power plant.

Hannah Lindberg, a stitcher at the R.B. Grover & Company shoe factory, was one of 55 people who lost their lives in the great explosion and fire that destroyed the five-story building on Monday, March 20, 1905. Born in Sweden on October 18, 1873, she left three children: Helen (who was with her in Brockton), Martha Elizabeth, and Lars Olaf (both of whom remained in Sweden). Martha Elizabeth immigrated to Brockton some 15 years later and, for 25 years, operated a beauty parlor in the Vasa Hall building, only two blocks away from where her mother had been employed.

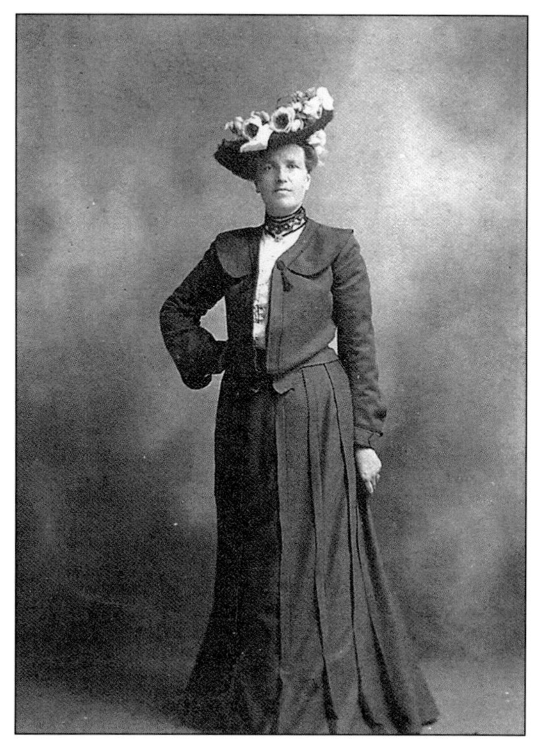

# IN MEMORIAM

*Mrs. Hannah Lindberg.*

**The Brockton Central Labor Union** mourns its loss in the sacrifice of the lives of the Union women and men, our sisters and brothers, who finished their Earth Pilgrimage in the wreckage, smoke and fire which followed the explosion of a boiler in R. B. Grover & Co.'s factory, between 7.55 and 8.15, on the morning of Monday, March 20, 1905.

Words cannot express the deep sympathy we feel for those whose homes are darkened by this sudden tragedy. Our prayer is that faith in the Highest Power may soften the blow to the bereaved. The finite cannot comprehend the Infinite.

**Resolved,** That these Resolutions be spread upon our records, published in our local papers, and a copy be sent to the afflicted.

E. GERRY BROWN,<br>THOS. H. FAIR,<br>JAS. E. KELLEY, } Committee.

*Emmet T. Walls* President.<br>*Joseph W. Kelley* Secretary.

Shown here is a memorial certificate presented by the Brockton Central Labor Union to the family of Hannah Lindberg.

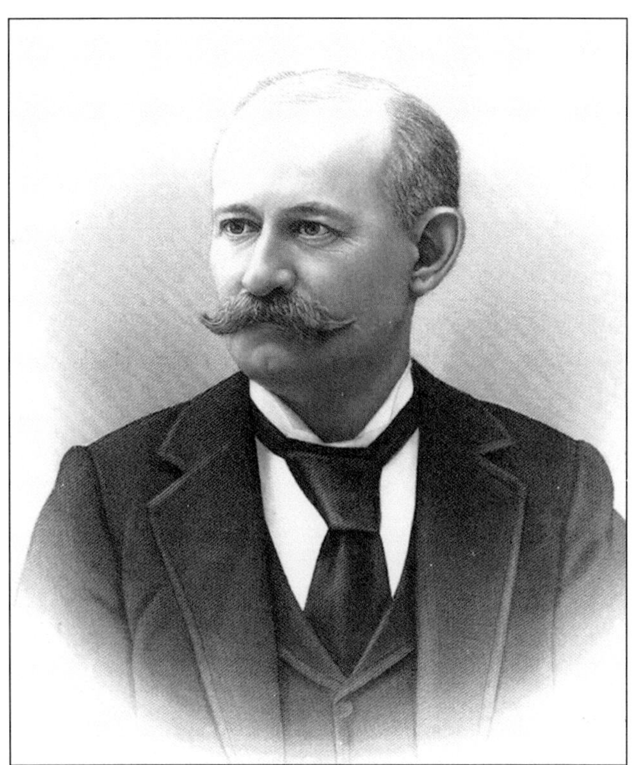

The history of the region's Swedish people would be incomplete without the inclusion of shoe magnate George Eldon Keith. In 1871, age 21, having worked at the bench since childhood, "George E" established a shoe-manufacturing business with $1,000 in capital and 10 employees. Instilled with his business acumen and personal integrity, the business flourished. By 1921, it comprised some 66 buildings totaling 1,166,260 square feet of floor space, 7,000 employees, and sales of more than $30 million. The famous "Walk-Over" shoe was sold in 102 countries.

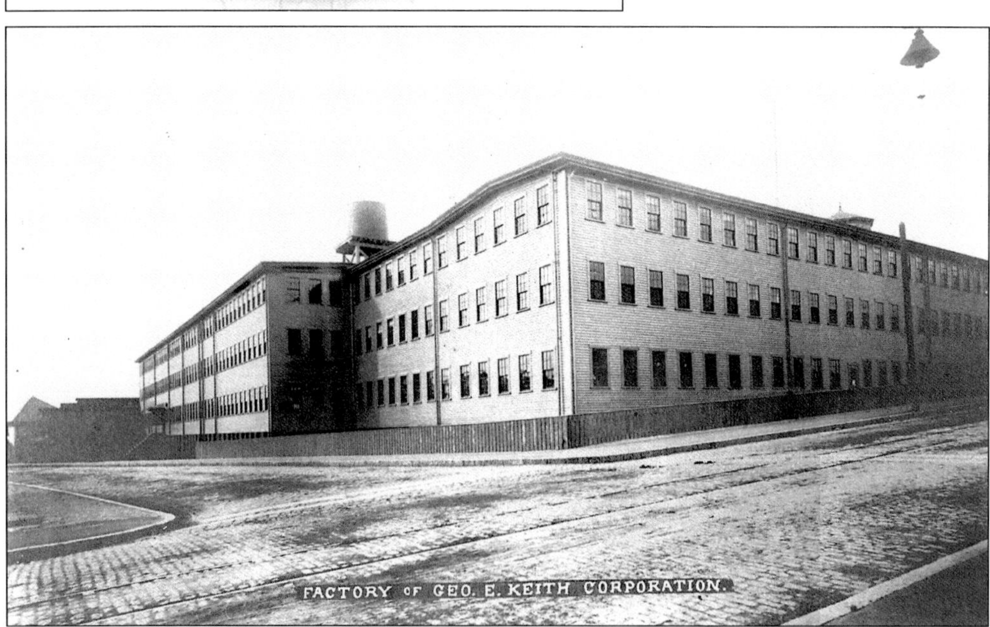


This early factory of the George E. Keith Company was a key place of employment for Brockton's Swedish population. Over the years, hundreds, if not thousands, of Swedish immigrants and their children worked in all areas of Keith's enterprise. The company's senior executive rolls included men of Swedish ancestry: Walter E. Johnson (treasurer and a member of the board of directors) and Emil Carlson (assistant treasurer of the George E. Keith Stores company).

THE ACHIEVEMENT OF THE PAST ~ SERVICE ~ THE ASSURANCE OF THE FUTURE

# Naumkeag Buffing Machine

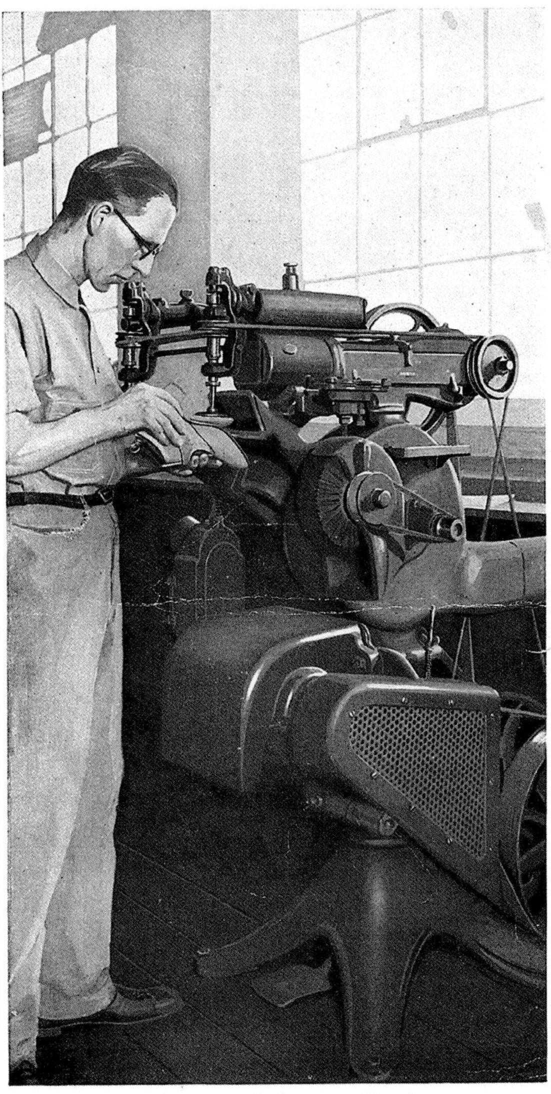

THIS machine produces that even, velvety surface on the bottom and shank of the shoe. It is equipped with two pad-holders, one for a coarse, the other for a fine abrasive. These pad-holders may be in two sizes if desired. The abrasives surround air-cooled rubber discs, which allow the machine to be operated at a high rate of speed. There is also a revolving brush to remove any dust that may accumulate on the shoe . . . It also has a blower which may be used if it is not convenient to connect the machine to the factory blower system. Operated by either factory power or individual motor.

FRANK E. JOHNSON . . . For the past five years Frank has been smoothing the bottoms of "Walk Over" shoes with the Naumkeag Machine in the George E. Keith Co. Factory No. 11 Brockton, Mass.

USMC

ONE *of a series of advertisements illustrating up-to-date shoe machinery in modern factories*

UNITED SHOE MACHINERY CORPORATION

BOSTON, MASSACHUSETTS

For 25 years, Frank Johnson was an edge trimmer and finisher at the George E. Keith Company. He had arrived in America from Västergötland at age 12 and had traveled to the Midwest, where he worked on a farm, and then traveled to New York City, where he drove a horse-drawn trolley. Finding this not to his liking, he was attracted to Brockton by its reputation for having good jobs with good pay. He came, but his greatest fortune was to be found when he met and married Agda Langden, employed at that time by C.W. Otto Lawson, a well-known businessman and vice president of Packard & Green Coal Company.

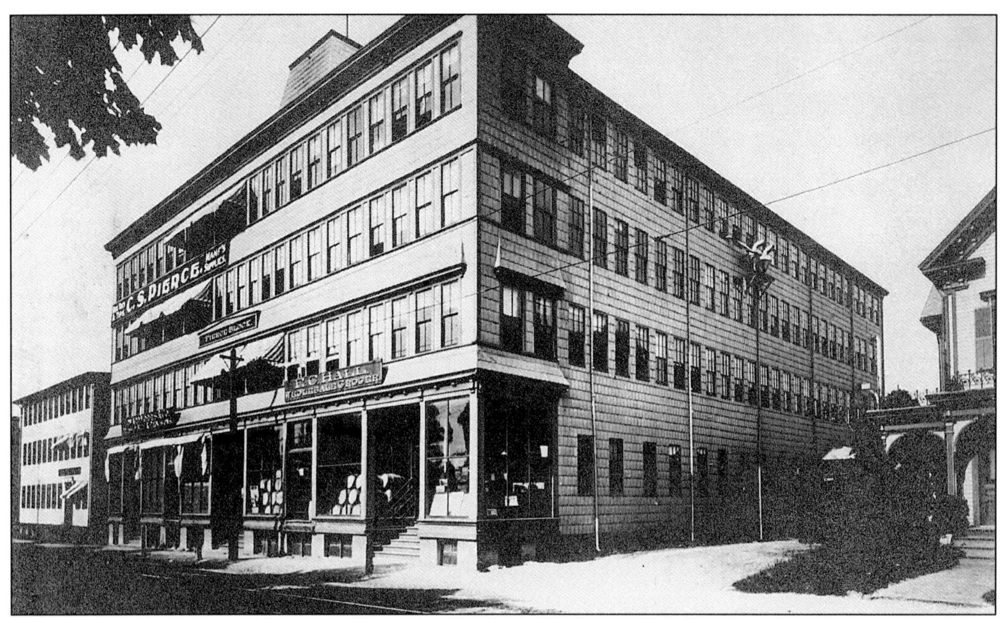


John M. Berglund purchased the C.S. Pierce Company in 1931 after being employed there during his high school years. Mr. Berglund, a graduate of Bentley College, and his partner Bernard Sabian manufactured shoe lasts, shoe dressings, and boxes. More than 150 people were employed in this company, known for quality of its products and pleasant working environment.

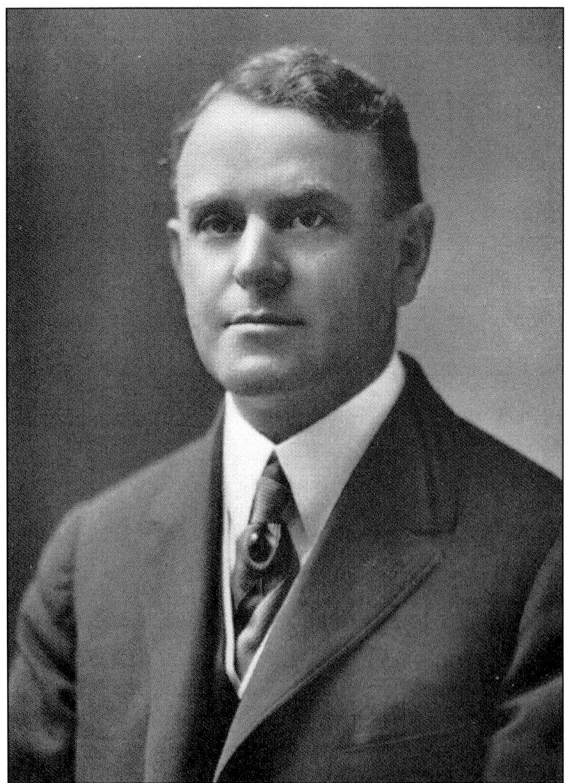

Albert F. Nelson was born in Brockton in 1877 to immigrant parents and educated in the local schools. Upon graduation from Bryant and Stratton Business College, he joined the Brockton Edison Company as a bookkeeper in 1906. By 1927, he had risen to the highest position within the company, that of vice president. Very active in civic affairs, he was a director of the Brockton Fair and a vice president of the Commercial Club.

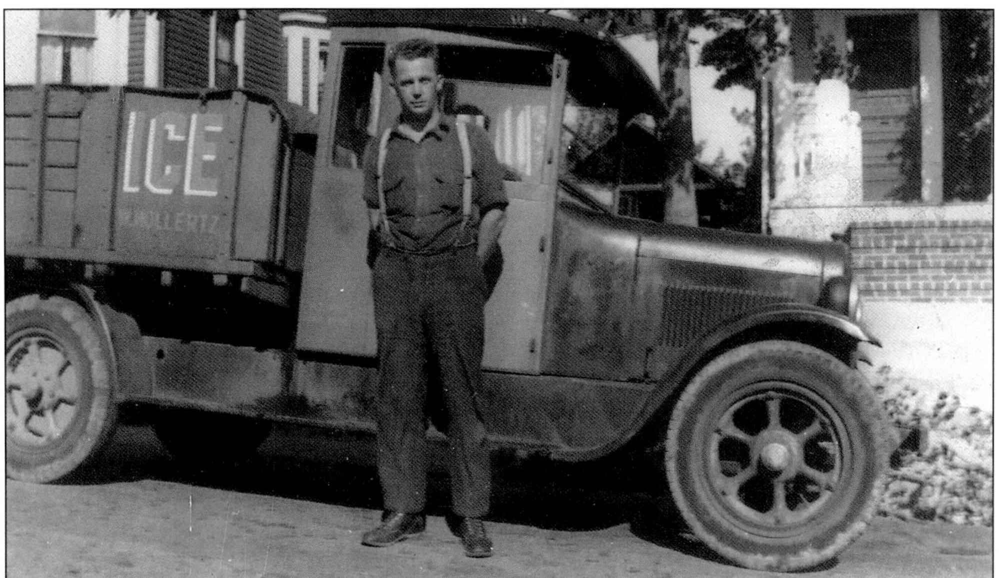


In the 1930s, the icebox was still the appliance of the times. When you needed ice, you would place a large "ice" sign in your front window. Walter Hollertz delivered not only ice but also coal, oil, and range oil. He ran the business from his residence at 20 Second Street. As the demand for ice dwindled, he concentrated on the fuel oil business. His green oil truck was a familiar sight on the streets of Campello for many years.

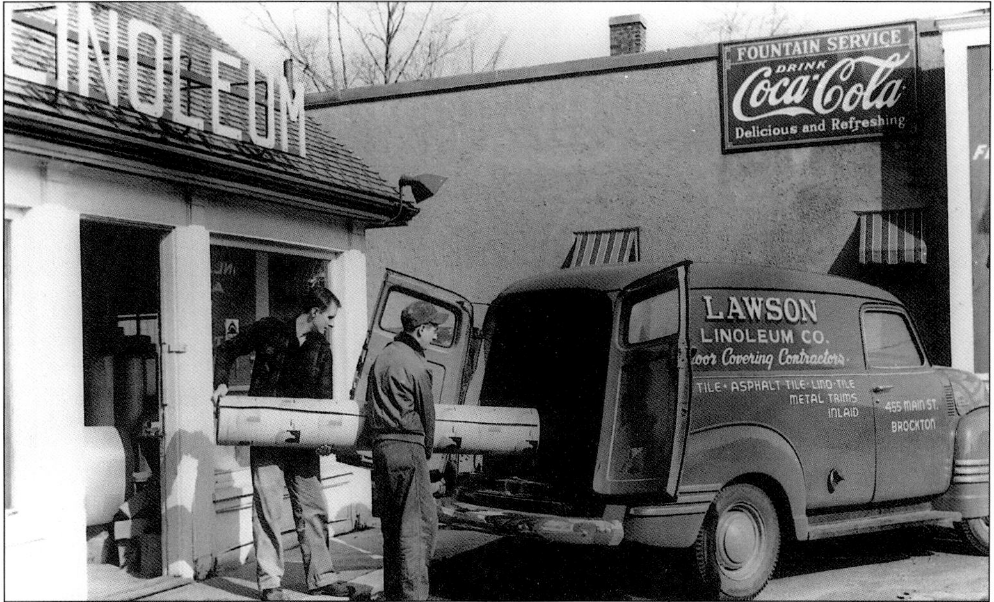


Lawson Linoleum was founded by Fremont and Lloyd Lawson shortly after the end of World War II on Lloyd's return from active duty in Europe. With help from younger brother Wendell (in the dark jacket) and older sister Myrtle, who kept the books and the brothers in order, a successful business was developed. Lloyd, standing nearest to their 1947 Chevy truck, is wearing the "good luck" flight jacket he wore during the war. A member of the 458th Bombardment Group, 8th Air Force, he flew 33 missions in a B-24 Liberator over Germany. He was a flight engineer and gunner in the "Martin upper" turret. (Stanley Bauman photograph.)

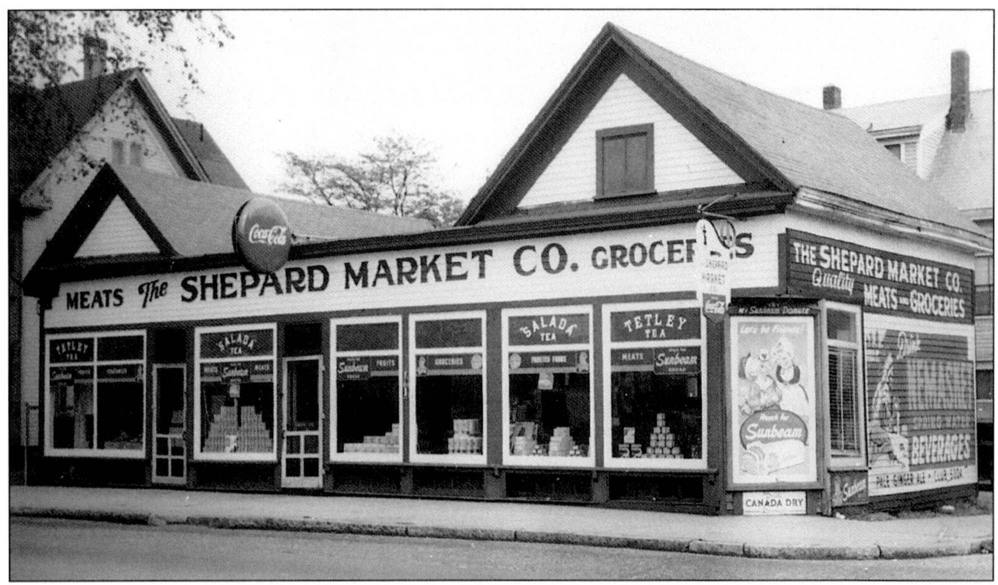


It may be hard to think of neighborhood grocery stores as institutions, but they were. Shepard Market was one of them. Founded by Knute Salander when he left the employ of Anderson & Nilson, the business grew to include three stores. These, and the many others, were centers of activity. Prime meats, vegetables, fruits, as well as American and Swedish groceries of all types were sold. Swedish foods were prepared on site, such as *kök-korv*, *kött-bullar*, and *sylta*. At Christmas, even *lutefisk* was prepared. Home delivery was free. (Stanley Bauman photograph.)

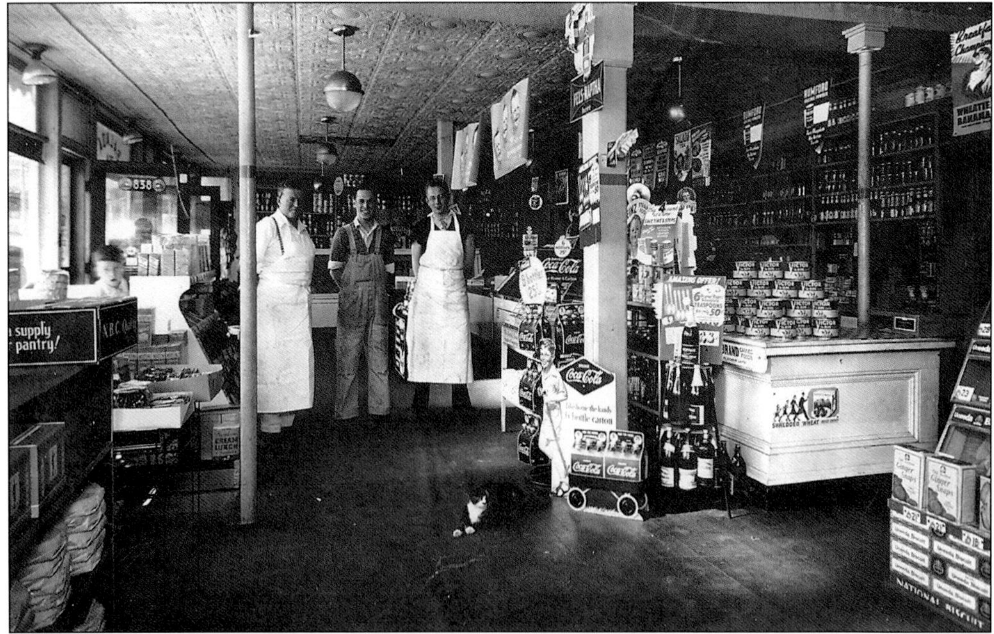


On May 13, 1928, Shepard Market founder Knute Salander was killed in a tragic boating accident that claimed the lives of nine prominent Brocktonians. His partner Elwin Bloomgren, who took over the business, is pictured here with two employees, Everett "Beanzie" Hedin and Alan Johnson. Until its closing in the 1960s, the store retained its character of friendliness, old-fashioned service with a smile, and quality products of the highest level.

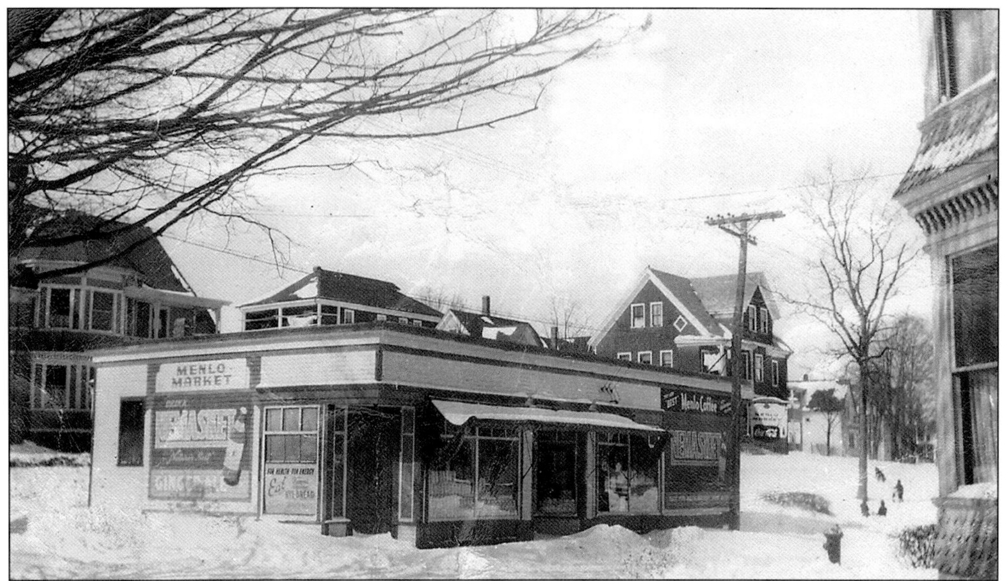


Originally known as Carlson & Lindblad, the Menlo Market was later owned and operated by Emmanuel "Manny" Holmander for some 40 years. Swedish foods were one of his specialities and, to this day, people still debate whether Manny made better *kök-korv* than Bloomgren. Menlo Market was a great place to shop and was also a great place for neighborhood kids. Many a Keith School student worked there—stocking shelves, making deliveries, running errands, and sweeping floors. Another item of interest is that Manny was the only merchant in Campello who sold Indian Gum, the original picture-pack gum, which contained "illustrations of Indian and Pioneer romantic days."

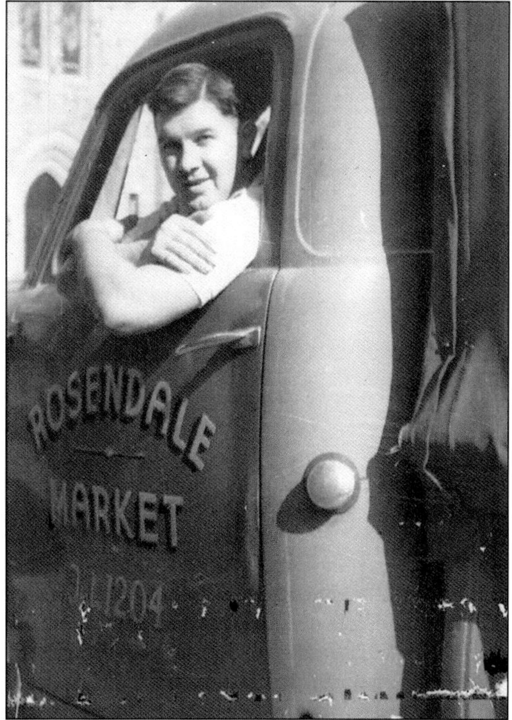


Albert "Ubber" Anderson is off to make his deliveries for Rosendale's Market in the firm's 1947 Studebaker panel truck. Edward A. Rosendahl, the original owner, was followed by Henry Thompson, a tall man with a big smile who ran this neighborhood enterprise at the corner of Nilsson and Main Streets. In 1929, there were 273 grocery stores in Brockton. After the Great Depression, only 95 had survived, with Rosendale's among them.

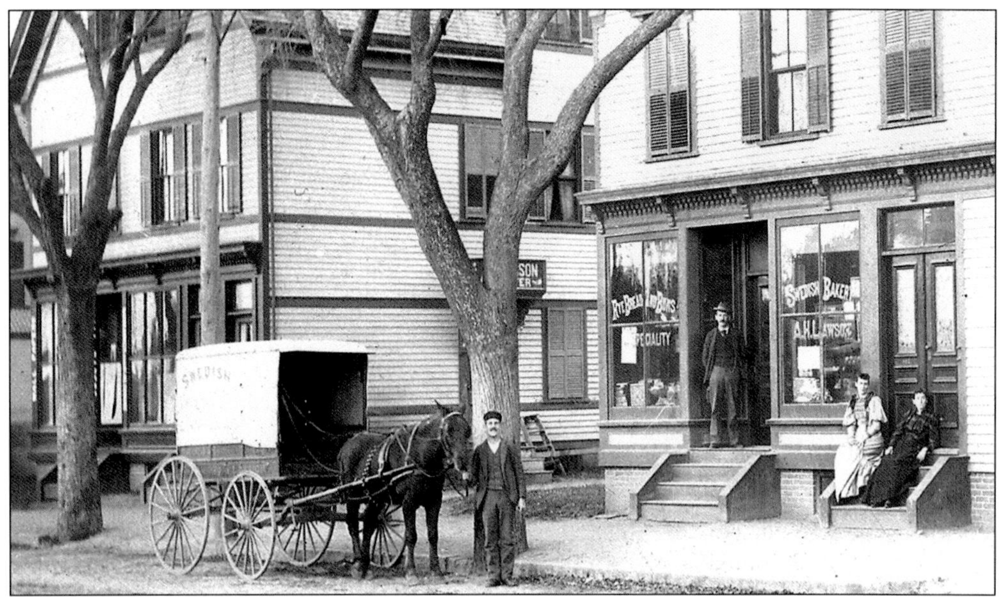


On arrival in Brockton, baker A. Herman Lawson opened Lawson's Swedish Bakery at 830 Main Street in the late 19th century. He died at the early age of 44, leaving his wife to run the business. Mrs. Lawson's untimely death left daughter Greta and the business in the hands of a guardian. Upon Greta's marriage to Ivar Pontus Benson, the couple ran the business, calling it Benson's Bakery, into the 1960s. People traveled from as far away as Duxbury to purchase Benson's famous rye bread. A. Herman Lawson is pictured in the doorway.

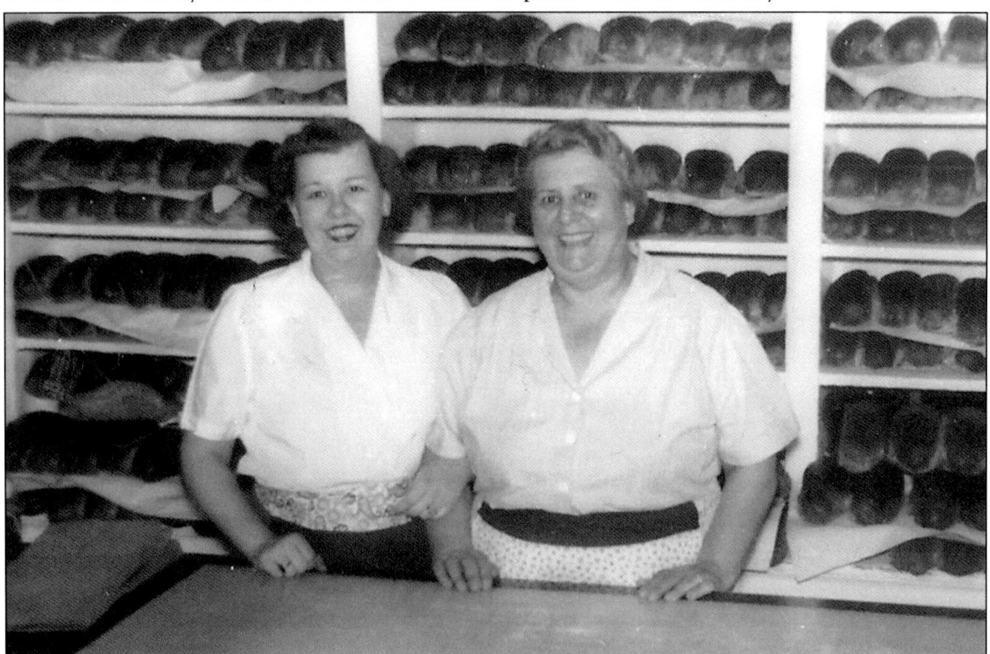

As the aroma of rye bread and cardamom filled the air of Campello, Greta Benson and daughter Hazel greeted customers with a smile. With shelves well-stocked with Swedish rye and cases filled with cookies and fancy pastries, they awaited their many customers, who on Saturdays would form a line that flowed onto the sidewalk.

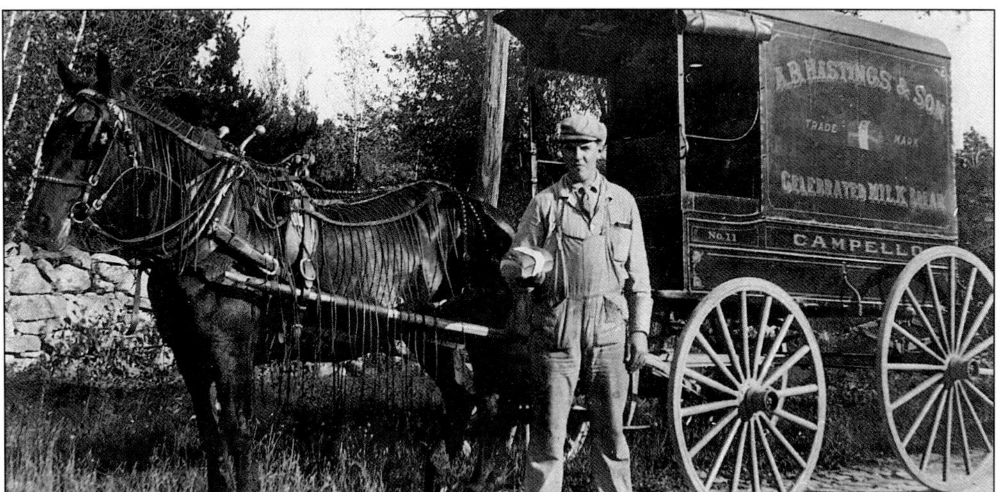


Paul Bernhard Holmes, a young immigrant, worked for the A.B. Hastings Bakery delivering his goods throughout much of Easton. From the days of the horse and wagon, Holmes grew in the business along with advances in transportation. When Hastings closed, Holmes went to work for Hathaway Bakers. Shown below is Holmes's sister Margaret.

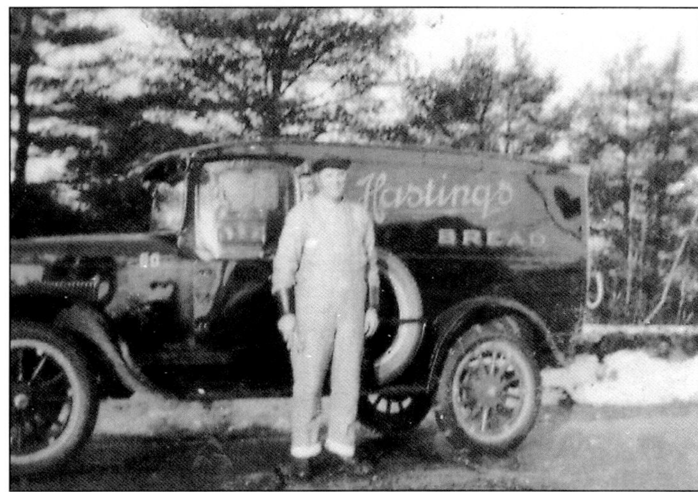


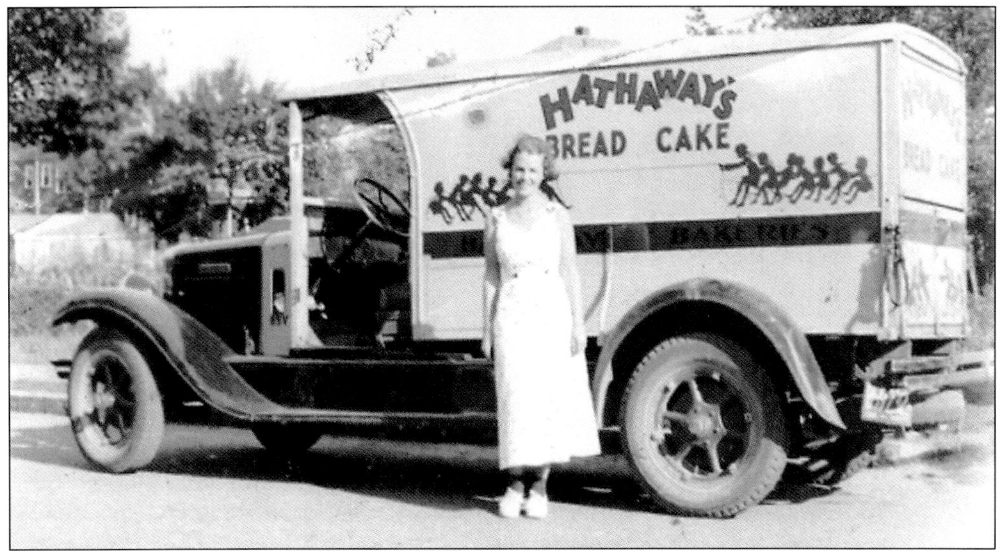

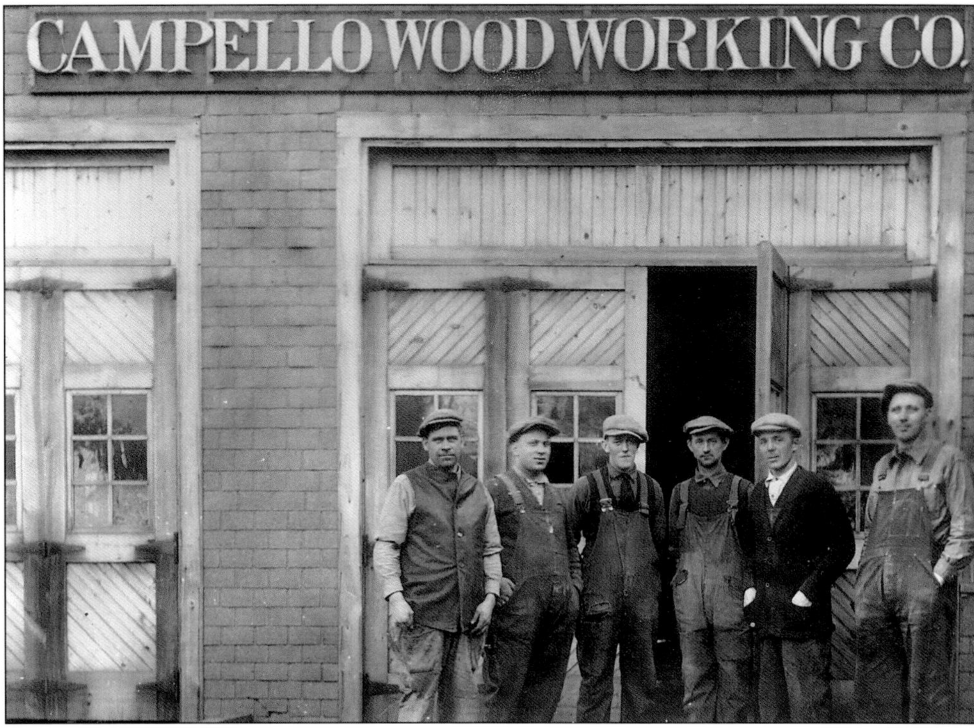

Woodworking is among the many skilled trades for which the Swedes are well known. The finest millwork and cabinetry in the region was produced by Campello Woodworking, owned by Anton Anderson, second from the right. Fred Benson, one of his master carpenters, stands at the far right.

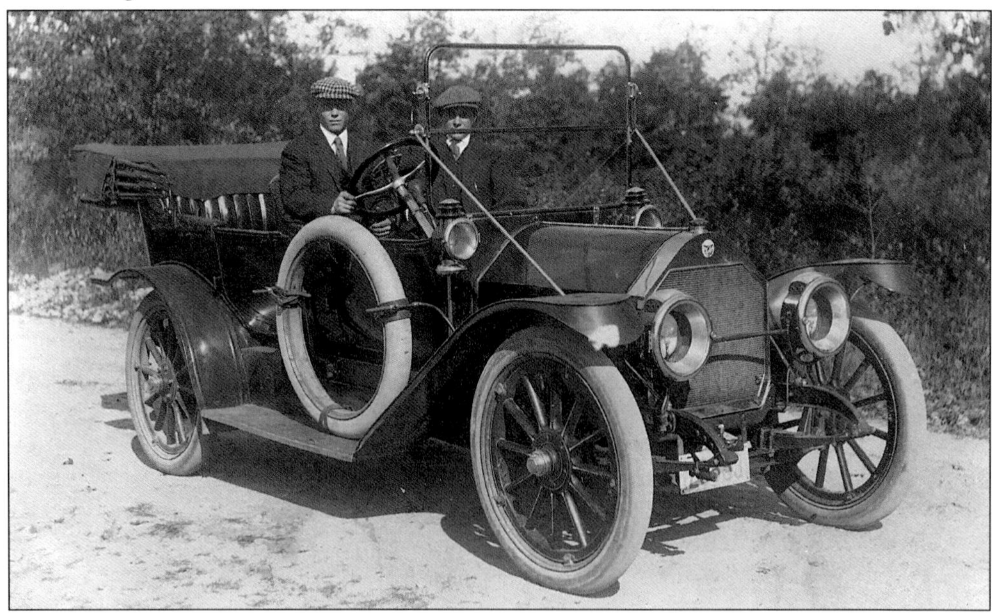

Per Eric Bergstrom, shown behind the wheel of Daniel Tolman's Pierce-Arrow, chauffeured the Tolman family for several years. Owners of Tolman Printing at 71 Center Street, they were the first company to print labels for shoe boxes.

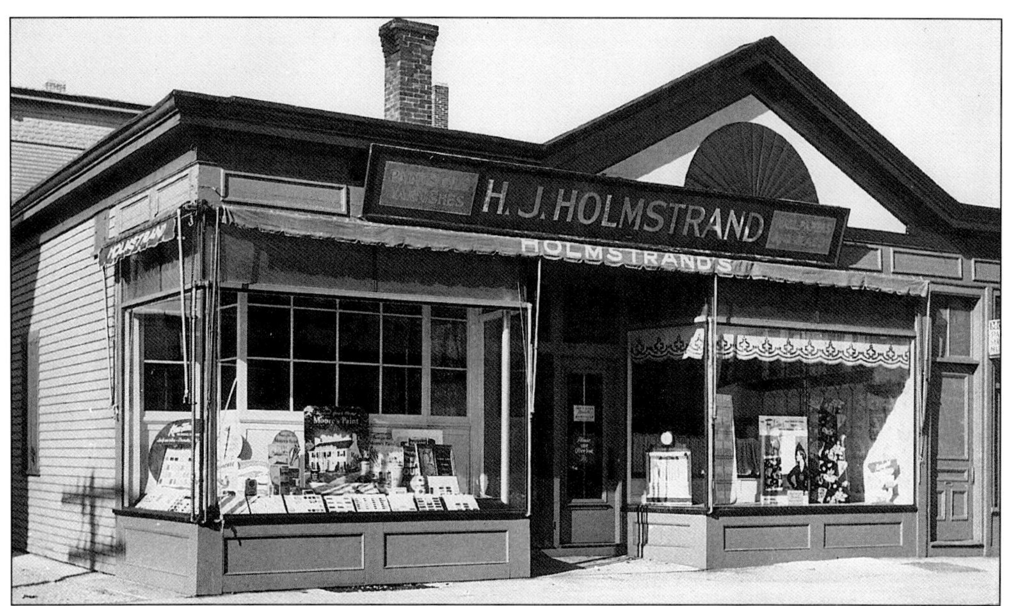


A painting business was started in the late 1800s by a gentleman named Lindskog. Ownership of the business changed to Charles H. Forsberg in 1914 and then to Harold J. Holmstrand in 1936. H.J. Holmstrand Paints was another Campello institution. Holmstrand worked in the business for 50 years, first as an apprentice painter and then as owner. He employed 12 painters and 3 paperhangers, who were busy every day (except during the Great Depression). Holmstrand's literally sold everything a professional painter or homeowner needed and, when you needed it, George Burgesson, an employee of 40 years, would get it for you. (Stanley Bauman photograph.)

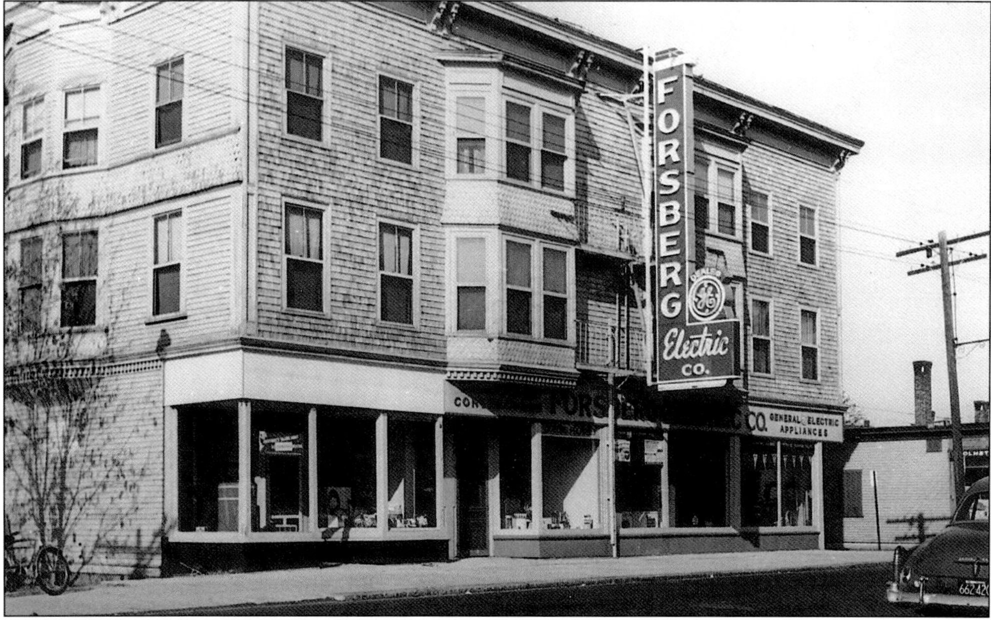


Forsberg Electric was founded by Carl Forsberg in the basement of his family's home at 8 Denton Street. At the dawn of the television age, people would gather outside the store and eagerly watch programs on the small round-screen sets. (Stanley Bauman photograph.)

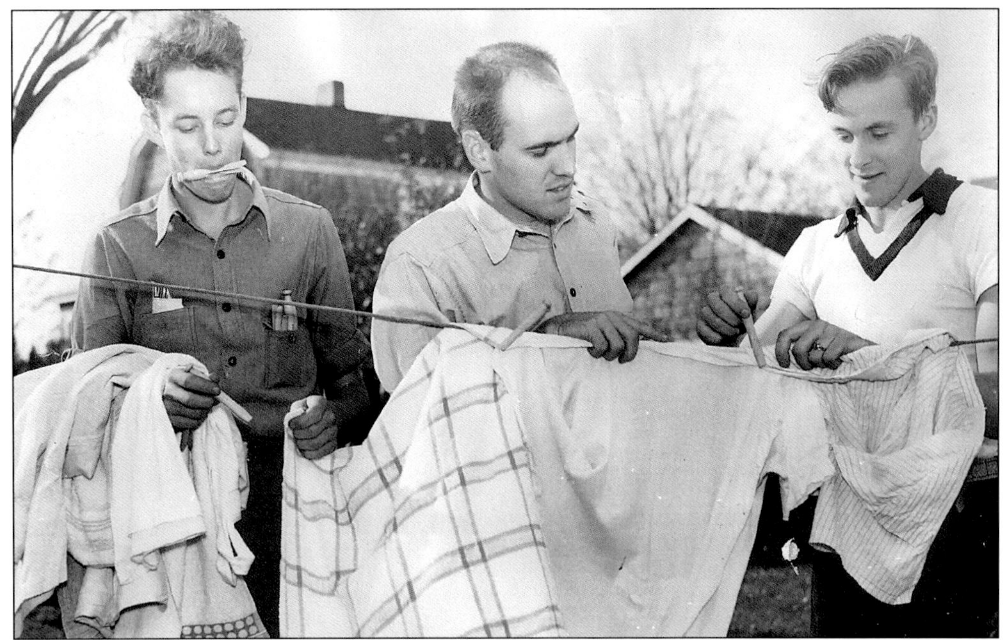

Enterprising youths Alan Ortendahl, Roland Brooks, and Lloyd Fihlman set out to lick the Great Depression through determination and hard work. They established a creative little enterprise, the firm of Fihlman, Ortendahl and Brooks. "We Do Anything and Everything" was their slogan, and they did just that. The boys' first big job came when they were asked to rebuild a sun parlor destroyed in the Hurricane of 1938.

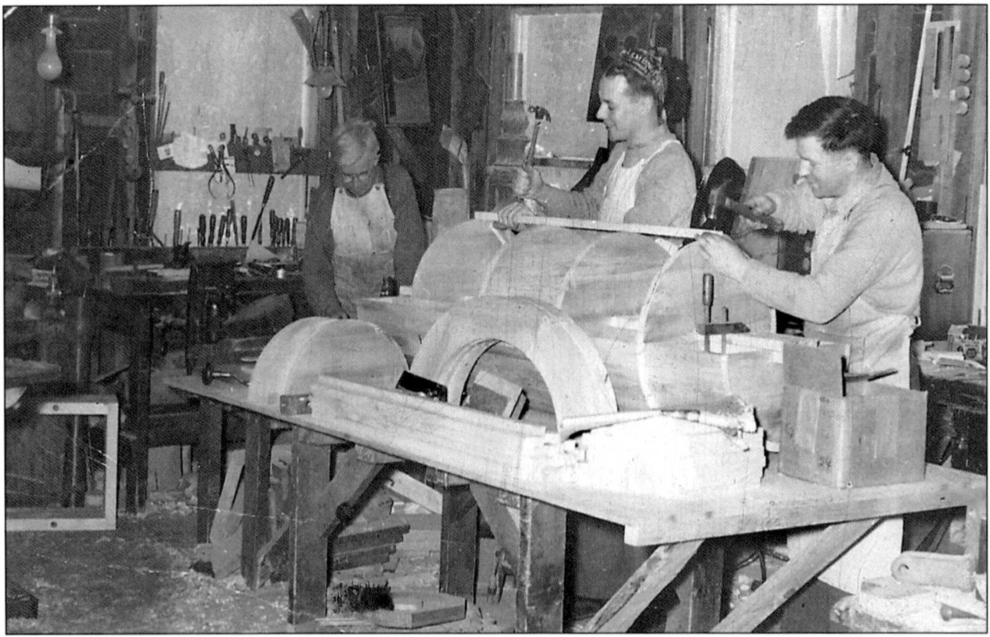

With Marcus Holmgren as his partner, Allan Ortendahl (center) formed the pattern-making firm of Patterns., Inc. These highly skilled craftsmen were responsible for scores of intricate and artful designs ranging from altar rails to fine cabinetry. This *c.* 1949 photograph is the only known visual record of the company's shop interior.

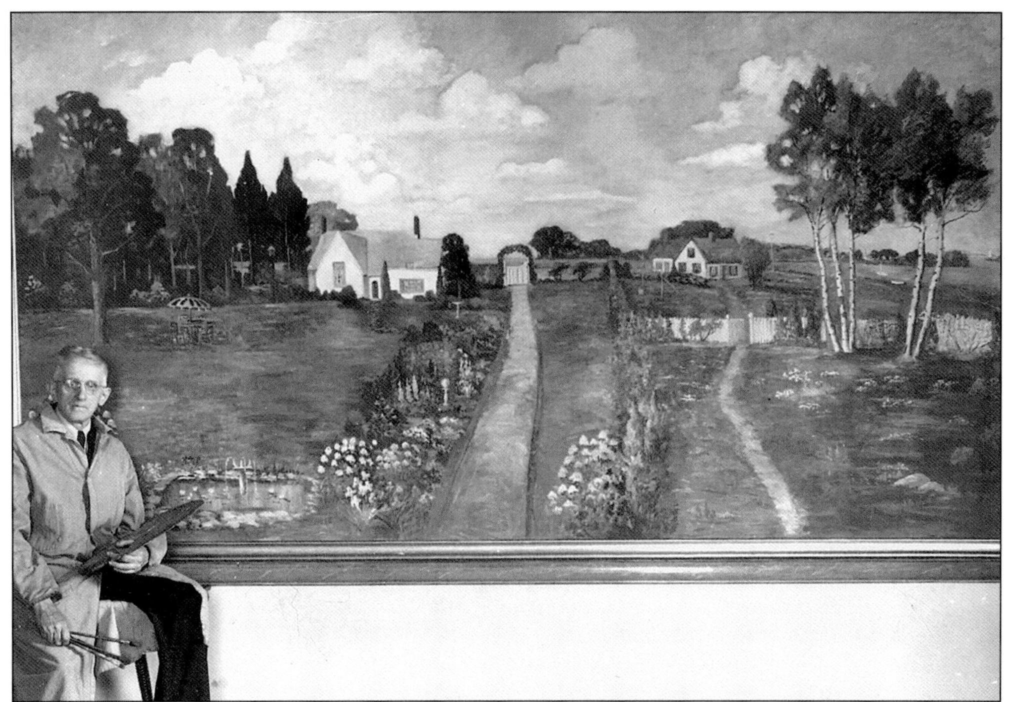

A self-taught and accomplished artist, Victor Lawson is seated in front of a mural he painted in the vestry of the Swedish Congregational Church. Lawson, the church sexton and retired shoeworker, was a prolific painter whose work remains displayed in the homes of many local residents.

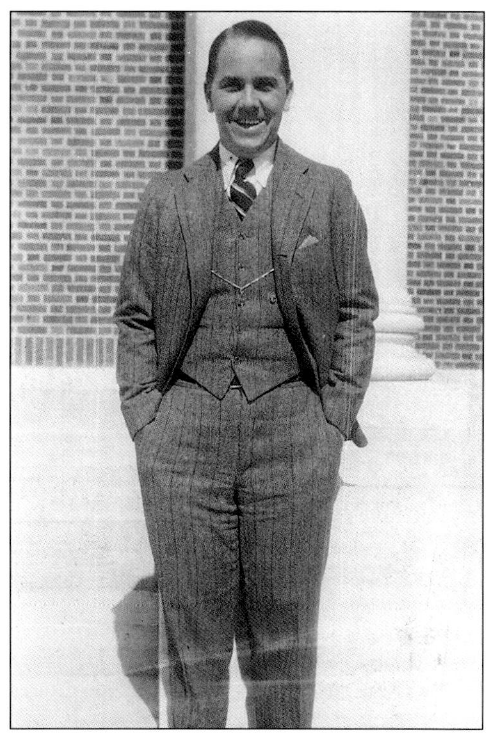

Prof. Kenneth Lagerstedt, son of an immigrant shoeworker, was at first a reluctant scholar. However, after one summer of gluing heels at the Eaton Shoe factory, school looked very appealing. Professor Lagerstedt followed his brother to Duke University, where he earned A.B. and A.M. degrees. He then went on to Harvard for a second master's degree. A language specialist, he did postgraduate work at Columbia University, Tuebingen and Heidelberg Universities in Germany, the Sorbonne in Paris, and Middlebury College in Vermont, where he became an associate professor.

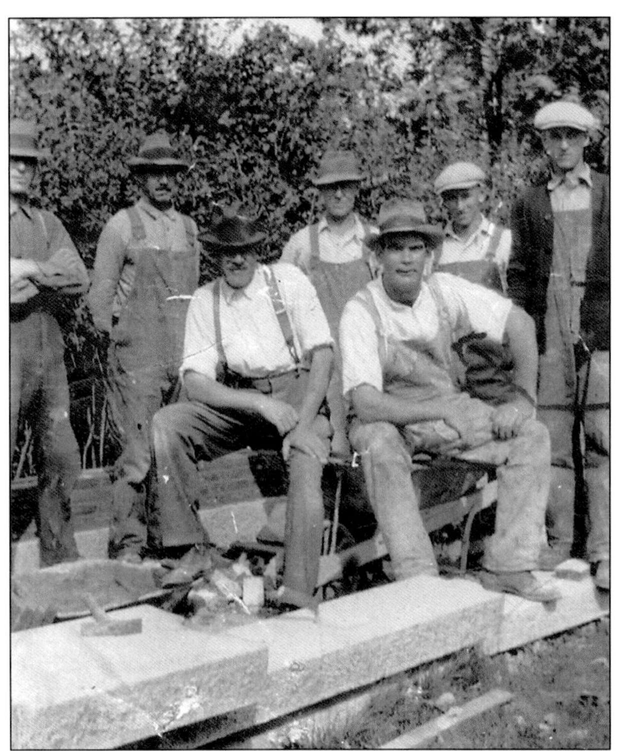

Brockton was indeed fortunate to have Daniel Waldo Field, whose philanthropic legacy lives on in Brockton's D.W. Field Park and through charities. The man who carried out several of Field's plans was Carl O. Johnson, a master stonemason. Shown here surrounded by fellow tradesmen, Johnson was the designer and builder of the stepped waterfalls at Thirty Acres Pond, the entrance pillars to the park, and the stone tower atop "Tower Hill." Field personally selected Johnson for these projects because of his fine his reputation as a craftsman.

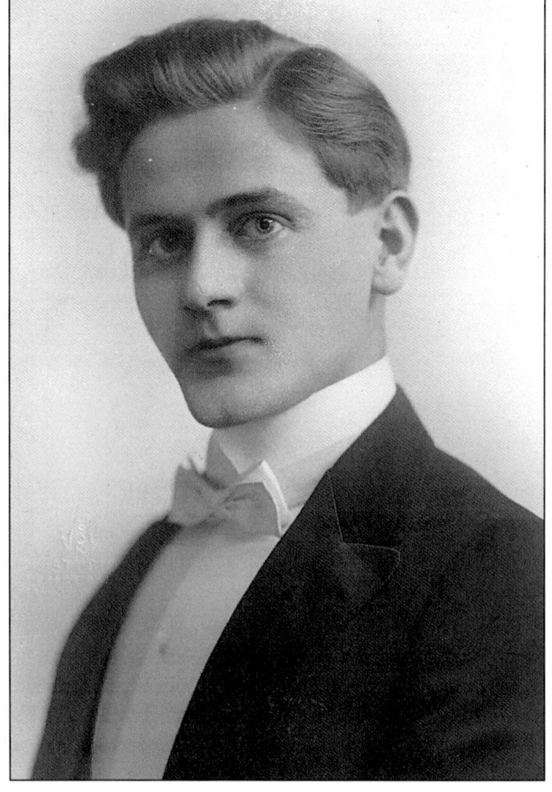

Truls Lagerquist, well-known musician and teacher, was known throughout the region for his violin virtuosity. Another renowned musician, composer, and lecturer was Frank E. Johnson, nephew of Brockton's first Swedish settler, Daniel Lawson. Brockton produced many other musicians. Among them are Hartley Erickson and Larry Gustafson, enterprising youths whose orchestra, the Rhythm Makers, brought the sound of the big bands to social functions of all types.

The Brockton Machine Company, located at 55 First Street, was founded in 1922 by Arabam Lagerquist (second from left), J.F. Oscar Burman, Herman Anderson, and Emil Jacobson. The company specialized in mechanical rubber molds and employed many Swedish men from the neighborhood.

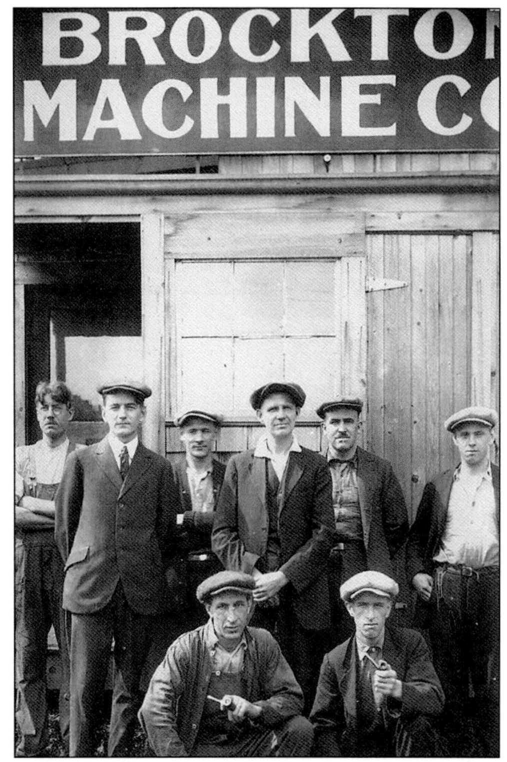


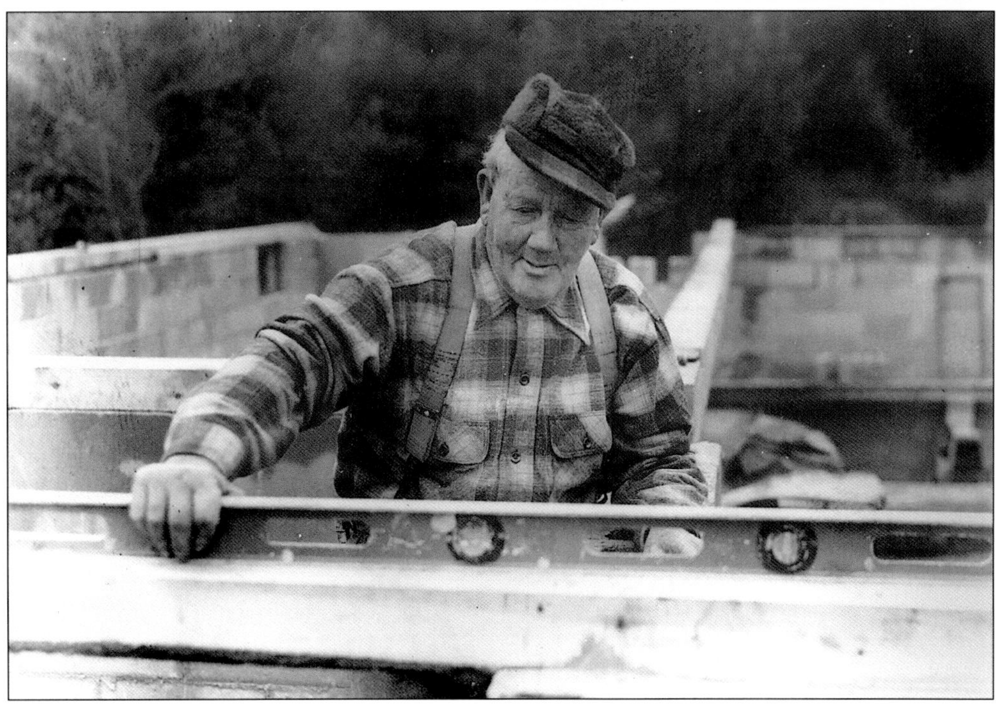

Master carpenter Oliver K. Ness was one of the first builders to develop subdivisions of custom homes. Norman Avenue in the Matfield section of West Bridgewater was one of his ventures. (Stanley Bauman photograph.)

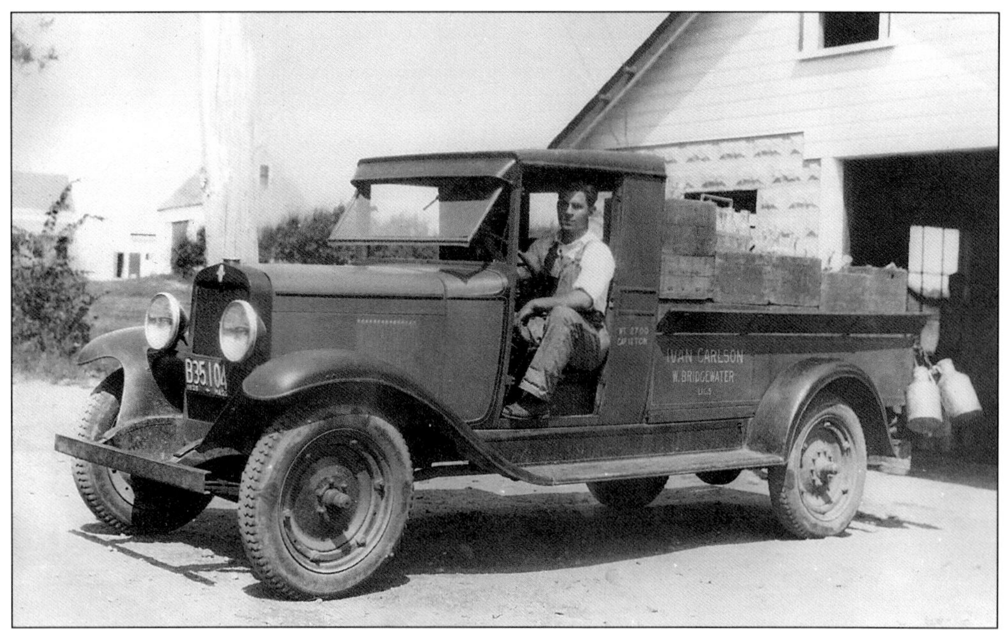


Many Swedes brought the farming tradition to America. Carlson's Dairy, on Brooks Place in West Bridgewater, was one such farm. Here, *c.* 1930, a young Ivan Carlson in his delivery truck gets ready for a day's work. Ivan often traveled his route about town with a dog named Booze.

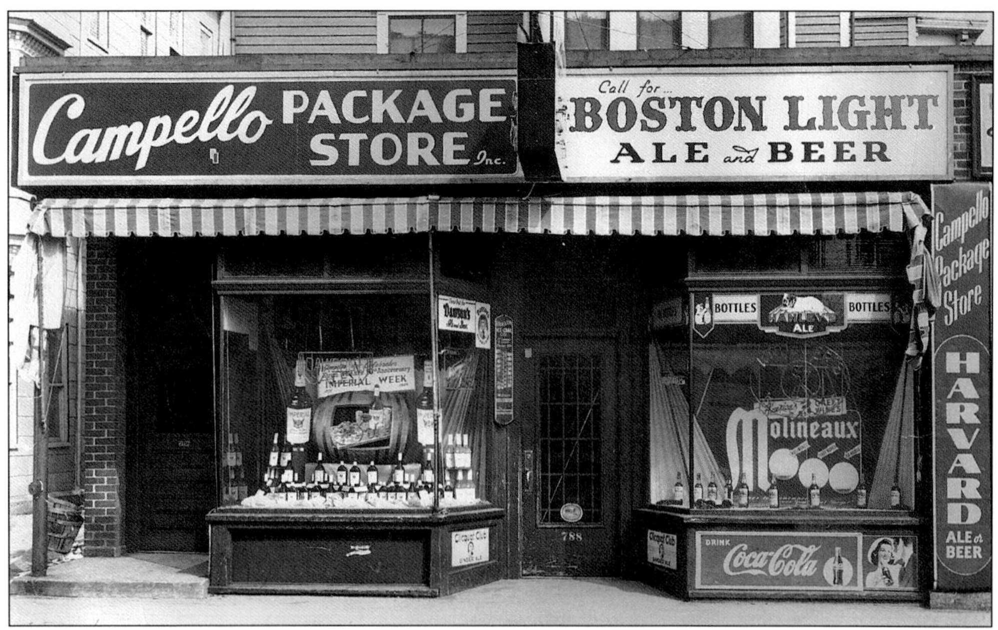


The Campello Package Store, which opened shortly after the repeal of the Volstead Act in 1933, was owned by Ralph Swift, Gus Olson, and Edwin Ozelius. Many such stores, as in this case, had apartments above them. (Stanley Bauman photograph.)

Gustaf Adolf Anderson, born in Björketorp, was a resident of West Bridgewater and a well-known teamster and farmer. At his death, it was written that "he could get more out of his team by talking to them than most could with whip or spurs" and "with his team and plow he was an artist."

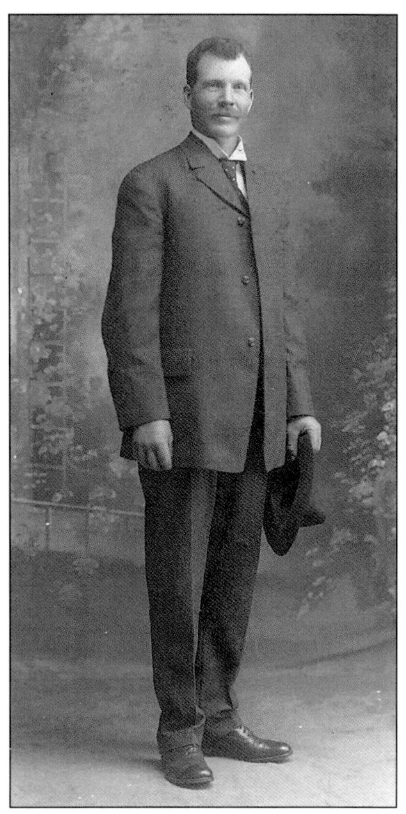

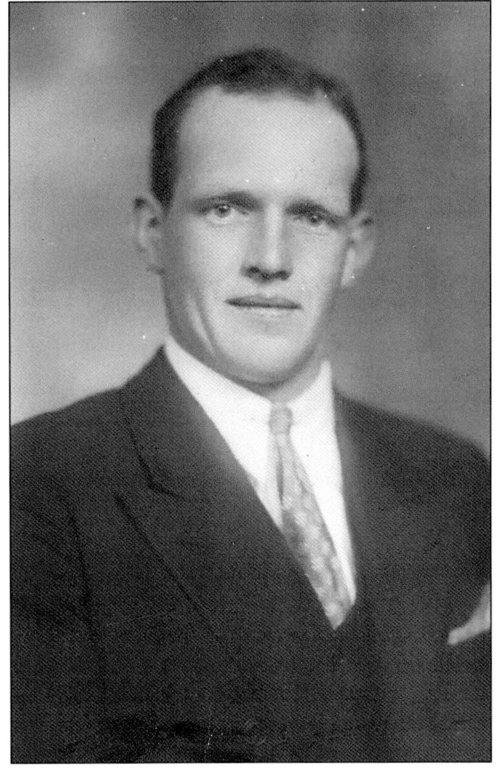

Howard Anderson—following in the footsteps of his father, G. Adolf—established Anderson's Dairy Farm in West Bridgewater in 1941. Anderson ran the farm with his sons Richard and Howard and was a member of the Producer's Dairy Co-operative. The farm, along with Anderson's Farm Restaurant, continues to this day.

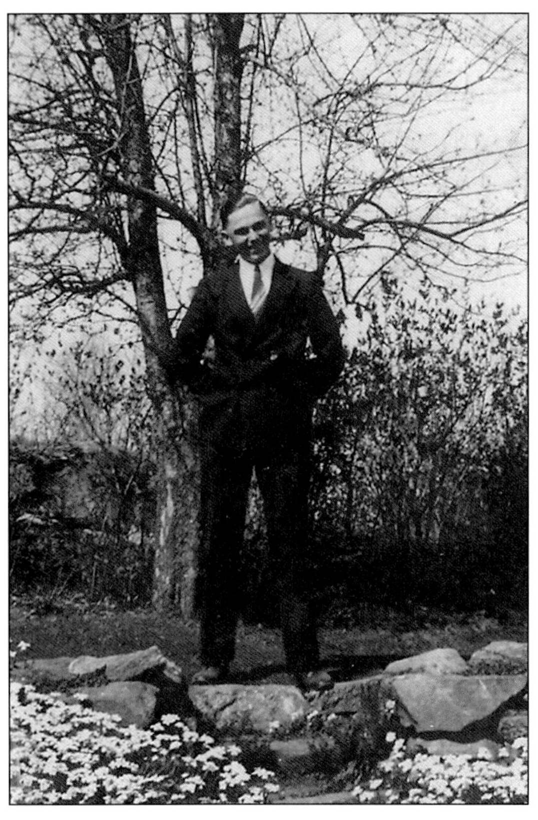

Looking more like the lord of the manor than a student, Lloyd F. Thompson stands amid one of the many gardens on the Rock Estate in Littleton, New Hampshire, which he tended during a summer internship. Graduating from the Stockbridge School of Agriculture at Massachusetts State College in 1933, he started Thompson Florists at the family homestead. Mr. Thompson served as Brockton's city forester from 1952 to 1956, was a coach in Brockton's first Little League, and coached the Brockton All-Stars at the 1953 and 1954 National Pony League Championships in Washington, Pennsylvania.

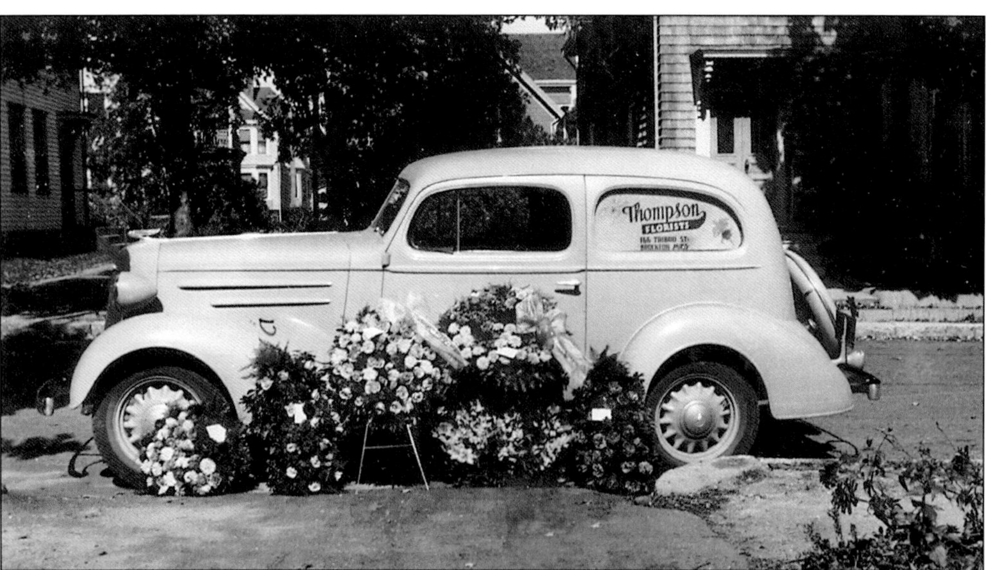


A cream-colored 1937 Chevrolet sedanette was Thompson Florists's first delivery vehicle. With a $400 loan from his grandfather (together with $200 from his fiancée, Martha Erickson), the business moved into a store at 879 Main Street, adjacent to Rosendale's Market and Frederickson's, later "Arlene's." Sixteen years later, the business was relocated to 426 Plain Street, where the Thompsons built a new home, store, and greenhouse.

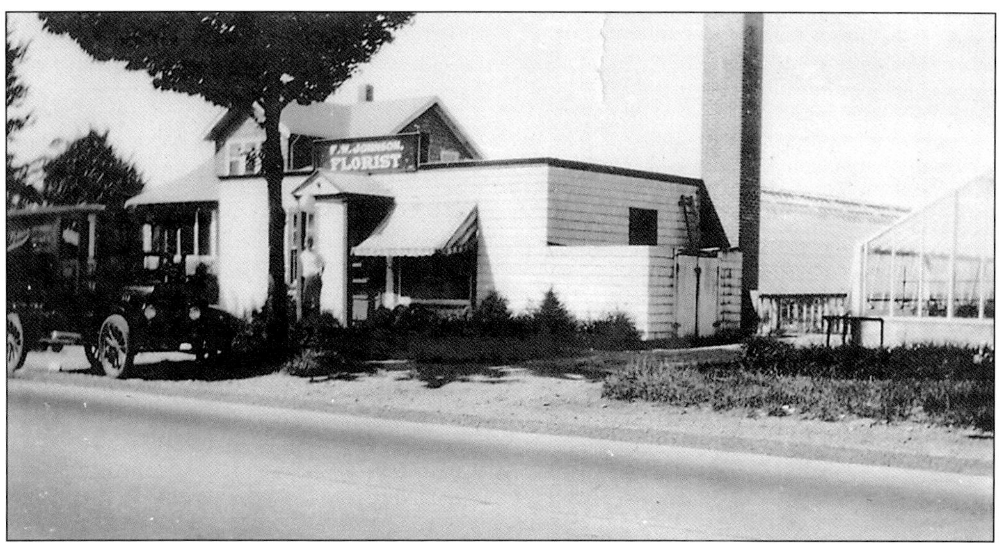


Fred Johnson operated a large florist and greenhouse business on South Main Street. A grower of some note, Johnson sold carnations, roses, and snapdragons to other florists in the region.

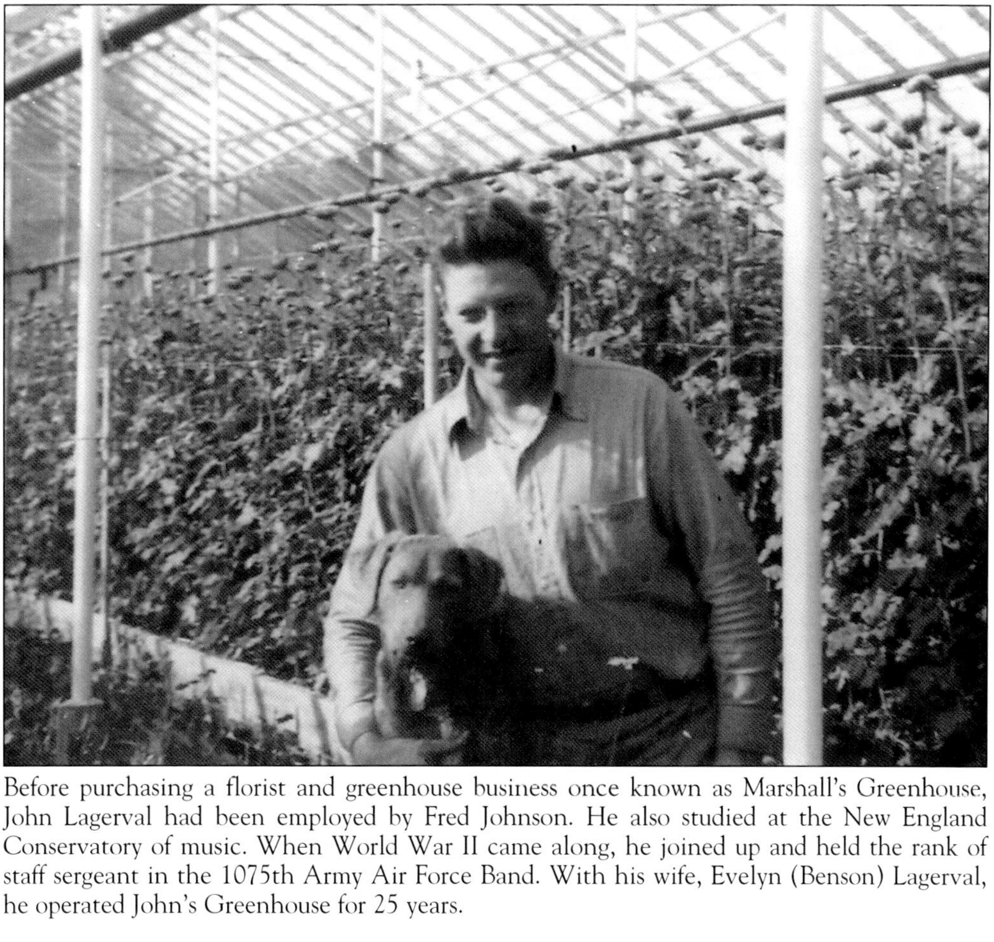

Before purchasing a florist and greenhouse business once known as Marshall's Greenhouse, John Lagerval had been employed by Fred Johnson. He also studied at the New England Conservatory of music. When World War II came along, he joined up and held the rank of staff sergeant in the 1075th Army Air Force Band. With his wife, Evelyn (Benson) Lagerval, he operated John's Greenhouse for 25 years.

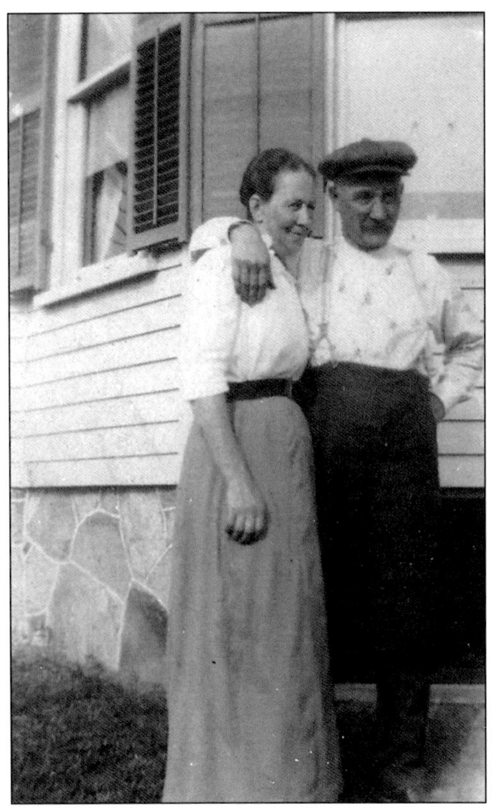

Possibly the finest shoemaker in all of Brockton, Carl W. Sundstrom plied his trade in a small shop, about 8 by 10 feet, in the backyard of his home at 115 Hillberg Avenue. His customers were the women of the elite families: Keith, Packard, Douglas, and many others. Mr. Sundstrom's shoe designs and craftsmanship were unequalled. These elegant high-button shoes were fashioned with a combination of brown and black leathers. His wife, Hannah (Larson), was a cook for the Moses Packard family and was mother to five children. As a note of interest, his Hillberg Avenue neighbors were Truls Lagerquist, Edward Dahlborg, and John Lind.

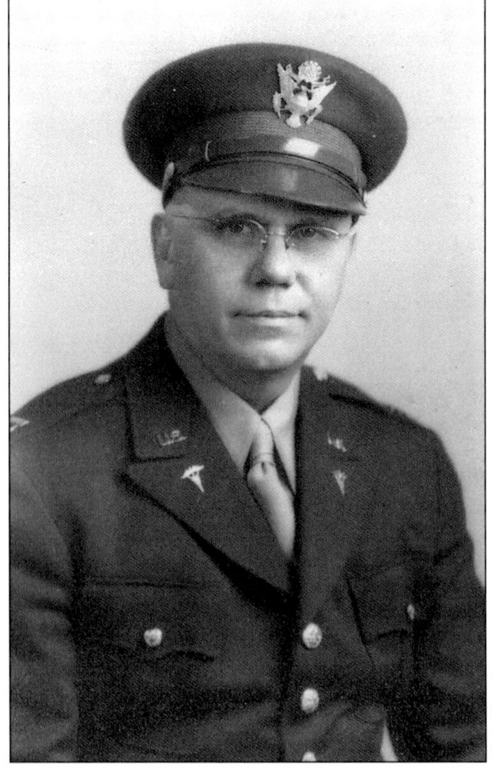

A graduate of Duke University, where he was a star football player, Dr. Edward William Howard Lagerstedt served as a captain in the Medical Corps at front-line hospitals in North Africa and France during World War II. "Pinney," as he was known, conducted his practice in Nilsson Street and, for many years, served as city physician.

A wonderful humorist who could convulse people with laughter or move them to tears quite as easily is an apt description of Nan Lagerstedt. She specialized in character portrayals of "People You Know," which included the *The Old Maid's Ride*, *Hubby Has The Grippe*, and *The Irish Widow*. For more than 20 years, her artistry delighted audiences throughout the East Coast. She and her husband, Harold Winston Churchill, lived in Hanson, where she operated a gift shop after retiring from the stage.

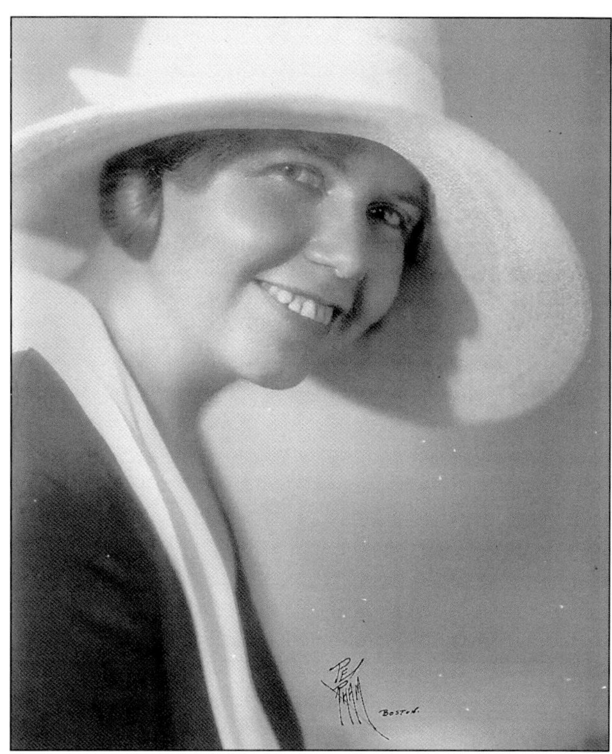

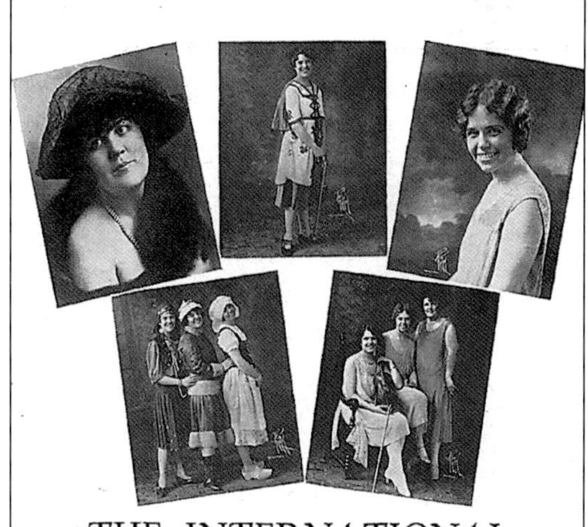


This 1930s handbill of *The International Artists* features Nan Lagerstedt. Exclusively managed by the White Entertainment Bureau of Boston, Nan Lagerstedt, Theresa Sprague, and Nina Spaulding offered "a fascinating program of soprano solos, pianologues, and stories with many novel costume features."

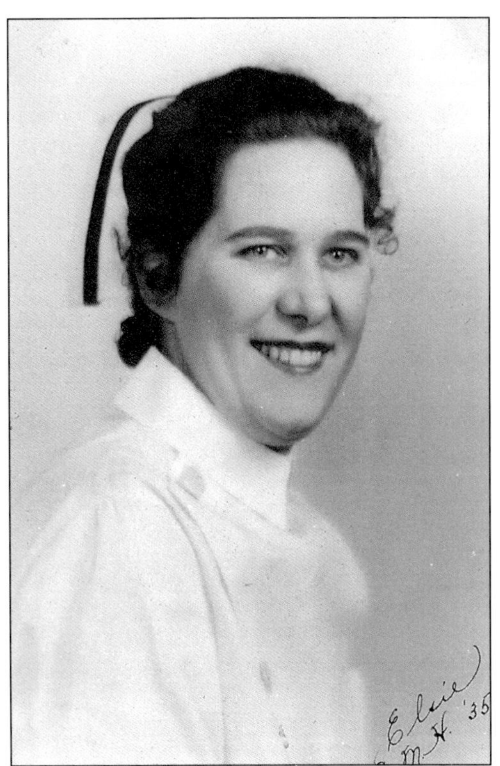


Elsie (Olson) Stevens, daughter of Swedish immigrants Sigfrid and Hanna Olson, graduated from the Chelsea Memorial Hospital in 1935. During the Great Depression and through the early years of World War II she worked at a small, fourteen bed, doctor owned hospital in Holbrook, where she served as charge nurse and scrub nurse in the operating room. Here, she met her husband to be – "an appendix case." They were married in 1942, just two weeks before he left for a four year tour of duty in the Southwest Pacific.

Her long career included being school nurse for the Town of Holbrook, and head nurse at the Lutheran Nursing Home in the Montello section of Brockton. A mother of three and grandmother of nine, Elise retired from nursing in December 1978.

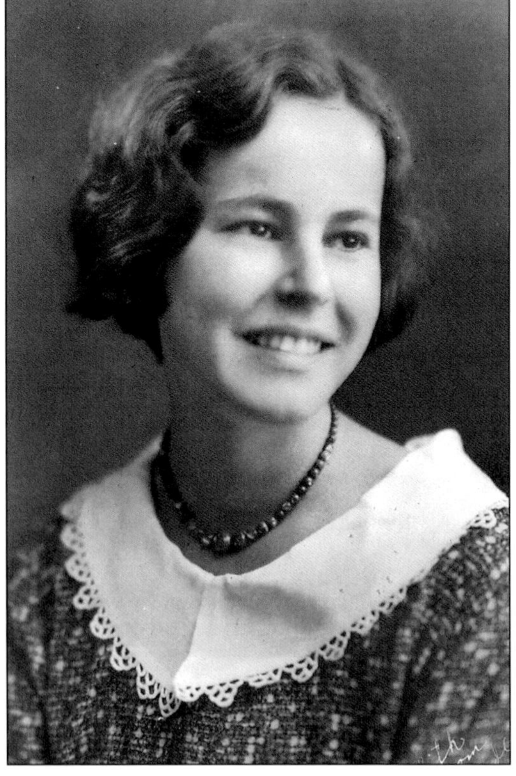

For more than 40 years, Gertrude Forsstrom faithfully served as secretary for First Evangelical Lutheran Church working with pastors Froeberg, Olander, Spong, Lundeen, Willis, and Fruth. Miss Forsstrom's diligence and "save everything" approach to her job resulted in the church having a comprehensive historical archive, for which the authors are grateful.

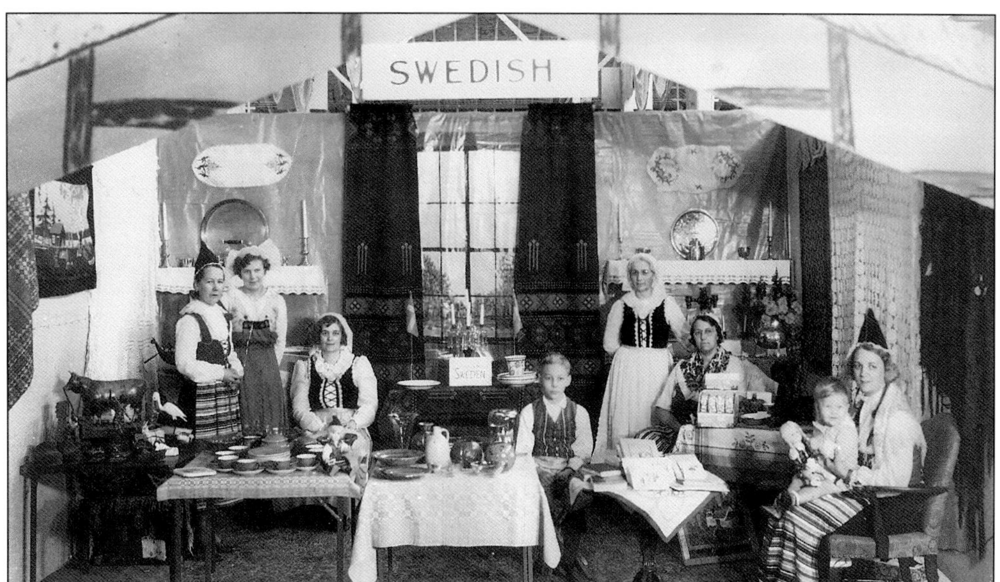

An annual attraction at the Brockton Fair, was the "food tent" sponsored by the the First Lutheran Church. The extensive preparations included moving several gas stoves from the church, on which the ladies prepared turkeys, hams, and roasts, and, of course, their famous Swedish coffee, cookies, cakes, and coffee bread. Shown in this rare photograph taken inside the tent (*c.* 1936) are, from left to right, Persis (Lagerstedt) Genacco, Sylvia Broman, Naomi Anderson, Dale Anderson, unidentified, Mrs. Truls Lagerquist, and Pearl Thorell. The hardworking church women turned a profit of $3,000.

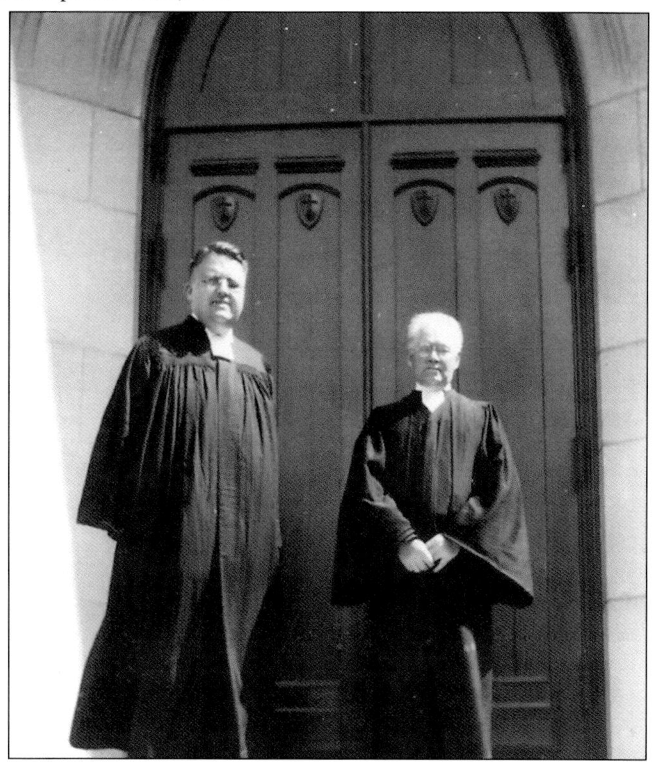

Looking presidential and scholarly are the Reverend Dr. Evald B. Lawson and the Reverend Dr. Peter Froeberg. Dr. Froeberg was the second president of Upsala College in East Orange, New Jersey, and left that position in 1918 to come to First Lutheran Church. Dr. Lawson, a son of First Lutheran, became Upsala's fourth president in 1936 and served for 27 years. It should be noted that Peter Froeberg, a young Swedish immigrant, was the first student to enroll at the newly founded Upsala in 1893.

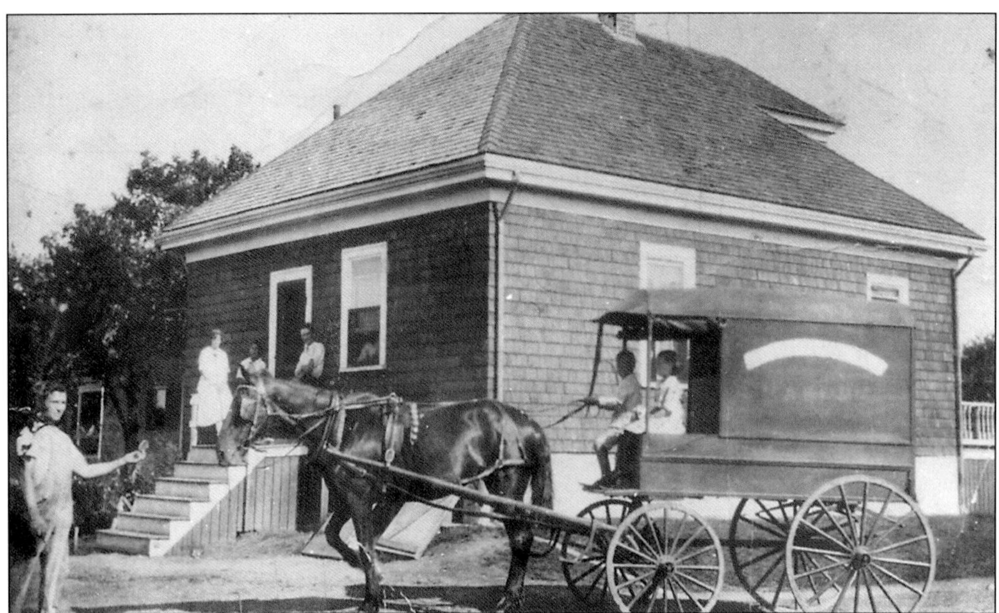

The bakery of J. Anton Anderson and Sons at 1 Woodard Avenue was a neighborhood institution from 1915 to 1940. One of their wagon drivers, "Kaffeman" Johnson, was also an institution in his own right. It is said that he consumed a cup of coffee at every house on his delivery route. Enterprising Swedes, the Andersons on Sundays would take the week's leftovers to a small storefront near St. Patrick's Church and sell them to parishioners.

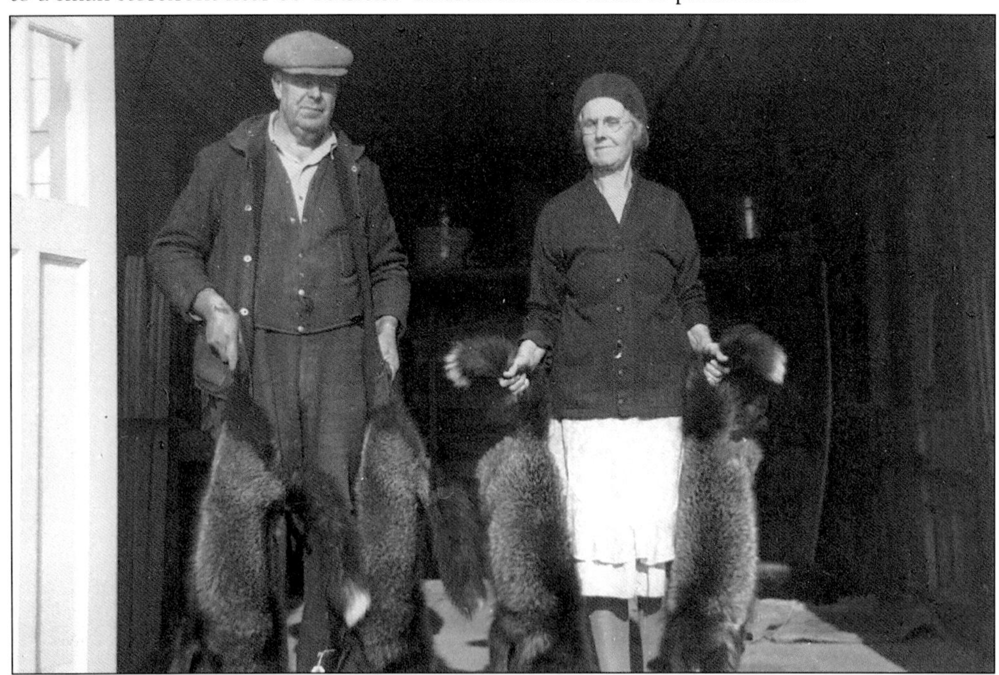

Often belying its position as an industrial city, Brockton was also the home to several farms. Conrad and Signe (Pearson) Peterson operated Chestnut Hill Farm at the corner of West Chestnut and Ash Streets. Among the many animals and crops they raised were minks and foxes. Here it appears the furs are tagged and ready for market.

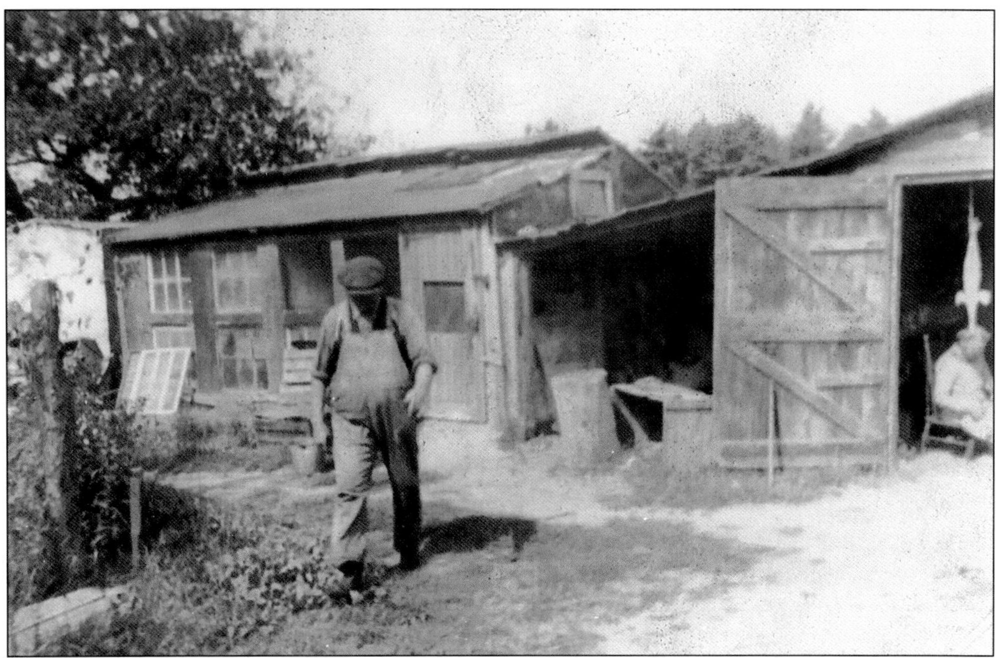

During the jobless days of the Great Depression, Joseph and Anna Johnson went to Brockton City Hall, took out a peddlar's license, and began a house-to-house delivery business of fruits and vegetables. This candid shot shows Anna (far right) "dressing" a chicken on their small farm in West Bridgewater. Before long, the couple's income, which they tithed, had gone far beyond what they had earned in the shoe factories.

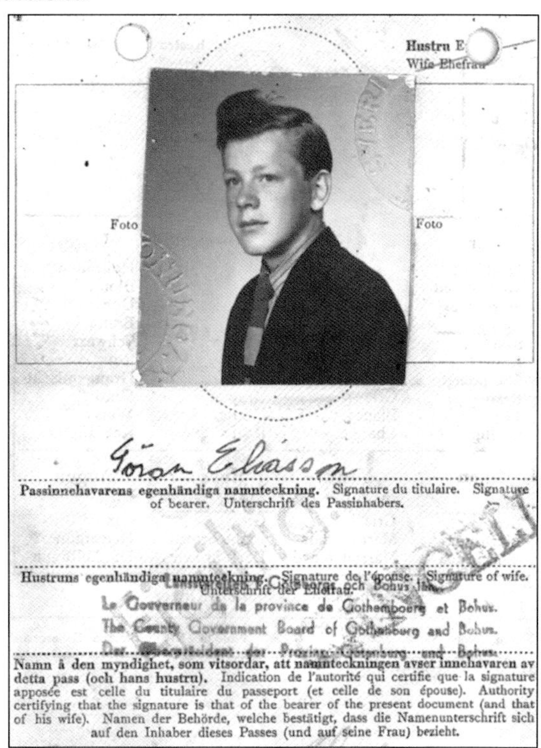

Hustru E
Wife Ehefrau

Foto Foto

Göran Eliasson

Passinnehavarens egenhändiga namnteckning. Signature du titulaire. Signature of bearer. Unterschrift des Passinhabers.

Hustruns egenhändiga namnteckning. Signature de l'épouse. Signature of wife. Unterschrift der Ehefrau.

Le Gouverneur de la province de Gothembourg et Bohus.
The County Government Board of Gothenburg and Bohus.

Namn å den myndighet, som vitsordar, att namnteckningen avser innehavaren av detta pass (och hans hustru). Indication de l'autorité qui certifie que la signature apposée est celle du titulaire du passeport (et celle de son épouse). Authority certifying that the signature is that of the bearer of the present document (and that of his wife). Namen der Behörde, welche bestätigt, dass die Namenunterschrift sich auf den Inhaber dieses Passes (und auf seine Frau) bezieht.

Shown is Swedish émigré Lars Göran Eliasson of Surteby-Kattunga. He arrived in New York City in 1955 aboard the Swedish East Asian liner MS *Mongalore*. While a chef at the Stockholm Restaurant, he made plans to return to Sweden via the SS *Stockholm* to visit his family. Luckily, he changed his plans. On the voyage he nearly took, the *Stockholm* collided with and sunk the *Andrea Doria* off Nantucket. A future journey would prove more fruitful—he bicycled across the United States to raise money for the Jimmy Fund. He is now the owner of Gary's Restaurant in West Bridgewater.

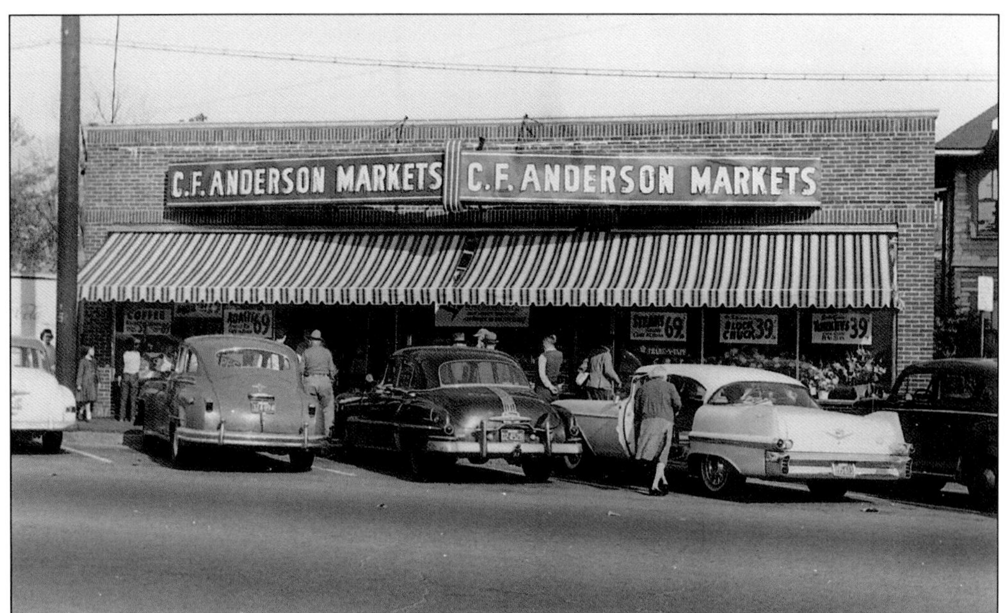


With a store on Union Street in Rockland and seven others throughout the Greater Brockton area, C.F. Anderson was a major force in the retail grocery business prior to the onslaught of the supermarkets.

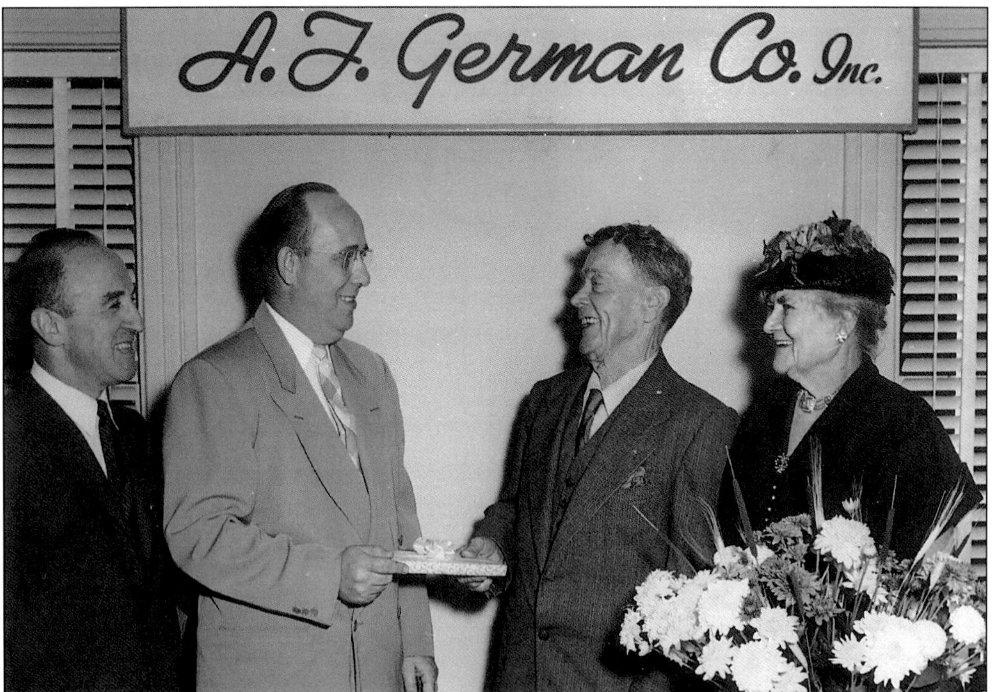


Harold A. Gullbrantz (age 79), of 74 South Leyden Street, was honored on October 7, 1957, at a testimonial dinner given upon his retirement as the street sweeper in the Campello business district. Sponsored by the Campello Businessmen's Association, he was feted for his more than 30 years of service to the city. Pictured here are Martin Fireman of Martin's Furniture; Carl R. Bystrom of Taft Jewlers; Mr. Gullbrantz; and his wife, Georgina.

# *Five*

# Those Who Served

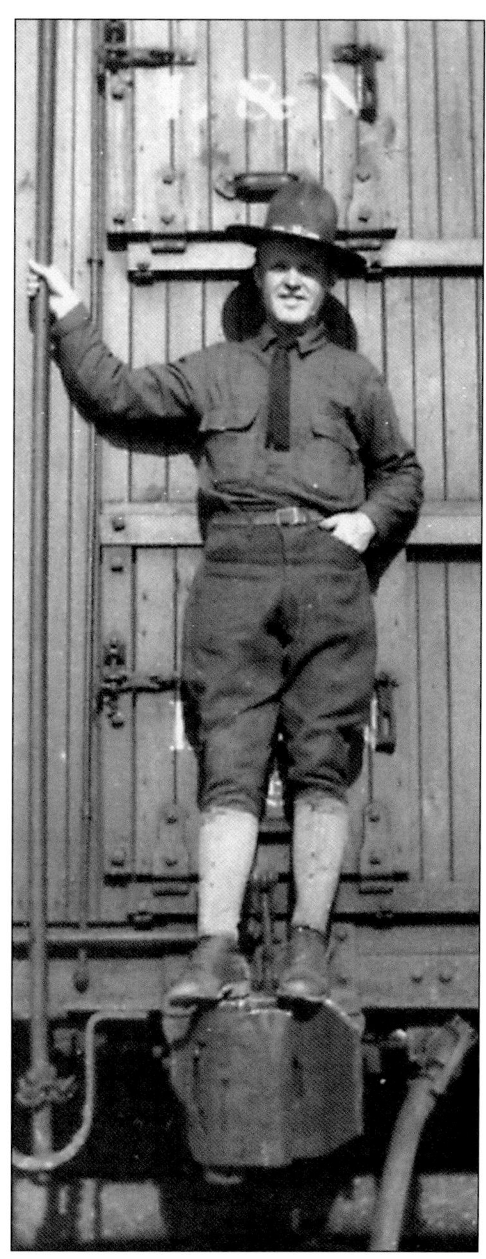

Scores of Swedish immigrants from North Bridgewater served in the Union army in the Civil War. Among those who served were Malcolm F. Dahlborg, Peter Johnson, Swan P. Colberg, F.T. Benson, Charles A. Gustafson, Oloff M. Holmberg, Axel F. Ahlstrom, Daniel Lawson, and Otto Carlson.

During the world wars, thousands from this region answered the call to service. These citizen soldiers were shoeworkers, clerks, bakers, doctors, delivery men, machinists, pipefitters, lawyers, ministers, nurses, teachers, carpenters, pharmacists, pattern makers, farmers, and florists. Most of them were kids—some as young as 17—who were asked to do extraordinary things. They were sent to places they had never heard of, such as Krinkeld, Lorient, Anzio, Kiska, Uttweiler, the Ardennes forest, Saipan, Okinawa, New Guinea, Guadalcanal, Tinian, and Iwo Jima. They were sent to places with code names like Omaha and Utah Beach and to places with infamous names like Buchenwald, Auschwitz, and Dachau.

Two Campello boys—S.Sgt. Walter Carlson and WO Everett A. Swanson—were at Pearl Harbor when the Japanese attacked on Sunday morning, December 7, 1941. Capt. Harry Carlson, PFC John O. Nelson, T3. Wallace Johnson, Cpl. Carl A. Lundin, PFC Warren Samuelson, Pvt. Alton Nelson, Sgt. Lennart Plahn, Ph.M./1C Alton W. Lawson, and S.Sgt. Herbert Johnson participated in the great invasion of Normandy. Ptr./1C Carl Newburg was aboard the carrier USS *Wasp* when it was torpedoed and sunk off Guadalcanal in August 1944. Lt. Harry Benson received the Distinguished Flying Cross after flying 25 missions over Europe in a B-17.

These and countless other descendants of the Swedish immigrants have a proud record of service to their country.

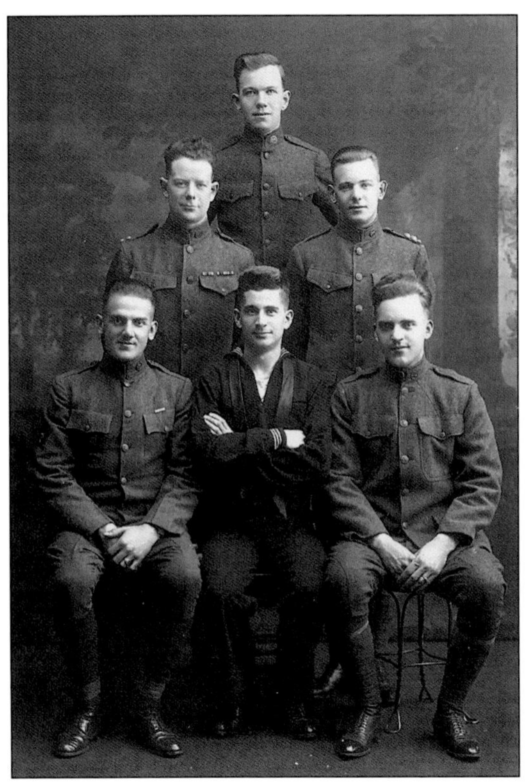

A large contingent of Greater Brockton Swedes served in the "war to end all wars," as World War I was proclaimed by Pres. Woodrow Wilson. At home on leave in 1917, these Campello boys took time out for this photographic remembrance. They are, from left to right, as follows: (front row) Martin Engstrom, Henry Fries, and Gust Anderson; (middle row) Harry Johnson and Walter Sondeen; (back row) Fred Hylen.

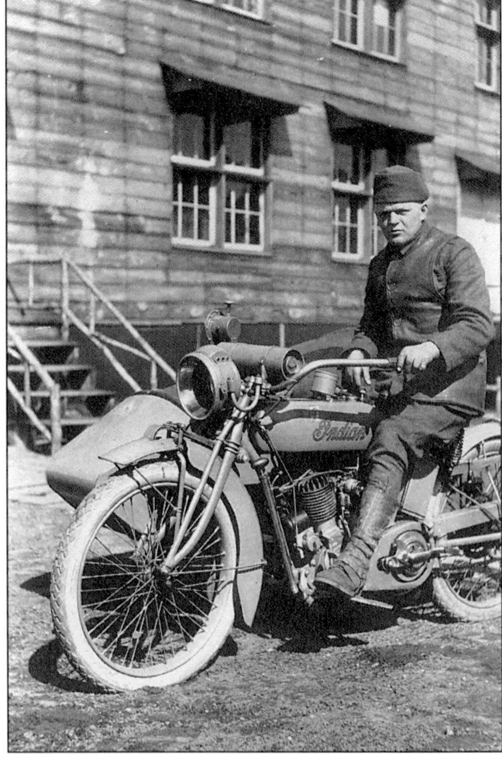


The sidecar on Pvt. Harry D. Gustafson's Indian motorcycle was used to transport "the brass" around Washington, D.C., during World War I. The experience he gained in the Motor Corps proved beneficial many years later when, on May 23, 1935, he piloted the last trolley in Brockton (car 6064) to the terminal on School Street. Along the route, the songs of the few last passengers pierced the midnight air.

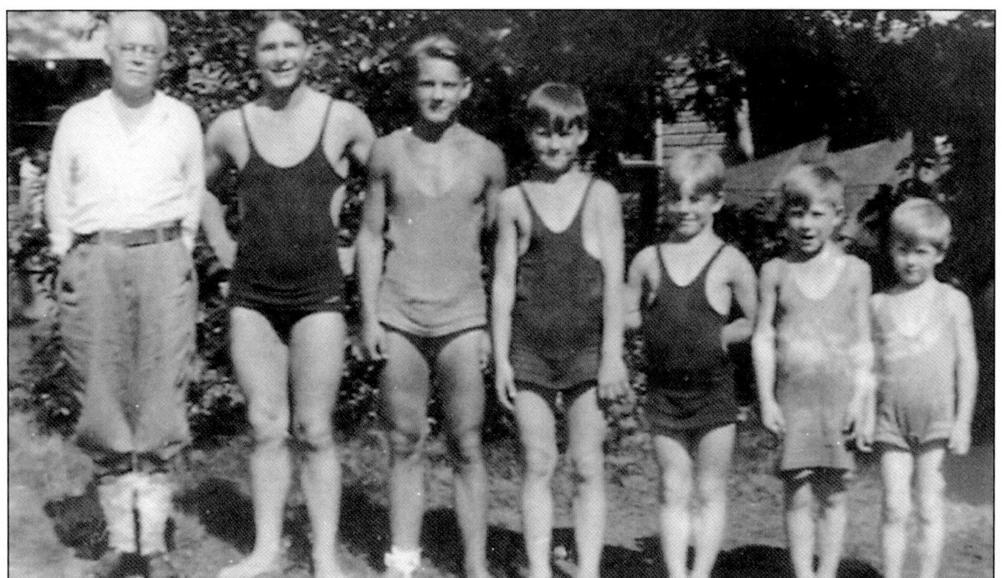

Shown here in casual dress is the Reverend Dr. Peter Froeberg with his six sons—Theodore, Joseph, Bertil, LeRoy, Kenneth, and Paul. Five of these six boys were on active duty in the U.S. military during World War II, and all returned home. Theodore, an engineer, did not serve in the military but was engaged in defense work during the war. Joseph, T/R G., 8th Air Force, designed and built the first automatic radio bomb release used in the European Theatre. Bertil was a Marine Corps captain and commander of 1st Marine Aircraft Wing. LeRoy was an aviation-machinist mate, U.S.N.R. Kenneth became an aviation cadet. Paul, the youngest, served stateside in the U.S. Army.

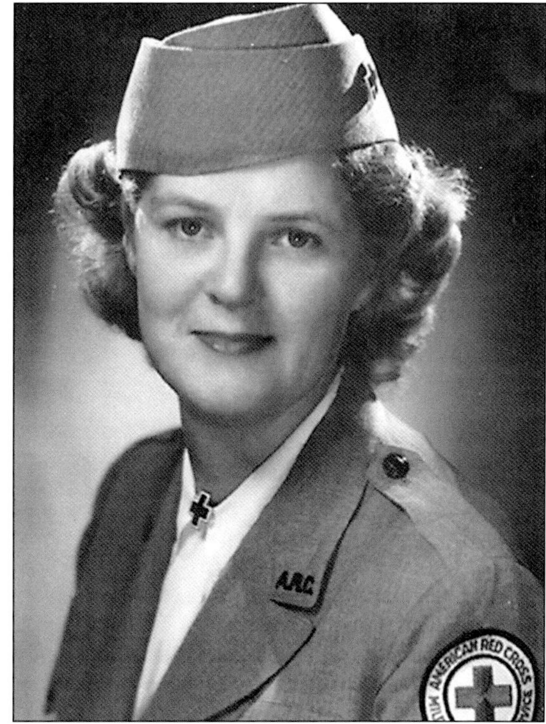


Verna L. Moberg was a staff assistant for the American Red Cross, Military Welfare Service. She was stationed at Batangas, Luzon, in the Philippines, and ran "clubmobiles" for the GIs. After V-J Day, she was sent to the Japanese cities of Osaka and Kyoto—the first Brockton woman to enter Japan after the surrender.

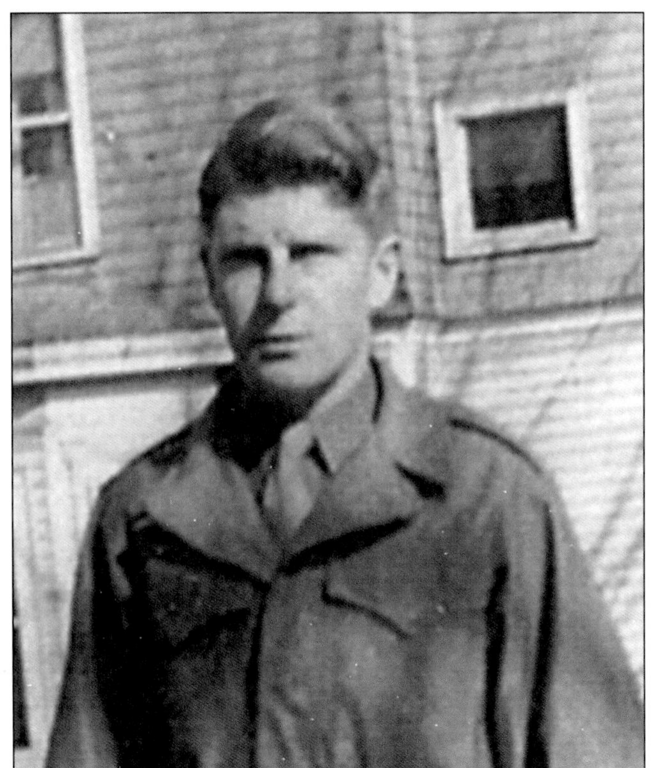

Cpl. George A. Moberg, U.S. Army, was a combat wireman in the 69th Infantry Division and operated a wire truck for the Artillery Hq. Battery during the entire drive through Belgium and Germany. When they landed at LeHavre on January 24, 1945, his battery mate Charles Chapman proclaimed, "Lafayette, we are here!" On February 11, 1945, they entered combat for the first time at Krinkelt and relieved U.S. troops. In the town of Pegau, Moberg and two German prisoners dove into a shell hole to avoid mortar fire. When it ended, they discovered that a mortar shell had landed only a few feet away but had failed to explode.

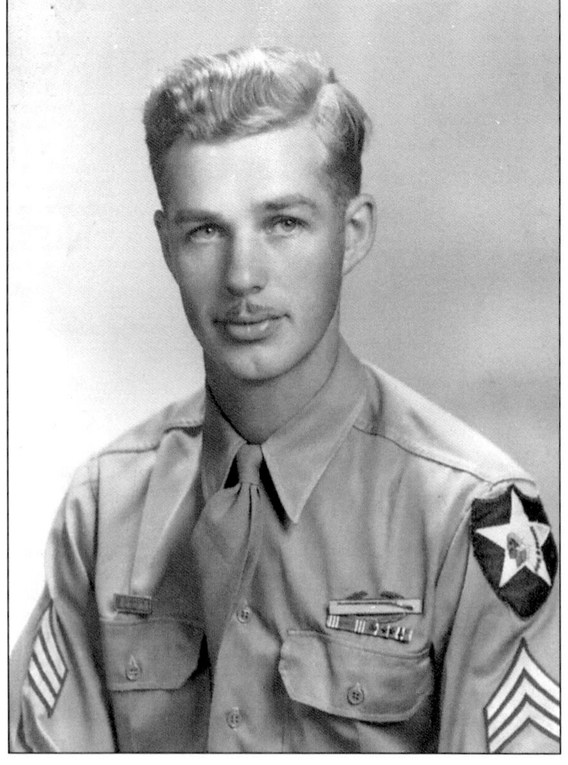

S.Sgt. Donald W. Broman was a member of the 2nd Infantry Division and served in "I" Company in numerous battles, including the bitter fight at Fourneuf Hills for the fortress City of Brest and Brest Airfield. Broman left Brockton on January 24, 1944, to enter the service of his country, along with the young man pictured above, George A. Moberg.

Cpl. Bertil Holt, U.S. Army Engineers, served in England, France, Belgium, Holland, and Germany. Nearing Berlin at the close of war, he was wounded when his truck drove over a shell, which exploded and overturned the vehicle.

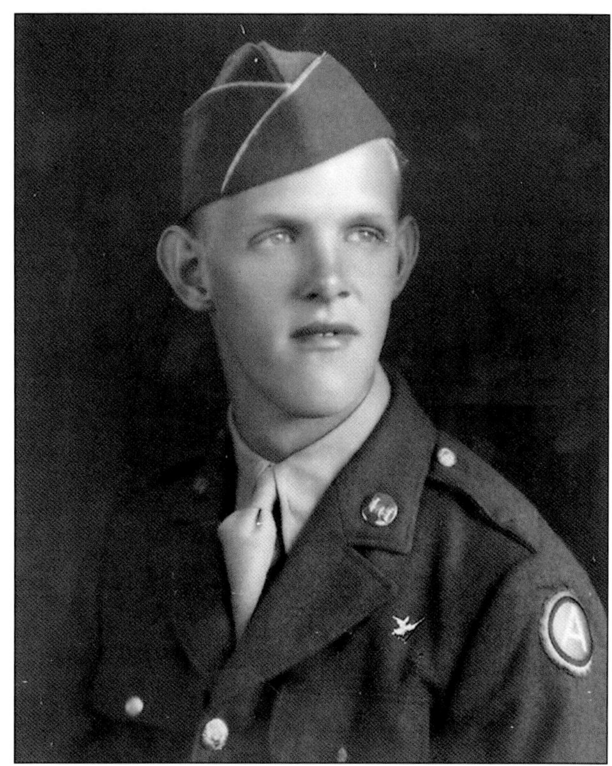

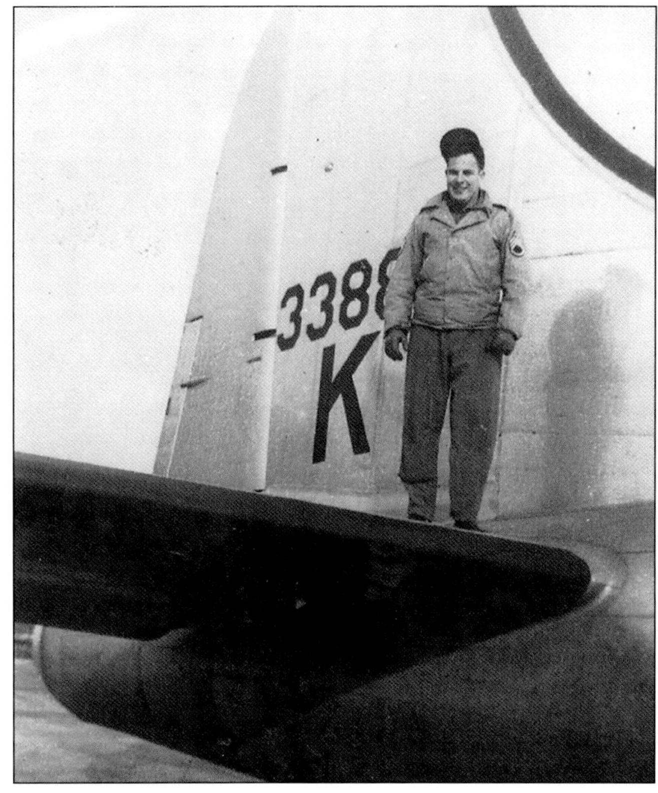


T.Sgt. Harvey G. Freer, 652nd Bomber Squadron, 8th Air Force, arrived in England in April 1943. He was initially assigned to a B-24 Liberator as an engineer and top turret gunner. Later, he was assigned to a B-17 Flying Fortress, in which he flew 33 missions. Sgt. Freer participated in a raid, originating in North Africa, on the Ploesti oil fields in Romania, one of the most heavily fortified targets in Europe.

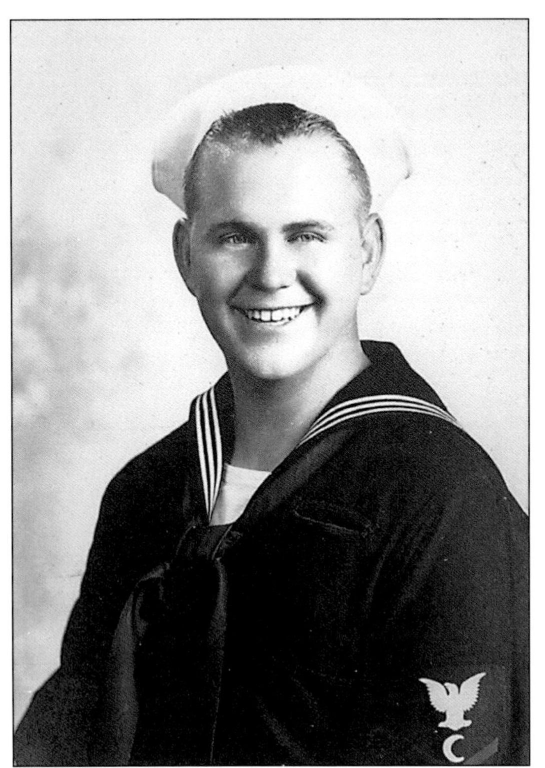

Like so many of his generation, Winston Bolinder's college career came to a halt when the United States entered World War II. Leaving Boston University, he enlisted in the U.S. Navy Seabees. As ship's cook (SC2c.), he saw action on the Marianna Islands and on Guam. At war's end, Bolinder capitalized on his cooking skills and became the chef at the famed Hampton Beach Casino.

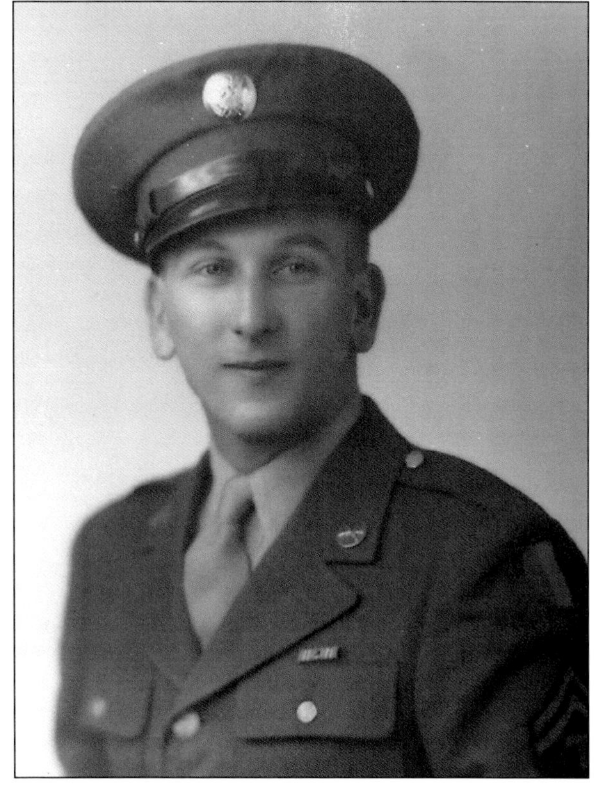

T5. David A. Johnson was inducted into the U.S. Army on July 31, 1942. On June 3, 1943, he traveled aboard Kaiser Wilhelm's Yacht, which had been gutted and converted to a troop ship, to Dutch Harbor in the Aleutian Islands and then to Adak. Their mission was to invade and take the island of Kiska, which had been captured by Japanese forces. With their fortunes falling in the Pacific, the Japanese had hurriedly left Kiska, and the Aleutians returned to U.S. control.

Fireman 1c. Eugene W. Carlson, U.S. Navy, served for two years aboard the USS *Greyhound* (repair service) with the 6th Pacific Fleet. Homebase was Bremerton, Washington. He worked on several battle-damaged naval vessels to return them to combat, including the USS *Pittsburgh*, USS *Shangrila*, USS *Quincy*, and the USS *Canberra*. The photograph was taken aboard the USS *Boston*.

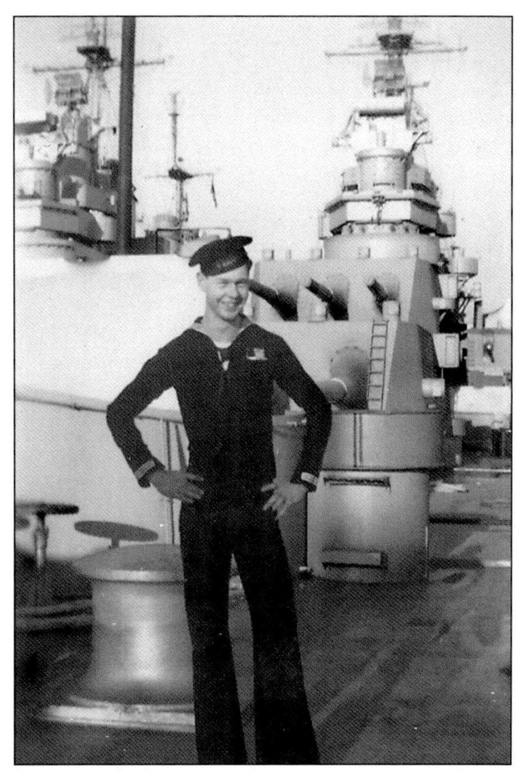

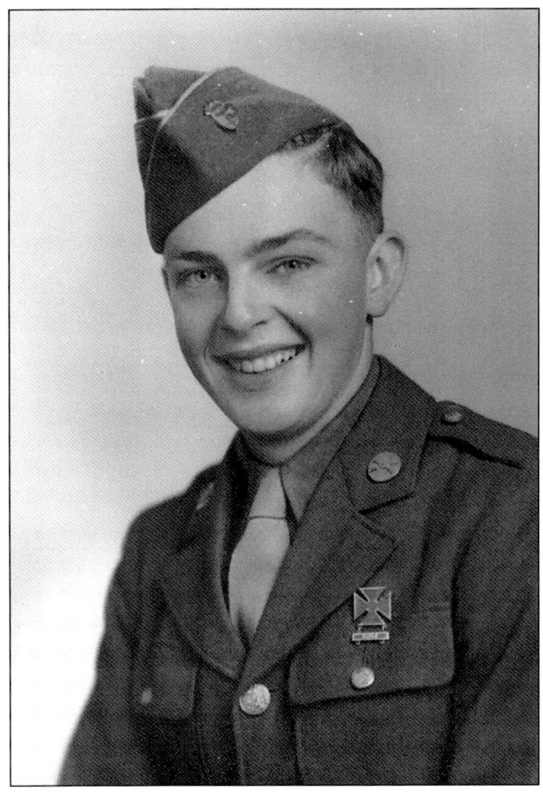

On August 8, 1944, 18-year-old Donald E. Lundquist entered the service of his country. A member of the famed 79th Infantry Division, he saw combat action in three major battles, including the crossing of the Rhine River. At the end of World War II, he was transferred to the 1st Infantry Division. Working at headquarters, he was able to finagle a pass to the Nuremberg Trials of the Nazi leaders of Germany and attended two sessions. "I was a witness to history although at the time I did not fully appreciate the importance of this event. We were all just happy the war was over, and that we were victorious," commented Mr. Lundquist.

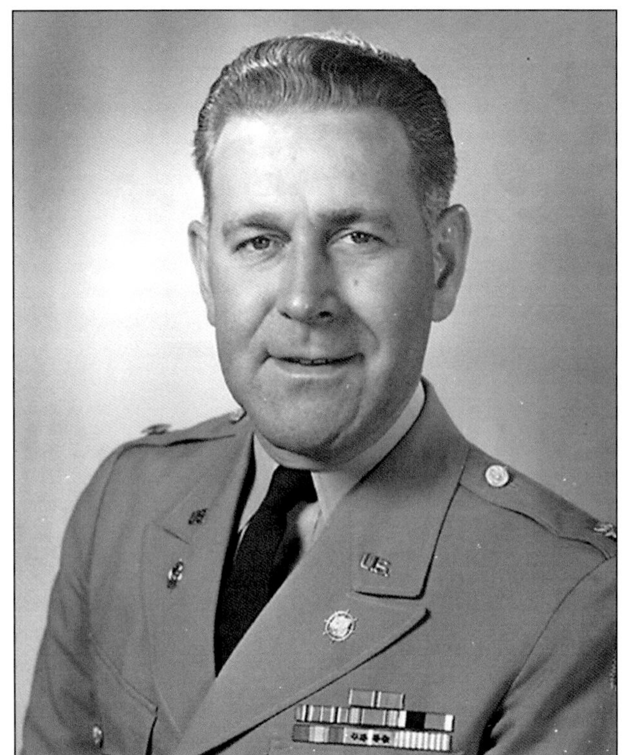

A graduate of the U.S. Military Academy at West Point, Harold C. Werner served his country with distinction for 23 years. Throughout his military career, which included service in World War II and the Korean War, he rose steadily to the rank of lieutenant colonel. Because he was a specialist in logistics, his assignments took him to posts in Germany, Japan, Korea, Thailand, and Spain.

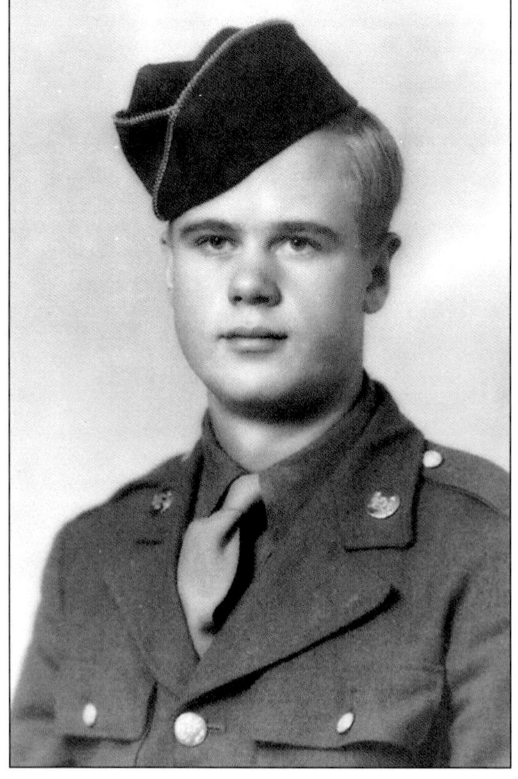

PFC Alton E. Nelson, U.S. Army, served in the lst Army under Gen. Omar Bradley. He landed at Omaha Beach on June 7, 1944, where his company's job was to clear underwater and land mines along the Normandy Coast and the Cherbourg Peninsula. The last day of the Battle of the Bulge, January 25, 1945, he was found wounded on a frozen field. Nelson was sent to a hospital in Paris, where, quite coincidentally, one of his nurses was a Brockton girl, Lt. Norma Surgens. Returning to combat, his unit was the first to build a bridge across the Elbe River and the first to advance on Berlin.

PFC Ernest R. Johnson, U.S. Army, was in the 66th Infantry "Black Panthers" Division. On Christmas Day 1944, he was part of a convoy crossing the English Channel as the first leg of the journey to reinforce troops in the Ardennes Forest. Tragedy struck during the crossing, as one of the troop ships was torpedoed and suffered a loss of 800 lives. A close friend, T5. Robert Anderson, also from Brockton, was aboard that ship but survived the ordeal. The division was instead sent to St. Nazaire with orders to contain the German submarine bases.

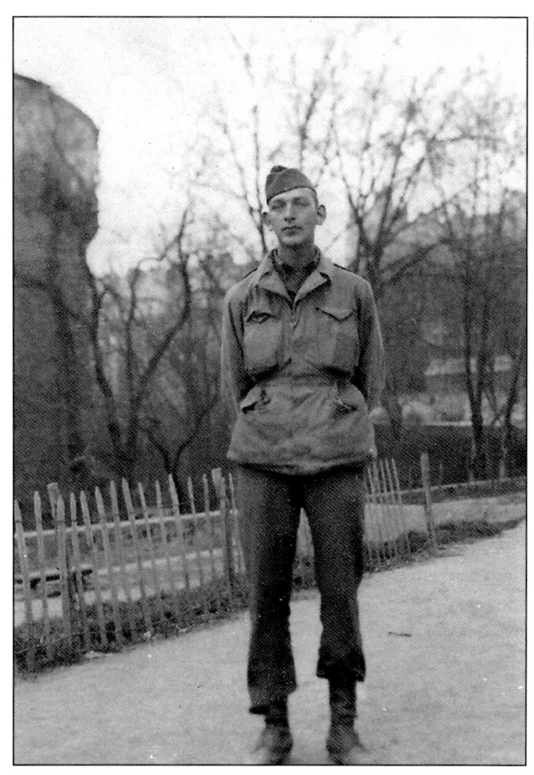

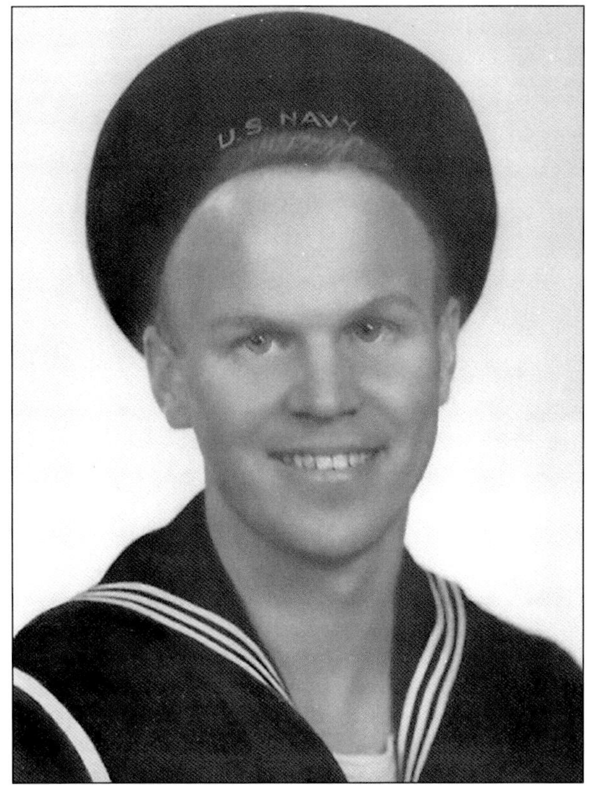


Shown here is MMOM3c. Robert A. Sigren, U.S. Navy. Sigren served aboard the USS *Magoffin*, on which, in one year, he traveled more than 50,000 miles traversing the Pacific. On April 1, 1945, his ship arrived at Okinawa, part of an armada of 1,213 warships carrying a force of more than 170,000 men. For five days during the invasion, he stood behind a 30-caliber machine gun on a Higgins Boat, a 35-foot wooden landing craft ferrying men of the lst Marine Division ashore. At the war's end in August 1945, Sigren remembers a remarkable sight: "All of the lights on the ships came on, there was no more darkness."

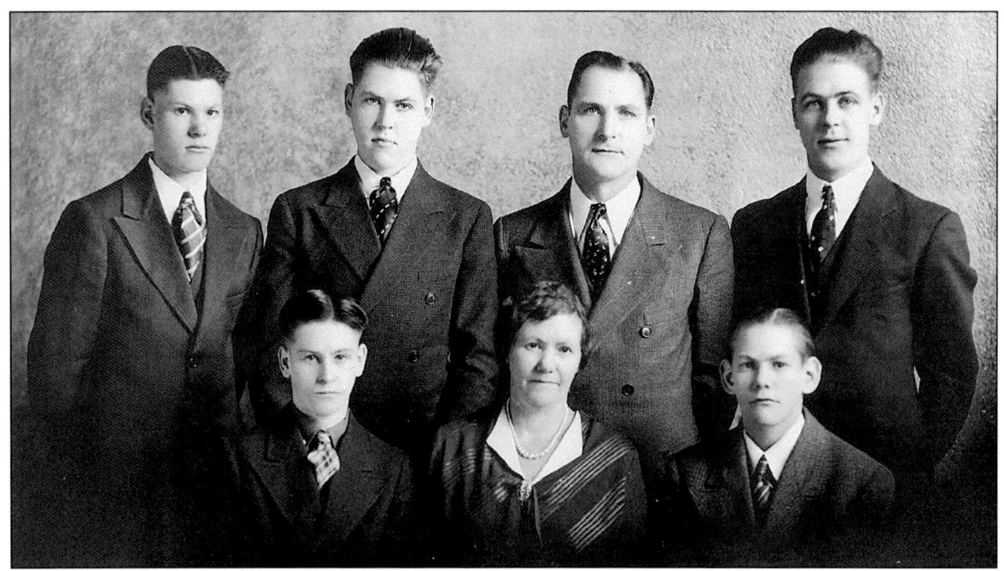

Oscar and Ida Lyman sent three of their five sons—Victor, Carl, Andus (back row) and Otto and Ivar (front row)—off to war. The oldest, Carl O. Lyman, to the right of his father, served in the Yankee Division of the 3rd Army under General Patton. In France, he was wounded and received a Purple Heart. On December 30, 1944, some 20 days after his release from the hospital, he was killed in action near Edelbrook, Luxembourg. Only days before, he had spent time with Alton Nelson and others from Brockton who were bivouacked nearby. Victor, to the right of Carl, was a torpedo specialist aboard the destroyer USS *Bremen*. Ivar, seated to the left of his mother, served in the U.S. Army in England and France.

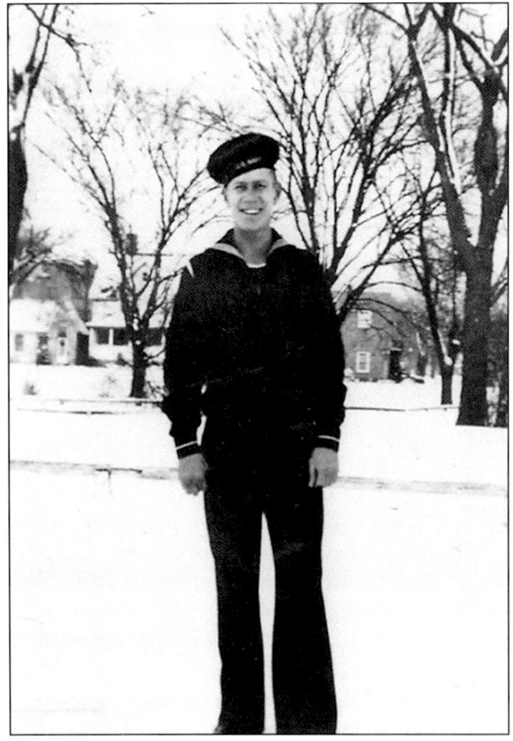

EM2c. George W. Peterson served in the U.S. Navy for three and one-half years engaged in transport duty to various South Pacific islands and Australia. He was aboard the USS *Mayrant* at Iwo Jima, where he was critically wounded. He was sent to the Brooklyn Naval Hospital but was unable to recover. He died in early 1946.

On December 28, 1944, T5. Arnold W. Halvorsen lost his life in a fierce artillery battle near the Belgian-German border during the Battle of the Bulge. Capt. Orville A. Lorenz, chaplain of the 26th Field Artillery Battalion, 9th Infantry, wrote the following words to Arnold's mother: "I wish to use these humble means to express to you my own deep sympathy. I can assure you that Arnold was held in high esteem by the officers and men of the battery in which he served. He was well liked, always very helpful, and had many friends."

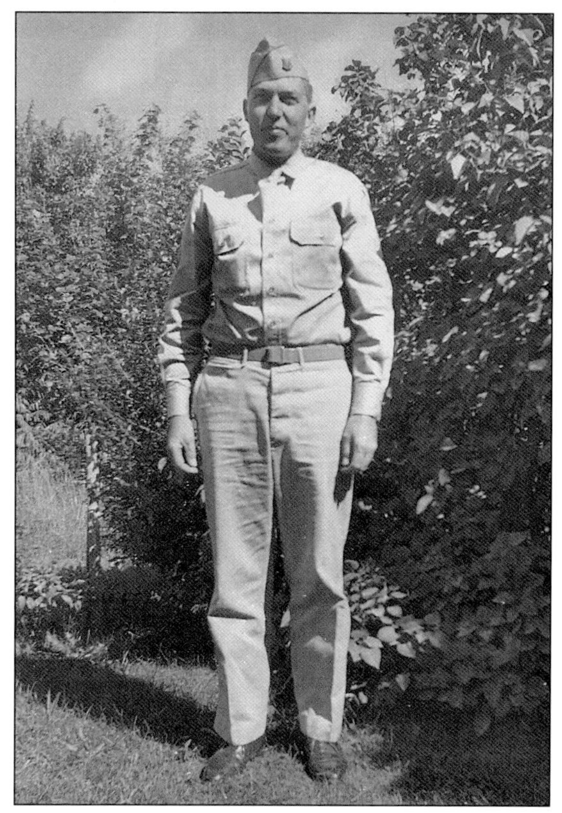

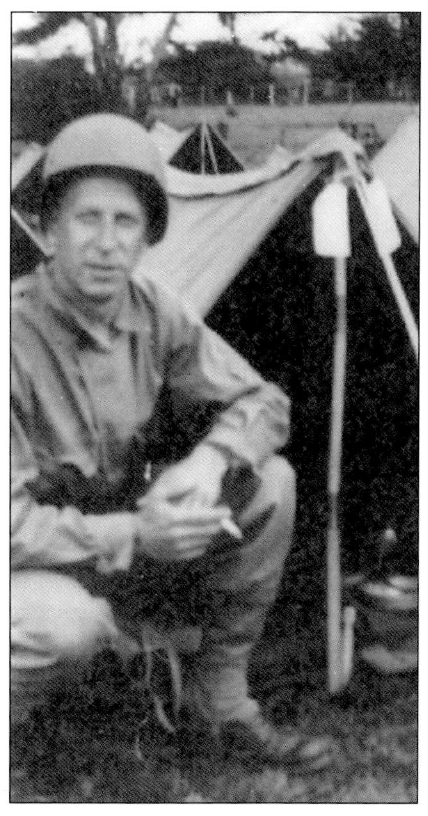

Shown here is 2nd Lt. Roger C. Peterson, U.S. Army. He served in the 39th General Hospital Medical Corps in Auckland, New Zealand, where he ran the post office for the entire hospital. He was accepted for OCS and, on June 9, 1945, received his commission in the Corps of Military Police. Peterson was then assigned to a German prisoner of war camp in Tallulah, Louisiana, where 425 troops of the Afrika Corps were imprisoned.

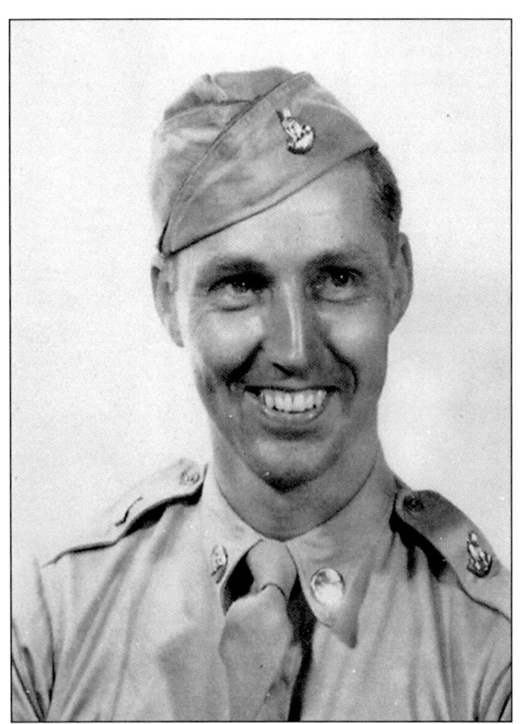

Sgt. Lennart B. Plahn served in the U.S. Army, Battery E, 101st Field Artillery, 26th Division. He had spent seven years in the National Guard prior to World War II. His unit was federalized in February 1941. After training, he was sent aboard the USS *Dickson*, part of a 185-ship convoy that sailed from Boston to the Firth of Clyde, Scotland. Plahn served 285 days in frontline combat from June 6, 1944, at Utah Beach, to the end of World War II. A member of Patton's 3rd Army, he was a forward combat observer engaged in heavy fighting. He was awarded the Silver Star, five battle stars, the World War II medal, the French Croix deGuerre, and the Belgian Croix deGuerre. Plahn received his Silver Star for pulling a comrade from a burning half-track, which exploded seconds after the rescue.

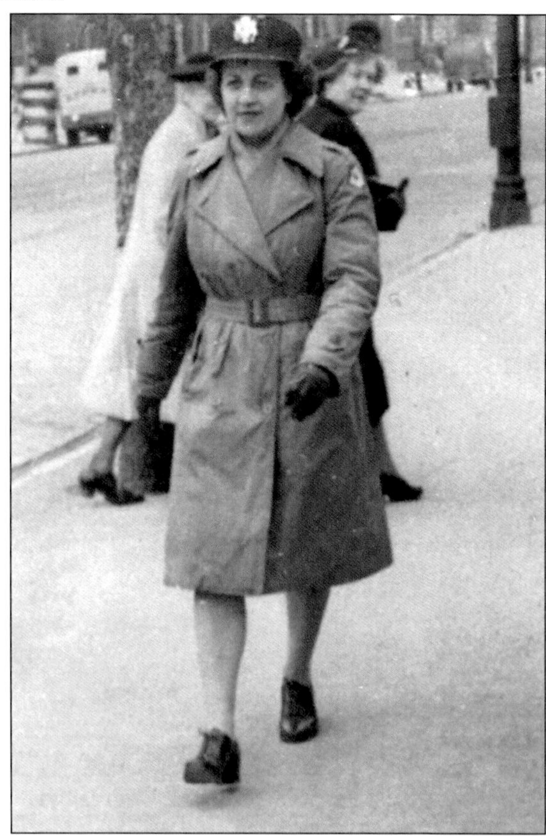

First Lt. Virginia (Johnson) Dunlap, U.S. Army Nurse Corps, saw duty for two years in England and France. She served in several hospitals, the last being at the 68th Station Hospital at Compiegne in Northern France.

Sgt. Eldon H. Ekman, U.S. Army, was in the thick of the battles in North Africa and Italy. Ekman received a citation from Lt. Gen. Mark Clark for meritorious service on the beachhead at Anzio for keeping weapons in firing order during the invasion by U.S. forces.

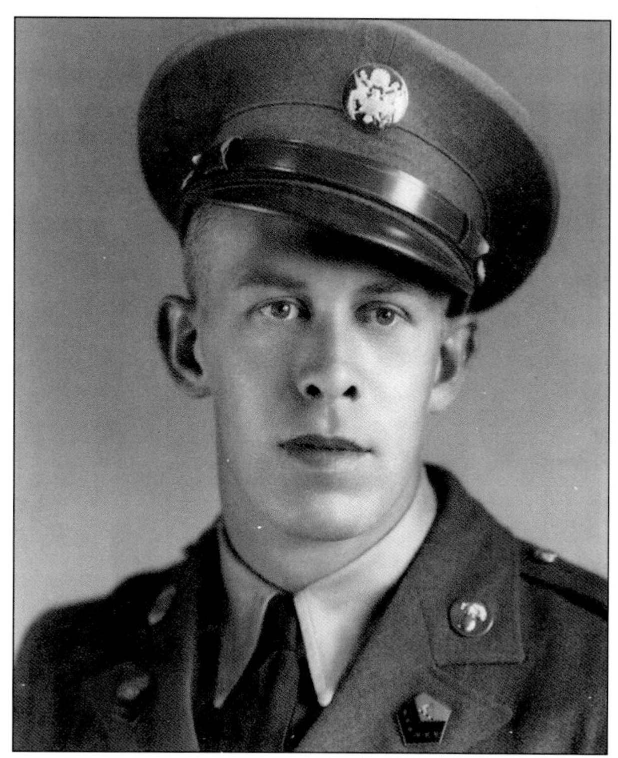

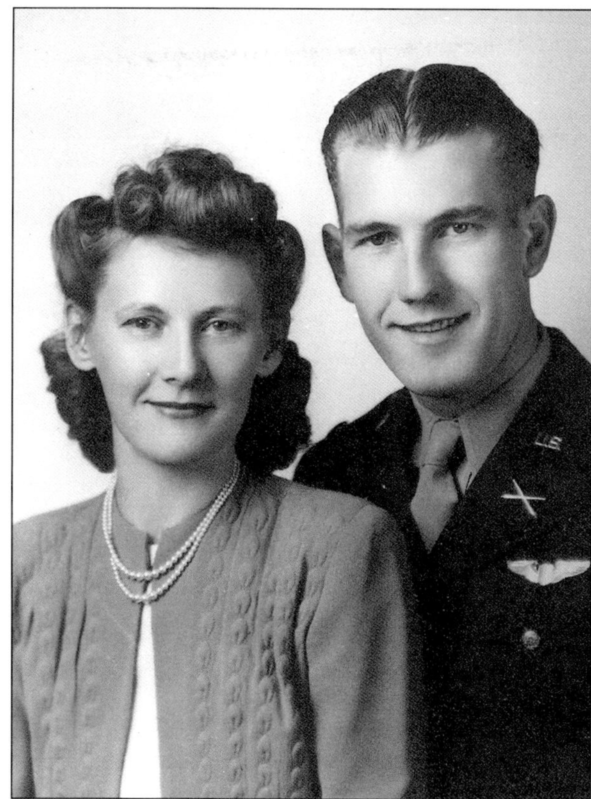

"The mothers and wives were also heroes," commented 1st Lt. Lester R. Johnson, shown here with his wife, Edna Winberg. Johnson was a member of the 12th Armored Division, known as the "Hellcats." Flying above the battlefields in a Piper Cub aircraft, he directed artillery fire and provided strategic information on enemy positions and strengths. He flew some 131 missions, losing five aircraft to enemy fire, and was wounded several times. He was awarded a Purple Heart and five Air Medals for his service. On May 6, 1945, the German army group in his sector surrendered. "We fell to our knees and thanked God we were alive. For us it was finally over," he remembers. Three Johnson brothers—Lester, Herbert, and William—saw service in World War II.

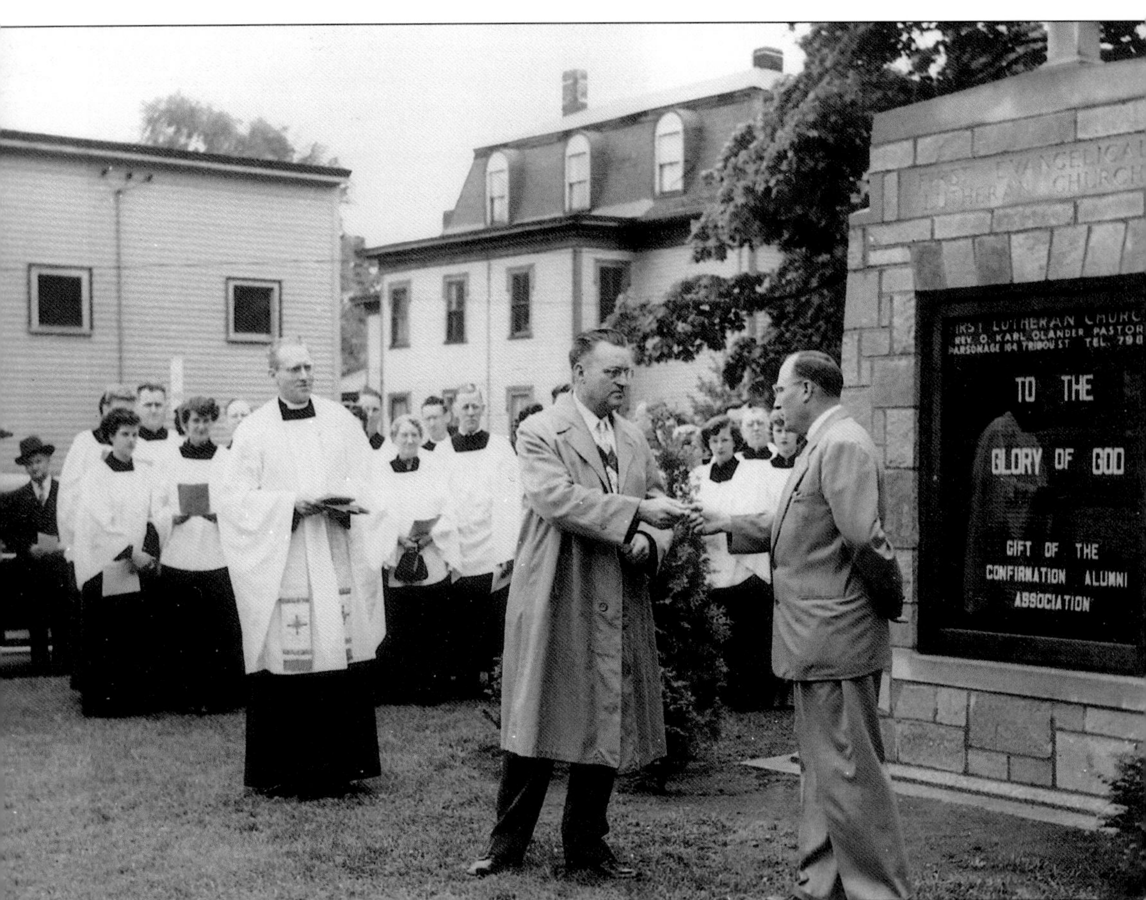


At the First Evangelical Lutheran Church, a memorial to the Brockton men who gave their lives in World War II was dedicated in memory of Sgt. Carl A. Carlson, PFC Carl O. Lyman, and EM2c. George W. Peterson. Shaking hands are Confirmation Alumni Association president G. Arthur Moberg and First Evangelical Lutheran Church Council chairman Roy Anderson Sr. Looking on is pastor O. Karl Olander, himself a combat veteran of the Pacific Theatre. Dr. Olander served as chaplain aboard the USS *Princeton*, a carrier that, in his words, "saw plenty of action before being lost near the Philippines."